DAVID'S
INFERNO

My Journey
through the Dark Wood
of Depression

DAVID'S INFERNO

My Journey
through the Dark Wood
of Depression

By

DAVID BLISTEIN

Foreword by KEN BURNS

Hatherleigh Press is committed to preserving and protecting the natural resources of the Earth. Environmentally responsible and sustainable practices are embraced within the company's mission statement.

Hatherleigh Press is a member of the Publishers Earth Alliance, committed to preserving and protecting the natural resources of the planet while developing a sustainable business model for the book publishing industry.

Library of Congress Cataloging-in-Publication Data is available upon request.
ISBN 978-1-57826-429-2

David's Inferno is available for bulk purchase, special promotions, and premiums. For information on reselling and special purchase opportunities, call 1-800-528-2550 and ask for the Special Sales Manager.

Cover and interior design by Dede Cummings/DCDESIGN

10 9 8 7 6 5 4 3 2 1

Printed in the United States

All photos by the author
Author photo by Beowulf Sheehan

The author would like to thank the following authors for permission to quote from their work:

Peter Schjedahl, Jerod Poore, Susan Orlean, and Sid Mukherjee.

"Born to Run" by Bruce Springsteen. Copyright © 1975 Bruce Springsteen, renewed © 2003 Bruce Springsteen (ASCAP) Reprinted by permission. International copyright secured. All rights reserved.

Jane Kenyon, excerpts from "Credo" and "The Suitor" from Collected Poems. Copyright © 2005 by The Estate of Jane Kenyon. Reprinted with the permission of The Permissions Company, Inc. on behalf of Graywolf Press, www.graywolfpress.

Harriet Rubin Excerpt Reprinted with permission of Simon & Schuster, Inc. from *Dante in Love* by Harriet Rubin. Copyright © 2004 Harriet Rubin.

Visit us at www.hatherleighpress.com and register online for free offers, discounts, special events, and more.

For Wendy

ॐ

Together Wendy we'll live with the sadness
I'll love you with all the madness in my soul.

—Bruce Springsteen

"Beyond the obvious—that it's a travelogue of an emotional journey, a Fodor's Guide to the troubled soul—the great insight of *David's Inferno* is that life and literature are interwoven, that we can look to even ancient books for wisdom, diagnoses, and hope. Blistein's frenetic, torturous—and surprise, funny!—tale offers all three in just the proper dosages."
— J.C. HALLMAN, author of *Wm & H'ry: Literature, Love, and the Letters Between William and Henry James*

"Why would I want to read so much about another person's life except that it's self-revealing, honest, illuminated with humor, and urgent. It has a reason for being; a perfect storm of a book."
— KABIR HELMINSKI, Shaikh of the Mevlevi Order of Sufism and Co-Director of the Threshold Society

"There is no hushed reverence, no self-aggrandizing, no simple tried and true cures...just a shared battle and a stunning honesty."
— WILL ACKERMAN, Grammy Award winner and founder of Windham Hill Records

"Warm and compassionate, often hilarious, and full of hope and encouragement...If you love someone who is depressed (or who you think might be), read this book."
— CAROLINE CARR, author of *Living with Depression: How to Cope When Your Partner is Depressed*

"David Blistein takes depression—something scary and overwhelming—and makes it approachable through this remarkable new book. He brings to his story a great deal of practical and scientific information without ever losing sight of the human element."
— REBECCA JONES, MD, Founder of the Vermont Greenprint for Health, and Vermont Director for Doctors for America

"This record of a writing life, a talented man's self-examination, a marriage, all enduring the scalding tides those beset by depression know, stands out particularly for its articulated wisdom and graceful prose. It is plain-spoken, funny, and at times almost heartbreaking. But insight is what gets us all by and the most insightful writing is always help in need. *David's Inferno,* with its wit and thoughtfulness, is a gift to be cherished."
— ROBERT STONE, winner of the National Book Award for *Dog Soldiers* and Pulitzer Prize Nominee for *Bear and His Daughters*

Contents

౪

Foreword

⁊

NOT FAR from where David Blistein lives in southeastern Vermont is a pretty good Chinese restaurant. It moved to its current location near the interstate a few decades ago, taking over from a failed business, also an eating establishment. For years before the good folks from China took over the place, on a large yellow sign with black letters visible for a least a mile, the old restaurant owners advertised their strong suit with just one word: "STEAK." When the new owners came in, they very simply removed the "S" and the "K." (That leaves "TEA" for those of you not paying close attention.)

Both David and I have long recognized, in big ways and small, the importance of *subtraction;* that is, less equaling more in most things connected to the odd set of events we all call the human experience. But there are times when more is…well…more—and a good thing. This happens most often when we need each other. I need David Blistein.

Over the more than forty years we've known each other, we've shared many things: LOVE, good times, laughs (lots of them), women (no comment), alcohol, drugs, and GOD. But our madness or our depression—"Black Care," Theodore Roosevelt once called it—has been something we've had to endure mostly alone. Not that we weren't without help. We had it. Not that we didn't help—or try to help—each other. We did. But we were essentially alone. All alone.

I'm not surprised that his brain betrayed him so mercilessly. (Or perhaps, all of this has also been the best blessing ever for him—and for us.) His mind works so wonderfully, so differently, so fast, and so generously that it was bound to trip over itself, bound to need a spare part not easily found in the usual places, bound to need a bit of rewiring, rebooting. But it was the depth of it that scared us, the way it cancelled out his own superb cleverness, the way it usurped his own strengths and sapped his normally prodigious life force, the way it scared *him*.

It took a lot of hard work, and a lot of love from others and from David himself, but he did get better. And the hard work he did was a marvel to those of us who love him so unconditionally. Because he has always been *for* the world in a way too unique to accurately describe here in a few words, his way out of his hell had to include helping others out as well, without judgment, without making someone or something wrong. That is this book. It takes us deep into the mysteries of depression, and its power to transform our relationships, our creativity, and our very selves—a remarkable achievement.

Courageously and honestly, he has revisited the terrifying places, and while not smothering the terror in bromides and platitudes (it is really frightening—and should be), he has given us all a map and some basic instructions for doing the hard work we may need to summon when the inevitable vicissitudes of life threaten even the most controlled and controlling among us, i.e., when shit happens.

In this book, David often evokes Dante, who shares with my friend a sustaining curiosity about the places most of us hope we never encounter, the circles of Hell we trust will not be our lot. During the Great Depression (get it?), Franklin Delano Roosevelt, no stranger to overcoming demons and afflictions of his own, himself quoted Dante at his acceptance speech for his party's re-nomination of him for the Presidency in 1936: "…Dante tells us that divine justice weighs the sins of the cold-blooded and the sins of the warm-hearted in different scales." David Blistein has written a warm-hearted book that can help deliver us all—thank God—from the cold-blooded fear that now and then invades the perfection of our own solitude.

—Ken Burns
Walpole, New Hampshire

Preface

∽

RIGHT NOW, I am *not* depressed, manic, hypomanic, dysphoric, bipolar, cyclothymic, or agitated. The stories and insights in this book are primarily based on experiences between 2005-2007. Except for the occasional blip, as long as I take my meds, I rarely experience the symptoms anymore. My official diagnosis is: Major Depressive Disorder, Recurrent, in Partial Remission.

I guess that means I'm a person *living with* major depressive disorder...in the same way that someone might be *living with* HIV/ AIDS, diabetes, high blood pressure, high cholesterol, or some combination.

Hey, we've all got problems, right? And most of us have cupboards full of supplements and prescription drugs to show for them. Until there are reliable one-step cures that work for just about everybody all the time—or, as futurists expect, can be customized to work for each individual virtually all the time—most people accept the fact that they need to keep taking their anti-virals, insulin, beta blockers, or statins indefinitely.

But many depressives, myself included, still consider major depression a temporary condition, not a chronic disease. I don't see myself taking these drugs for the rest of my life. Instead, I think about when it would be a good time (spring) and a good year (well, not this one...) to start tapering off. Although, if I'm ever convinced the apocalypse is right around the corner, I *will* rush downtown to the drugstore to stock up on all my meds—at full retail if necessary—before I bother with milk and eggs.

Unfortunately, while there are fairly objective ways of measuring HIV, insulin, blood pressure, and cholesterol, depression is just too subjective a disease to define what it would mean to be "cured." That doesn't stop people from trying: In an independent, double-blind study of website results (i.e., I just did it), "Depression Cure" beats "Coronary Cure" by 30 million results, and even "Breast Cancer Cure" by 15 million.

So, I suppose, whether I realize it or not, I'll always be living in depression's shadow. Then again, maybe we all are. Considering how little we know about the brain's potential—and the rich complexity of human intelligence and creativity—that may not be such a bad thing…within reason.

∞

People have asked me if I really want to write this book. If I really want to expose my neural endings to the memories of that time. As if the very words carry a contagion. One to which I am particularly susceptible.

For the most part, I cavalierly brush off their concerns, saying that it doesn't affect me to write about it. That, if anything, it puts me and the avenging angel—yes, angel as much as devil—on an equal footing. That I'm a storyteller and this is a story I have to tell; a story I have to stitch seamlessly into the other stories of this life… every holographic moment, from the everyday to the ecstatic.

At the same time, I knew I was on the right track when people who have been down or are still on these roads told me they *couldn't* read it. For while I have practiced and deeply appreciate the detachment of meditation, dispassion and compassion remain only mental experiences without *passion*.

On October 10, 2006, exactly a year after this journey began, I emailed a friend:

> *Yesterday, I just became edgier and edgier throughout the day at work. Got into the car, sobbed all the way home, and continued for a while after getting there. I'm spent, buddy.*

They say that life passes before your eyes when you die. If I'm going to squeeze the last drop of humanness out of this life, I hope it also passes through my heart.

—David Blistein
East Dummerston, Vermont

THE
DARK
WOOD

HOW WILD THE FOREST WAS, SO TANGLED AND OVERGROWN
I STILL SHUDDER TO THINK OF IT.
BUT TO REVEAL HOW I WAS TRANSFORMED THERE
I MUST TELL YOU OF EVERYTHING I SAW.

Inferno, Canto I (5-9)

Midway upon the journey of our life,
I found myself in a dark wood,
For the straightforward path had been lost.

ᘓ

T HREE OF THE MOST FAMOUS LINES IN LITERATURE.
The mid-life crisis against which all others are measured.

Dante's not in Hell yet. Hell, he's not even in Limbo yet. But he's lost his way. Big time.

For starters, he's being tormented by a lion, a leopard, and a she-wolf. And those are just the symbolic threats. His real life is much more perilous:

He's been continually undermined in his attempts to mediate between Rome and the city-states, the nobility and the bourgeoisie—until he gives up and declares himself a "party of one."

He's been forced into exile from his beloved Florence, and reduced to wandering the solitary roads of Northern Italy, France, and maybe England—living off the kindness of patrons and occasional work as a tutor or scribe.

He's wrestling with a philosophical split from his former mentor and friend Guido Cavalcanti. (Dante's also feeling a little guilty since, back when he was in political favor, he was one of the Florentine magistrates who banished Guido—who died of malaria shortly thereafter.)

He's continually disillusioned by the reigning popes who are guilty of the worst kinds of manipulation and greed. But Catholicism remains embedded deep in his genes.

He's estranged from his wife and children. More significantly, Beatrice, the famously unrequited love of his life, has gone to Heaven and, it turns out, is in no mood to hear any excuses from a sinner like Dante.

He's also driven by a conviction that transcendent Truth and Love can be experienced on earth; and that *his* mission is to reveal The Way by writing a masterpiece that will capture all the hopes, foibles, and dreams of man in a way that nobody else ever has. In fact, his original title was *The Vision of Paradise, Purgatory, and Hell.*

In the midst of this tangle of woes, Virgil shows up. And makes it perfectly clear that the only way out is in. And the only way up is down. Way down.

Words Fail

Nothing happens to any man that he is not formed by nature to bear.

—MARCUS AURELIUS

∽

O N MONDAY MORNING, October 10th, 2005, I took a 40 mg tablet of Celexa, cut it in half, and swallowed. Presumably with juice or cold coffee. Or I just put my mouth under the faucet to wash it down—one of my less civilized habits.

This, unlike many things which followed, was not a particularly crazy thing to do.

Since 1999, Celexa had been a potent ally in my balancing act between streams of creative energy and a tendency to disappear into black holes. A cycle that I'd, previously, been able to "self-medicate" by using various combinations of exercise, cigarettes, diet, alternative therapies, liquor, meditation, and several varieties of non-prescription drugs. By taking Celexa, and at times Wellbutrin, I didn't have to be so concerned about my shifting moods…about which version of myself would show up the next day…or hour.

During the summer of 2005, I decided to take a little break from Celexa. It seemed like a good time. My life was about as good as it gets. I'd just left a fairly stressful job. My wife and I continued to successfully negotiate the slings and arrows of a 30-year marriage. We owned our own home, and had virtually no debt as well as adequate savings. Plus, I'd begun doing the writing I'd waited many years to do. Why not take the summer to see if my depression was primarily caused by circumstance, stress, or both?

But, that fall, after nine months of creativity unleashed, my energy plummeted, my enthusiasm dulled, and the darkness began its inexorable descent. Clearly, my depression was chemical. Perhaps seasonal. But if the past were any indication, summers could be just as hard. And, while I had experience with many non-pharmaceutical ways to treat it, none of them had ever proved as reliable as a small pill two times a day. So, as the familiar foreboding sensation arrived—a soft, pre-gag sensation in the throat that flows up into the tear ducts and down through the chest to the pit of the stomach—I knew this was no time to take any chances.

The previous spring, I'd slowly reduced my dose over about six weeks: from 60 mg every day, to 60 mg one day and 40 mg the next. Then 40 mg both days. Then 40 one day and 20 the next. Then 20 each day. Then 20 every other day. Until eventually I stopped altogether. It went smoothly.

I planned to go back up the same way. 20 mg once a day for a few days, and so on. Maybe stopping around 40, or continuing up to 60. I knew the drill. I didn't even bother telling my psychiatrist I was starting up again. I had a refill left over from the spring and figured he wasn't going to tell me anything we hadn't discussed before.

But, by Sunday, I was sitting on the floor with my head in my hands, my agitation barely managed by Valium, telling a long-time friend that there was no way I could get on a plane and join him for a business trip to California.

I could barely talk.

∞

The phrase "nervous breakdown" is inadequate. The experience is way beyond "nervous." It's a rampant agitation that careens from constant low-level anxiety to gut-wrenching, dry-heaving despair. After the worst attacks, I'd feel like I'd just been spit up, Jonah-like, on the shore, wondering if next time the whale would be a shark.

Breakdown is way too static a word. Every day is spent on roiling waves. Occasionally—for an hour or two, maybe even a day—those waves buoy you up high enough for a gasp of blessed air, only to sweep you back down into such a fierce undertow that drowning, while terrifying, at least holds out the promise of peace.

For the next two years, only my own desperately flailing will and the determined surround of family, friends, and guides kept me from being institutionalized or far worse.

As I wrestled with this relentless onslaught, a procession of compassionate and insightful healers: doctors, psychiatrists, acupuncturists, astrologers, tarot readers, homeopaths, Craniosacral specialists, medical intuitives, and a dear friend who guided me through soul-rendering wails in the Southwest desert, did everything they could to help me stay on the treacherous path that I'd chosen—yes chosen, whether subconsciously or karmically—without wandering so far into the wilderness that I'd never find my way back.

LIMBO

TRULY, I FOUND MYSELF AT THE EDGE
OF AN ABYSS OF INFINITE GRIEF
FILLED WITH THE ECHOES OF ENDLESS LAMENTATIONS.

◦ *Inferno, Canto IV (7-9)*

HAVING FOLLOWED VIRGIL OUT OF THE DARK WOODS, Dante arrives at the infamous Gates of Hell. This is a pretty chaotic place. Most people are waiting to catch a ferry while trying to ignore a sign telling them to abandon all hope.

The docks also swarm with lost souls who, during their lives, were unable to choose between good and evil. They're joined by a host of cowardly angels who couldn't decide which side to root for when Lucifer rebelled against God. (That would seem to be a no-brainer.) They're not even allowed on the boat. Instead, they're running around naked, carrying meaningless banners, and screaming their lungs out as stinging insects swarm all around them.

To make things worse, while Virgil is persuading a reluctant Charon to give them a ride across the River Acheron—in spite of Dante's less-than-gung-ho attitude and the minor detail that no living person has ever made this crossing before—the ground begins to shake and the wind starts blowing something fierce. If I found myself in that God-awful place, I'd reach for the nearest benzodiazepine. Dante does the next best thing. He faints. When he wakes up, he's in Limbo.

Limbo is one of the most convoluted theological constructs in history. The early Fathers (the Mothers probably knew better) took a simple suggestion by Matthew that Christians should be rewarded or punished based on performance, and transformed it into an organizational chart only a consultant could love. As if that weren't bad enough, at some point they realized that they hadn't set aside a safe place for unbaptized babies or perfectly good people who had the misfortune to be born before baptism was invented—like Socrates, Plato, and Hippocrates.

Limbo—neither here nor there, neither damned nor saved—

was their compromise. It's the first stop in Hell. Yes, Hell. Even though, counterintuitively, people don't really suffer there. At least not in the gory ways people in the other realms of Hell do.

People in Limbo are depressed. Really depressed. They sigh all the time. For the simple reason that they can't experience the pure light and love of God—or, to put it in non-denominational terms, be graced with inspiration and enthusiasm. This type of yearning is the hallmark of pure depression—i.e., depression without any apparent cause. Or, as Dante puts it, "Sorrow without torment."

In Limbo, you can feel Dante trying to clarify his own vision and questioning his ability to pull it off. In fact, while there, he consults with four great classical poets: Homer, Horace, Ovid, and Lucan. Oddly, he says he shouldn't repeat the things he talked with them about. Why not? They're totally supportive. In fact, the whole scene is a backhanded way to get their blessing. So, what's the big secret?

It's not that he shouldn't talk about his dialogue with four of the greatest minds in the history of the Western World. It's that he can't. He doesn't know how yet. He says that his words aren't equal to the experience. This problem—which has tormented writers throughout history—will plague him for the entire twenty years it takes to write *The Divine Comedy*. And probably continues to plague him to this day.

The poor guy is wrestling with shadows. Very real shadows. Dante may share top billing with Shakespeare as the best writer of all time, but he faces the same challenges all writers face:

He has to find his voice.

He has to make the tools of his trade conform to his vision. In his case, that means eschewing Latin and, instead, trying to bash together a mess of regional dialects into a single vernacular that all his compatriots can understand.

He has to find a way to convince people his stuff is worth read-ing...maybe even good enough to toss a couple of florins or hunks of bread and cheese his way.

He also has to find a way not to overly antagonize the Powers-that-Be—powerful men who are more than willing to toss any suspicious writing into the flames (and sometimes the writer along with it), as well as potential patrons who might give him a few months or years of peace so he can get this thing written.

In the Dark Wood, Dante learns there's no turning back. At the Gates of Hell he sees that you're either on the boat or you're not. By the time he makes it through Limbo, he is fully aware that his life's work is to be a clear channel for an illusive, inchoate, ineffable—all these adjectives are necessary—vision that will make him a medium for something far more transcendent than even he can grasp. And that, with all due respect to Virgil and the other great writers who've gone before him, he's on his own.

He accepts the challenge. He accepts enduring an indescribable, cataclysmic personal experience. For what? To come back to tell the world so that they, too, can discover what LOVE really is.

He begins the descent.

Fifty-Three Years, Four Months, and One Helluva Week

It is quite true what philosophy says: that life must be understood backwards. But then one forgets the other principle: that it must be lived forwards.

—SØREN KIERKEGAARD

☙

THERE'S A FINE, but significant, line between intense creative focus and fanaticism. And an equally fine, but significant, line between contemplation and creative despair. Lines that I've criss-crossed with reckless abandon since I was a kid.

In many ways, hypomania (mania-lite...hold the psychosis) has made me what I am today. Symptoms include the pressure to keep talking, thoughts racing out of control, and easy distractibility. Or, as psychiatric manuals officially put it: "involvement in pleasurable activities that may have a high potential for negative psycho-social or physical consequences." All of which I've always considered charming personality traits. (Inflated self-esteem is another symptom.)

Many professionals would probably consider the phrase "controlled hypomania" a contradiction in terms. But, thanks to an academically-disciplined family and a lifelong obsession with being, or at least appearing to be, perfect, I've usually been able to harness it to my advantage—whether it was graduating with high honors from Amherst or running a successful ad agency with, typically, about a dozen employees, twenty clients, and 50 to 75 projects.

In fact, a little hypomania is virtually a job requirement for the latter.

In any event, by managing/juggling my periods of depression

and mild hypomania, I was able present myself to the world as someone intelligent, trustworthy, confident, *and stable*.

⁂

Even during periods when the job became all-consuming and I had to squint to see a flicker of light at the end of the tunnel, I resisted taking antidepressants. I took solace in the knowledge that I was part of a distinguished line of brooding, whiskey-drinking creatives. Maybe someday I'd even have my own table at a café on *Boulevard St. Germain*. In the meantime, I'd just take some B vitamins, work out really hard, drink a little more coffee, tea, or alcohol, and try to be clever and amusing enough so that, even on my worst days, my family and friends liked having me around.

When those days stretched into a week or more, I'd get a massage, have an acupuncture treatment, or go to a homeopath. All of which would at least help temporarily.

And during the periods when I was "wired"? It just made me more productive. Plus, I'd been meditating every morning since I was 18. So I experienced at least a little calm every day.

These mood swings did have their drawbacks. I hated deadlines because I had no idea if the creative guy would show up in time. (Even though I'd usually do the job right away because I'd obsess over it until I did.) I could be annoyingly ambivalent about going out to movies, having friends over, or even going for a walk. I tended to resist requests—whether it was coming up with a new headline or stopping by a store on my way home—even if I enjoyed doing whatever it was. Because my drive to please—not just other people but my own strict inner critic—could make the simplest of those requests a burden.

Owning the ad agency didn't make it any easier. It's a business that can career from being really exciting and inspiring to oppressively worrying and frustrating—often in a matter of minutes. Especially when one of your employees is your unpredictable self.

I figured a lot of my emotional problems were due to what they call Seasonal Affective Disorder, or SAD—an acronym I've never liked because if you've really got it, you're a lot worse than *sad*.

Long before I ever took an antidepressant, my version would appear with heartbreaking clarity every year in late September or early October. I'd be on my daily commute—a 20-mile, full-fall-foliage ride with few cars and no traffic lights. As I rounded the corner at the top of the highest hill shortly after sunrise, I'd be overwhelmed by illuminated color, a crystal-clear view of Mount Monadnock, the *thought* that all was all right in my world, and a sinking feeling that started in the back of my brain and flowed like a viscous dark ooze into the pit of my stomach. The experience of it being so unspeakably bright *out there* and so dark *in here* is one of the most humiliating aspects of depression. As if you've failed the universe itself.

Still, I figured that as long I could count on things getting better in the spring, I could "tough it out" with the help of my tried-and-usually-true forms of self-medication.

This delicate balance finally fell apart one day in January 1999 when I made a presentation to a very skeptical audience. I was fearless. Inviolable. I swayed them with hyper-articulate rants. People who asked challenging questions wished they hadn't. Back at the office, I heard one of my employees say to another, "I wish you'd been there. It was remarkable." She later confessed it was also kind of scary.

That afternoon, I was in the conference room reviewing an interesting project with a client I really liked. Yet I spent the whole meeting trying not to bolt from the chair, rush back to my office, close the door, and start screaming.

That's when I accepted the obvious: I never knew who was going to wake up in the morning, walk into the office, show up for meetings, drive home, walk back in the house at the end of the day, or eat dinner that night. Would he be charming or sullen? Talkative or monosyllabic? Warm and gracious or irretrievably remote?

My wife Wendy had been encouraging me to have a psychiatric evaluation for years. But I had resisted. That night I came home and said I surrendered. I'd had enough. By then, the classic indicator of depression—*interferes with your normal functioning*—would have been a walk in the park. Interferes? Interferes? We're talking a major blockade.

A few days later, I saw a psychiatrist and started taking antidepressants. It took a few months for me to really stabilize, but, for the next six years, they worked as advertised.

☙

Fast Forward: 2005. I sold my business in 2001, continuing as Creative Director until the end of 2004. I also regularly did some work for an import business I'd started many years before with a friend. But he pretty much ran it, so I had a lot of flexibility in terms of how involved I wanted to be.

In other words, after 20 all-consuming years in business, I was free.

The first eight months of 2005 were one continuous burst of creativity. Ever since college I'd been writing for *other* people, always saying that I'd do my own writing someday. Now there was no excuse.

I started by taking a six-week trip in a VW Camper down the East Coast, over to New Orleans, and back: a classic right-of-passage for any writer.

Adventures like that are never as romantic in the doing as in the dreaming. Much of the time you're just driving…driving…driving…not quite sure where you're going, and less sure where you'll stay when you get there. It's not so much lonely, as intensely solitary. Still, you get to meet people you've never met and will never meet again; stay in places no one you know has ever heard of; and have experiences that become legends in your own mind by the time you're five miles out of town:

There was the night in Appomattox when I was the only guest at a B&B owned by a very young, very sweet, and very Christian couple. That morning at breakfast, I was alone in their elegant antebellum dining room, eating a very large breakfast and reading a very large book about the Salem witches. Needing more coffee, and not wanting to bother them, I walked into the empty kitchen where I saw a Bible lying on a table opened to that day's scripture. The witches and I beat a hasty retreat.

There was the three-day weekend I spent at a Best Western next to I-95 in South Carolina, waiting for the local repair shop to track down a new fuel pump for my old van. It was a town where the women were large and strong, the coffee was small and weak and, since the weather was raw and my bike was my only form of transportation, options for food and entertainment were pretty limited. (By the way, what's the deal with boiled peanuts?)

There was the BBQ place at a campground in Mississippi with fantastic food, great blues, and character that wouldn't quit. I can still feel the heat of the raging fire pit I stood in front of, eating ribs and drinking beer, a Northerner from another planet, surrounded by exuberant dancing—a synchronized conga line of blacks in one group; a separate but equally enthusiastic group of whites in another.

That was just the beginning of how I took advantage of my newfound freedom.

In April, Wendy and I went to the South of France with friends for one week and then up to Paris on our own for another week. A week of Rodin, Picasso, and Chopin. A week of trees in shameless bloom, churches in fading splendor, and architectural details that nobody's noticed since some anonymous stone cutter chiseled the final touches hundreds of years ago. A week of strolling along the most famous river in the world, wandering the most famous cemetery in the world, visiting the most famous bookstore in the world...and having tea with its legendary owner. A week of bread, cheese, coffee, and wine. Bread, cheese, coffee, and wine. But, most of all, for both of us, a week of reminders that creativity is its own reward.

In June, I took another solo trip, meandering out west to visit friends and *rendezvous* once again with myself. I stayed at a dank, dripping campsite in Woodward, Pennsylvania, next to one of the largest stalagmites in the United States. At Waunee Bay State Park in Ohio, next to some kids who drank bad beer and listened to worse rock & roll. At a Super 8 in Madison, Wisconsin where I spent the evening at a bar near the state capitol, drinking gin with politicians and watched the NBA Playoffs. At the Municipal Campground in Adrian, Minnesota, where I biked to Iowa and back before dinner. At a long-forgotten motel in Pierre, South Dakota where I ate the most memorable dinner of the entire trip.

I gazed into the eyes of Thomas Jefferson and the soul of Crazy Horse. I watched the moon rise over the Mississippi in Bismarck, North Dakota, and morning light race before me across the plains of eastern Wyoming. I approached Big Timber, Montana, in the shadows of the Crazy Mountains.

One day I reached into the side pocket of my van, pulled out the receipt from a campground in Buffalo, Wyoming, and wrote on the back: "I cross borders. I traffic in ideas."

Through it all, I wrote with a vengeance. Day after day. Hundreds of pages.

When I wasn't writing, researching, or traveling, I was working around the house, going on long bike rides, doing a little bit of freelance work, and hanging out with Wendy and friends.

To say that all was right in my world would be an understatement. After all those high-stress years, I was pretty much doing whatever I wanted whenever I wanted to do it. I was an extremely happy camper.

☙

My calendar from late summer 2005 doesn't seem the least bit ominous: I went to a few meetings in New York. Wendy and I spent a long weekend with friends on a lake in Maine for our anniversary. I went to the horse races in Saratoga, won a few bucks, and knew when to quit. A large group of us went on our traditional Labor Day ±60 mile bike ride. I completed the first draft of a novel.

On reflection, I want to shake myself by the shoulders and yell, "Look out!" If nothing else, it would have shown solidarity with those in the process of being devastated by Hurricane Katrina. During August, I did notice some familiar suspicious shadows building up the area behind my eyes and cheekbones—although, like floaters, you can't see them unless you really look close, and even then they stay just on the edge of your field of vision.

Two appointments, however, catch my eye: August 17th and September 12th. They were with a bodyworker who combines a Zen master's unrelenting insistence on being in the "now"—a place I've always enjoyed visiting, but don't necessarily want to live—with the equally relentless work of an experienced Rolfer: 1½ hours of deep massage that can be so intense you see flashes of light.

At the end of both sessions—and for hours afterwards—my mind was quiet, my heart was open, and my body was completely relaxed. It felt like a whole lot of thought patterns had been shattered and visceral memories unleashed...ancient prison doors of the psyche swung wide open...the inmates, free at last, running every which way.

I've often wondered whether those two rolfing treatments helped trigger the inevitable series of synaptic disconnects that culminated in what I call my "breakdown." The idea of seeing the guy again still makes my *psoas* tremble. But at least that pain was fleeting.

∞

I also had a couple of appointments with my acupuncturist. I recorded the first session on August 28th. It suggests that my condition was already a little more fragile than I remember:

> D: The shadows are right there...it's physical.
> A: Are you sleeping?
> D: Yes. It's not manic.
> A: So right now it's depression about to cascade down on you. How long have you been off your meds?
> D: Since late spring.
> A: We'll check your pulses...
> D: I feel like I don't have any. [As she begins putting in needles I jump.] Guess I do.

16

D: So what is the Chinese medicine take on depression? They don't call it depression, right?

A: No, the blood storing that part of the spirit holds its consistency and intention.

D: Of the depression?

A: No, just of your engagement with life. There's so much in the blood that needs to be nourished to keep moving. So people use the depression as a buffer sometimes.

D: Because they can't get enough nourishment?

A: Yes, because they can't get enough nourishment so their blood gets congealed...this whole plexus of energy around your wrist is really opening up [from the needles] and the energy will flow better because by treating here we're actually treating your heart meridian.

D: What do you find with people on antidepressants...does the energy have to go around the meds? Or does it work with them? Does that make sense?

A: Hopefully, people get more use out of their antidepressants. As the stagnation and congealed blood heal up, they can take less and less of the meds. The point is to get the maximum use of the smallest amount of the chemical.

☙

Everyone has totems and talismans. Seashells, pieces of jewelry, ancient carved figures. Autographed baseballs, tickets to rock concerts, and mementos of all kinds. My totems not only speak to me, they tend to speak for me; as if representing perspectives I don't have time to represent myself—or, if you want to get neurotic about it, that I'm not quite willing to fully "own."

In mid-September I lost one of my long-term traveling companions, a small stuffed cat named Ferguson, on a trip to Washington, DC. Probably on a bench outside the National Museum of African Art. Ferguson was blessed with far more wisdom than those tiresome "bobble-heads," and as much compassion as the ubiquitous statues of the Buddha (my generation's version of plastic lawn ornaments). He was intensely curious about everything and assumed, with an uncommon degree of wisdom and guilelessness, that people were always well-intentioned…although perhaps occasionally a bit misguided.

Lest you think this too childish a subject for such a serious book, you should know that Ferguson's presence and insights were held in high esteem not just by me, but by all who knew him—and his fans were legion.

In the clutches of hypomania, being two minutes late for a meeting simply causes heart palpitations. Hearing a strange sound from the back of your car triggers thought patterns resembling those of a squirrel in a blizzard trying to remember where the hell he put that last acorn. Losing something irreplaceable adds an obsession that blocks out everything, *everything* else.

When I realized Ferguson was gone, I wrote to the Washington Convention Center, Smithsonian, Southwest Airlines, Manchester airport, and anyplace else I could think of. In these emails, I implied that this "toy" had belonged to a small child—to their credit, most people took my request very seriously.

In retrospect, the fact that, at the age of 53, I was sending emails *complete with pictures* to the Smithsonian Museum (your tax dollars at work) seems bizarre even to me.

They say that psychosis is losing your mind. When I lost Ferguson I lost a small, innocent, and stable part of mine.

෴

On Sunday, October 2nd, 2005, I managed to get up and speak briefly at a memorial service for my aunt…even though doing so felt like trying to single-handedly pull back a 20 foot–high curtain on the stage of a one-man show. There was no longer any question I needed to start taking Celexa again. But, the next day I was flying out west for a writing workshop, and didn't think it would be a good idea to wrestle with potential side effects while 2,000 miles from home—several hours of which would be at 35,000 feet.

On Sunday, October 9th, 2005, John Lennon would have been 65. (Imagine *that.*) I was 53 years, four months, and one day. I woke up early in the morning and got on a plane in Montana for the trip home, arriving in Vermont just before dinner—early enough to take a walk up the road, and dose myself with a little reassuring fall foliage.

The week that followed would prove to be one of the most devastating and transformative weeks of my life. But, at the time, I just wanted to have dinner, catch up with Wendy, go to bed early, get up early, start taking my meds, and get back to my writing.

On Monday morning, October 10th, I cut that half of a 40 mg tablet, swallowed, and went to work.

I did the same the next morning and went to the dentist. One cavity. I made another appointment for two weeks later to have it filled.

By Wednesday, October 12th, I was already getting a little edgy from the meds. That's a common side effect when starting up. Fortunately, I had already made an appointment with my acupuncturist, and figured a treatment and some Chinese herbs would help me stay calm as the Celexa kicked in. After the session, she warned me to be careful.

On Thursday, October 13th, I decided to up my dose of Celexa a little. This isn't as reckless as it sounds. Finding the right dosage is a matter of trial and error and often, as long as those side effects aren't too bad, increasing the dose can help get you past them and reach a therapeutic level. Since I wasn't feeling much except minor edginess from the 20 mg, I decided to ramp it up a bit. Fortunately, in spite of my increasing urgency to feel better (and legendary addictive personality), I simply took another 10 mg instead of a fistful, bringing my total daily dosage to 30 mg—just half of what I had been taking the previous spring.

By Friday, October 14th, I was beginning to suspect that things were not quite right. I knew that Selective Serotonin Reuptake Inhibitors (SSRIs) like Celexa can cause some weird flutters in your stomach, but I didn't realize it could feel like the string section of the New York Philharmonic was tuning up in your gut. So I went back down to 20 mg and double-checked the insert to make sure that my side effects were common, if a bit extreme. Unfortunately, I didn't have a lot of time to get past these "minor" symptoms because I was about to get on another plane—a business trip with my partner to California. And the idea of taking off while jumping out of my skin was somewhat troubling.

Figuring I probably couldn't reach my psychiatrist on a Friday afternoon, I called my regular doctor and, in my most matter-of-fact voice, asked if I might have some Valium to get me through the plane trips. He was kind enough to give me a prescription for a few 5 mg tablets.

On Saturday, October 15th, I called my partner and said I *might* not be able to join him on the trip to California.

By Sunday, October 16th, things had gotten totally out of hand. Even armed with my precautionary stash of Valium—most of which I'd already taken—I knew I couldn't go. It wasn't fear of flying. It was fear of *being.* On the way to the airport, my partner and his wife— two of my oldest friends—stopped by to see how I was doing.

A few years later, I asked her what she saw that day:

...You were in sweats and you looked like you had just pulled three all-nighters in a row, hair a mess, needing a shave, disheveled. That was just the outside. The inside felt even worse. You were having a hard time relating, a furtive look in the eye, like where is the closest rock I can hide under, and not a lot of eye contact. The sense I got was there was an amazing number of strings or cords of energy all around you and they were all tangled up in knots, so much so that I couldn't

clearly see you—both see you psychically and actually see you in the physical, like there was fog all around you.

Did you lie down on the floor, near the dining room table? Perhaps. Were we unsure what was really happening? Yes. Did we deep, deep down feel huge concern? Even fear? Yes.

I turned to Wendy to get a read and she was circumspect, protective. Perhaps she didn't really know either, and perhaps she was afraid and freaked. I remember her in the background that morning. I was unsure what was really happening, and remember feeling kind of fuzzy. It took me some time to really see the gravity of this situation. Some of it I dismissed because I didn't want to or couldn't process what was happening...we don't have any structures for when someone comes unhinged...I think it took months before I really understood (from the outside, of course) what was happening to my dear, dear friend.

Make Up Your Mind

He felt like somebody had taken the lid off life
and let him see the works.

—DASHIELL HAMMETT

☙

ON MONDAY, OCTOBER 17, 2005, I got up off the floor, called my psychiatrist, told him I'd gone back on Celexa and, in a masterpiece of understatement, reported that things weren't going very well. He asked if I was taking anything that might be causing an interaction. I told him about the Chinese herbs. He told me about serotonin overload.

"Serotonin overload?" a good friend asked disbelievingly a few days later—this being a guy who had done some serious self-medicating in his day…a day that continues up to the present. "Shouldn't that be a good thing?"

Perhaps…if all we were dealing with were the hippocampus and a few of the other animals running around in our brains. But there are a whole lot of other physical processes that involve serotonin, including little things like blood pressure and breathing. Plus 90% of all serotonin receptors are in your stomach where they play a major role in digestion and trigger things like "gut feelings." Thoughts really *do* affect our digestion, which can affect our moods, which can affect our thoughts again. In fact, scientists now consider your stomach to be like a "second brain."

So if you jack your serotonin system up too much too fast, both your first and second brains can start behaving the way that, well, mine were behaving.

This official diagnosis is "Serotonin Syndrome," and it can be fatal.

While my case was nowhere near that severe, it obviously triggered a significant imbalance. In fact, my behavior was remarkably similar to that of someone who "flips out" on LSD.

No knock on Chinese herbs, my psychiatrist explained, but there was a chance they were working synergistically with the Celexa in the serotonergic system (say it three times fast). He suggested I go off them, at least until I had stabilized on the SSRI. He encouraged me to continue taking the Valium if I needed to calm down and sleep. No encouragement needed.

So there we were. Me and Wendy. She wasn't working that day. I wasn't functional that day. Both of us were stuck in the house with someone who wasn't a whole lot of fun to be around. Someone who took up a huge amount of psychological space.

She suggested we drive to Northampton. Just to get out of the house. Go somewhere. Change of scene.

I sat in the passenger seat the whole way, hands folded, head down, monosyllabic responses—like grandpa being taken out of the home for a Sunday afternoon drive, physically incapable of dragging my awareness from the lump in my throat, darkness behind my eyes, and a tenacious agitation that could attach itself nettle-like to the most trivial sensation or thought.

I followed her into various stores. Did my best impersonation of someone who was interested in something…anything. Survived the terrifying decision of whether to have a cappuccino or a latte. And, in general, tried not to make Wendy's life any more distressing than I'd already made it.

Most masters of meditation would undoubtedly disagree, but being aware every moment isn't always all it's cracked up to be. One of the "blessed curses" of being in a state like this is that wherever you go, there it is. No special technique required.

☙

A week later, I called my psychiatrist back and told him that, even though I'd stopped taking the Chinese herbs and remained at a very low dose of Celexa, I was still extremely anxious, had frequent crying jags and, most important was running out of Valium. He said to stop taking the Celexa and come see him the next day. I arrived in his office, agitated, emotional, tearful. With that wired feeling in the pit of my stomach. Five pounds lighter than I'd been the week before.

There's a particular sensation when you're about to get something you crave. The mouth-watering anticipation of being mere inches from that first bite of your favorite dessert. The equally moisturizing sensation of being on the verge of some serious—or not-so-serious—sex. The gentle relief in the back of your throat when you pour yourself a beer after work and begin to lift it to your lips. The more intense urgency of being on the verge of taking that first drag of a cigarette or line of cocaine. (Those days may be well behind me, but just saying the words evokes the sensation.)

When you're that bent out of shape, watching your psychiatrist write a prescription is just as intense. You believe with all your heart that you're one trip to the pharmacy and a dose or two away from relief. Realizing he *isn't* going to write that prescription is heart-breaking. But my doctor, undoubtedly wisely, said I'd better stay off the Celexa until "I felt myself again." Valium was a consolation prize. It meant we couldn't even get to square one until we had a chance to sort out the pieces.

To my surprise, things got better immediately. In email after email I announced my return to the free world:

October 26: "I stopped taking the Celexa yesterday and actually got a real night's sleep."

October 27: "I am starting to feel 'normal' and am even considering joining you guys this weekend for that bike ride."

October 29: "While I hesitate to ever describe myself as 'normal,' I'm pleased to report that I am once again functional and, occasionally, even have a sense of humor."

October 30: "I've gone from the most excruciating mental state I've ever experienced to one of the calmest, most productive, optimistic. Jeez, the mind..."

On Halloween evening, I sat in the same chair as I had the week before, in front of the same fireplace, drinking what might as well have been the same glass of wine, and waiting with childlike (i.e., immature) anticipation for the first trick-or-treaters. We never get trick-or-treaters. We live too far out in the country. But it's an excuse to buy a bag of serotonin-boosting chocolate. After eating my fair share and asking Wendy to hide the rest, I reflected on how my every thought was a mirror image of the week before:

Last Week: Oh, God, how am I ever going to face another human being?
This Week: Maybe I'll go downtown and see who I run into.

Last Week: How can I possibly call to make an appointment to get snow tires?
This Week: How could I possibly have been too frazzled to make a simple appointment?

Last Week: I can't sleep. I can't sit still. The wind is howling. A tree might fall on the house.
This Week: What a great night's sleep. Wind whipping around...I could lie here forever.

Last Week: It's like every thought brings up a wave of emotional nausea.
This Week: What a relief just to be able to think straight again.

Last Week: How can I possibly live another 1, 2, 20 years with this inside me?
This Week: I will never, never, never, think that anyone with any kind of mental illness should ever "snap out of it."

In retrospect, my "Last Weeks" sound a bit melodramatic. And my "This Weeks" too simplistic. Regardless, when you're walking that razor-sharp line between the two, you can't help but be aware that behind each thought of opportunity, interest, or humor, lies a shadow of hopelessness, apathy, or sorrow. And, more happily, vice versa.

∽

When you bounce back from a major mind-altering experience, you get a "double shot" of pleasure from the most ordinary activity. You not only enjoy what you're doing, you enjoy the fact that you're enjoying it.

I was particularly thrilled that I was able to have interesting conversations with strangers in crowded rooms—a high-wire act of such courage and creativity that I received standing ovations from other parts of my brain: He walks! He talks! He makes sense! He doesn't have to rush off and go to the bathroom to pee or throw up! Chatting up the car repair guy? Piece of cake. Having lunch with friends who thought you were about to be committed? No problem. Contentious meeting? Bring it on!

In early November, our daughter was sworn into the bar at the Vermont Supreme Court. I approached this important event with a certain trepidation. While breaking down in tears could be mistaken for relief that the law-school loans were in her name and not ours, it would have been a tough sell. Obviously, this day was about *her*. I would have felt guilty if my emotions were in any way a distraction. Turned out there was nothing to worry about. I was able to enjoy the ceremony—even the part that involved standing in a crowded room for a half hour or so—unencumbered by emotional baggage. I was just a guy who was proud of his daughter. And loved her a lot.

Even on my annual Thanksgiving walk with my brother—our once-a-year, no-holds-barred download about parents, wives, children, jobs, health, and the fate of the New England Patriots and

Philadelphia Eagles—I cavalierly described my recent depressive/
dysphoric episode with the confidence of one who had worked his
way down a fairly treacherous slope. Someone who'd figured out
where the rocks were loose and likely to give way, where a hidden
spring could send you ankle deep into the muck, or an inviting
branch could lend a hand but might not hold.

I'll never be that cavalier again.

HELL

DON'T FORGET WHAT YOU'VE LEARNED:
THE MORE PERFECT SOMETHING BECOMES, THE MORE SENSITIVE
IT BECOMES TO BOTH GOOD AND EVIL.

∽ *Inferno, Canto VI (106–108)*

WE MUST GO DEEPER INTO GREATER PAIN...
FOR WE HAVE NO TIME TO WASTE.

∽ *Inferno, Canto VII (97-99)*

FOR A GUY ON THE PATH TO DIVINE RAPTURE, DANTE SEEMS mighty opinionated, if not outright malicious. In the course of descending through the nine circles of Hell, he condemns former friends and enemies, popes and princes, the famous and infamous—with a degree of vindictiveness that should earn him a prominent place in his own Fifth Circle of Hell, where the terminally angry mix with the sullen, slothful, and despairing.

Inferno is a young man's book. He isn't even forty when he first puts quill to paper, and he's been thinking about it for several years before that. At that age, your angers still feel justified…your frustrations of other people's making. All the major and petty inconveniences of your life are caused by external events, not your own inability to transcend them: If only she loved me. If only they paid me what I deserve. If only they'd change that law. If only he'd stop sabotaging everything I do.

And so Dante badmouths Cleopatra and Helen of Troy for the sin of Lust with as much hell-fire-and-brimstone passion as would any repressed soul (especially one who's in exile, continually exposed to temptation while separated from the wife he doesn't really like). He condemns three contemporary popes for fraud and a whole lot of faceless clerics for avarice with the same self-righteous indignation of a modern voter saying we should "throw the bums out." He unceremoniously tosses a former acquaintance into the Circle of Gluttony for no apparent reason other than it lets Dante use the guy to predict the results of political intrigue in Florence after the events, thereby painting the poet's actions in the best possible light. And he shamelessly scatters others he disapproves of into whatever hellish realm he feels is appropriate for their perceived sins of commission or omission.

Dante tries to pin these judgments on forces way beyond his control—including Virgil, St. Augustine, and the entire foundation of medieval Christian theology. He even throws his beloved Beatrice under the bus—claiming that the only real reason he's being allowed to witness these things is that she wants him to come back and tell people what awaits them if they don't shape up.

But the book is written in the first person. There's no way Dante can escape the fact that he chose the examples. The fact that one of the most judgmental people in the history of the world should get a "Get out of Hell Free" card defies logic.

There are, of course, two sides to every story—in Dante's case a whole lot more than two. He knows full well where his epic journey is heading. In fact, one of the most amazing things about The Divine Comedy is that he's able to carry this spectacular holographic vision in his head for twenty years—like a warrior who learns to run with a mouthful of water and not lose a single drop. Sure, the basic Hell-Purgatory-Heaven, sinner-penitent-saved storyline has been around for centuries. But the comprehensiveness of his vision and the vividness with which he presents it is unlike any attempted before. And he knows it.

It's a little prosaic to point out there's at least a little lust, gluttony, avarice, anger, and fraud in us all. And there is no way—I'm throwing down the gauntlet here—that you can write that intensely about the entire spectrum of human experience without embracing it in yourself.

Having your mind spin wildly out of control makes that a little easier. You begin to appreciate how other people's strange behavior may be rooted in similarly random brain chemistry. You may not approve. But you understand.

By the time Dante is working on Paradise, he'll be in his fifties, no longer a young man by the standards of those days. Unfortunately, copies of the Inferno and Purgatory will have already begun circulating. He has to endure the curse of all writers—he can't take it back. He's stuck with those judgments. He's still stuck with them 700 years later. It's the price he has to pay for planting the seeds of a new vision without alienating contemporary readers and patrons.

Still, he'll manage—particularly, later in *Purgatory*—to hint at the most glaring inconsistency in the entire Judeo-Christian vision: You can't get into heaven with duality boots.

It's all well and good to say that on the Day of Judgment, Christ will take the good (and appropriately penitent) with him to Paradise, while the evil remain in eternal Hell.

But who are we to judge what Christ or God or the Cosmos will ultimately do? How can we experience unconditional love if we put conditions on it? How can infinite mercy be so finite?

I understand that, for centuries, theologians have made careers of dissecting these points—frequently getting stuck, if not impaled, on them in the process. All I know is that a guy like Dante—a guy who so deeply understands the struggle to simply be a human on earth, a guy who knows both depths of despair and manic visions of rapture, a guy who knows the struggle between good and evil within himself (and how hard it is to reconcile them) would have never condemned anyone to suffer in eternal Hell.

He knows that he hasn't really been sent to put all these people in their place. He knows that, as the famous quote at the start of this chapter implies, the more he can experience and share their grief the more perfect we all become.

"Follow me! Follow me!" I hear him calling. "We'll get through this!"

The Church may have wanted those sinners out of the way for all eternity. But there was no way Dante would have abandoned them down there.

He wasn't going to abandon me there either.

Looking for Traction

You have to navigate your own personal catastrophe.

—Anonymous

⌒

By January 2006, I was completely back in the belly of the beast. Establishing a pattern that held, with occasional brief remissions, for more than a year:

At 4 A.M....5 at the latest, I'd awake in a panic. My throat and heart vibrating. Racing. Sometimes in my solar plexus, too. I was still exhausted but couldn't go back to sleep, although with enough sedatives I might get another hour or two. When I did get up, I'd get outside as fast as I could. Sometimes I strapped on snowshoes and headed for the woods. Usually I'd just go out the front door and start walking. Walking. Walking. Walking. Exactly a mile and a half down the road to where it forks, and then exactly a mile and a half back. Fast. Real fast. Sometimes breaking into a run. Back. Shower. Maybe ending with a blast of cold water. Coffee. Yeah, I know, but while physically stimulating, it was emotionally comforting. Usually decaf. But sometimes the real deal. Some days, I had places to go and people to meet. Which I managed to pull off with various degrees of success. All professional depressives have their own techniques. For me, it took a combination of careful planning (where I'd be and when), occasional rehearsal (oh yeah, this is how humans are supposed to behave), fairly constant dissembling (even to myself, if possible), and, when all else fails, enough willpower to fake it until you're alone again. Or at least back home. Where there was no need to pretend otherwise. Around 9:30 or 10 every night, having staggered through another day, I'd go to bed. My mind comfortably numbed by a drink or two and an hour or so of empty TV.

I'd sit up for a while against the pillows, listening to Wendy get ready for bed, knowing that for at least a few minutes my emotions wouldn't be a burden to either of us. I didn't want to read—it was too hard to focus anyway. I'd just sink into the luxurious sensation of knowing I could now rest from the battle, no matter how briefly. Like a piece of chocolate you keep rolling around on your tongue until the last taste bud releases its hold, I'd roll around in that drowsy state as long as I could—exhausted, but knowing that the demons were done for the day. They had no fight left. I could drift off whenever I wanted. As hypnagogic images arose, I'd rouse myself enough to enjoy a few more seconds of conscious relief. Those moments were delicious.

Unlike Hamlet, it was the sleep of sleep I craved (not death), but he nailed the feeling:

> ...by a sleep to say we end
> The heart-ache and the thousand natural shocks
> That flesh is heir to, 'tis a consummation
> Devoutly to be wish'd.

My sleep would be light. But that was okay. I also loved waking up...as often as possible...in the middle of the night: midnight, 1, 2, 3; the sweet realization that I could fall back asleep before the jitteriness again reared it's chaotic head in the early hours of dawn. Which, inevitably, it did.

⤫

Even though an unexamined life might not be worth living, an examined one can be too painful. One warm-ish day that winter, I sat on the screened-in porch in the back of my cabin, drinking a cup of chai tea, very spicy, a lot of cardamom. Trying to generate some inner fire. I went in to get my laptop and sat there, forcing myself to write...to dissect the moment, as if that would give me some power over it. Instead of cowering, I'd look it right in the eyes:

The soundtrack is the steady just-above-freezing and even-warmer-in-the-sun drip drip drip of snow melting off the roof.

A nuthatch is working upside down on the almonds in the cage-like feeder. Carefully avoiding the slightly rancid oat-cake cookies. The chickadees have taken over the platform feeder like they own the place—as if squirrels were figments of their imaginations. They wish.

I got my best bird feeder for $2 at a tag sale. I had to turn it around so I could see the birds better. This means they have to fly right at the window, stop, hover, and do a 180° turn to get at the food. At first, there were a few minor window collisions—no harm done. But now they do it gracefully.

Two or three chickadees work the feeder at a time, bickering a little as they make space for new arrivals. Drops of melting snow drip off the roof onto their heads. They don't seem to notice. One just scooted the nuthatch away to see what the problem is with oatcakes. Hmm. They don't taste all that bad. Well, on second thought, sunflower seeds are better.

Birds don't dwell on the fact that perfectly good bird feeders have been turned the wrong way by some oblivious human; they don't ask why any self-respecting bird would ever want to eat rancid oat cakes. They're sort of like ancient storytellers. Comedy. Tragedy. Whatever. There's always a good excuse to burst into song.

The sun is prism-ing some purples and blues through wispy clouds. It already seems a little higher in the sky. Maybe that'll help. Maybe. I doubt it.

I've been looking for some traction. I've been looking for some ground. I've been looking for a pill I can take or a thought I can have. Something that will last more than half an hour or so.

The opposite of depression isn't happiness, it's inspiration. Having your ideas and energy pour forth, instead of sitting there, stagnating, cut off from the world. The angels ascended and descended on Jacob's

Ladder. Circulating the energy of creation. Being unable to even put your foot on the first rung is, is, is…

∽

The scariest thing about Hell is that it's the same old same old. We may not remember exactly what those poor souls did to deserve being frozen in whirlwinds, whipped by horned demons, or dunked in boiling blood—let alone having their heads screwed on backwards…a punishment I consider particularly savage. But, whatever they did, it's the fact they have to endure their torments *for all eternity* that really gives me the heebie-jeebies. I mean even being enveloped in the arms of your beloved (see Second Circle of Hell—Lust) or eating maple sugar candy (see Third Circle of Hell—Gluttony) could get old after a while.

I don't mean to romanticize the state. There's nothing romantic about it. Our fascination with our own or other people's suffering is always a little prurient or, to be generous, like that of a child who is fascinated by something scary…in large part to reassure him or herself she won't be similarly afflicted.

Sometimes I'm concerned that, by writing this book, I'm "profiting" (wouldn't that be nice!) from my own pain. But when I ask Wendy whether, in retrospect, I've been overstating my symptoms, she says that, if anything, I've been understating them.

∽

In the Fifth Circle of Hell, the sad, depressed, and gloomy are eternally mired in the swampy mud of the River Styx. While I knew the feeling, I managed to cling to the assumption—then belief, then desperate hope—that my condition was temporary. While I'd never experienced this intense an episode of crazed instability before, I was confident that some medical intervention—Western, Eastern, Northern, Southern…who cared?—or act of cosmological mercy would soon end this particularly virulent journey into my personal Hell.

Over the first few months of 2006, I tried just about everything. Acupuncture, amino acids (SAM-e seemed to help a little—the others seemed to just make me more jazzed), B vitamins, Bach Flower remedies, t'ai chi, some yoga, avoiding caffeine, avoiding sugar, eating more protein, avoiding carbs, and so on. They all seemed to help and then not. Like my system couldn't get any traction. I was still spooked by the idea of going back on meds. All I wanted was a little light at the end of the tunnel. Moments of feeling normal would trigger irrational optimism, followed by heartbreaking crashes.

When you're in that state, rational thought seems incredibly naive. The world is riddled with minor glitches, each of which is just waiting to build hurricane-like into a Class V disaster: elevators whose doors pause a second too long before opening, people whose names you've forgotten walking toward you, appointments you're five minutes late for, checkbooks that don't balance.

Your car doesn't start? Forget it. You're toast.

Every few days I'd crack completely. Utter hopelessness. Crying jags. I'd scream my bloody head off. Play squash as hard as I could. Sit in the sauna too long and then go into the shower and turn on the cold water full blast. Anything to earn me a few minutes of peace.

All I remember is trying to act normal; trying to act normal; trying to act normal.

By early spring, however, it became pretty clear that my uninvited emotional tenants, whom I'd been trying to evict using those various medications and therapies, had signed a long-term lease, were beginning to rearrange the furniture, and had no intention of being evicted. It was time to get out of Dodge.

Road Trip

Black care rarely sits behind a rider whose pace is fast enough.

—THEODORE ROOSEVELT

☙

DRIVEN BY A LITTLE BUSINESS and a lot of mania, I got into my 1990 VW pop-top camper in March, 2006 and started driving towards southern California. I harbored secret hopes that some warm weather and spring sunshine would cook the agitated depression out of my system.

I was neither Jack Kerouac nor Neal Cassady. I was fueled by neither cigarettes nor amphetamines. I just had to keep moving. As if, in some kind of Einsteinian thought experiment, if I could drive as fast as my brain was racing, it might appear that the latter was standing still.

I typically drove 500 to 600 miles a day, during which I'd try to settle…settle on anything: which radio station to listen to, where to eat, when to eat, what to eat, where to pull over to nap, whether I *could* nap. When to call Wendy. *If* I should call Wendy. If I'd be able to call *anybody* without my agitated unease spilling over and drowning us both. Usually, I'd stick to emails at the end of the day. So I could edit out the more pitiful parts. Not that I was fooling anybody.

As I drove, I'd occasionally dictate random observations into a digital tape recorder, obsessively transcribing my words each evening. If only to feel I was accomplishing something, *anything*.

I think about people with PTSD. What do I know about their suffering?

I think of friends who have been incapacitated by drugs or mental illness. What do I know about their suffering?

I think about my own last 6 months, during which stringing together a few moments, minutes, or hours has been such a relief. Only in those moments—after maybe a week of constantly dealing with this physical anxiety-without-object—do I realize that I'm in pretty deep myself.

March 15, 2006: Dummerston, Vermont to Morgantown, West Virginia. 637 Miles. Beware the Ides of March. Snow flurries. Blue sky. White, puffy fair-weather clouds incongruously threatening. The sun rising over New Hampshire hills as I round the cloverleaf onto Route 91 South. Wind blowing hard enough to send a warning shot of adrenaline as I cross the bridge over the West River.

Sometimes I'm dealing with the agitation. Sometimes I'm breaking down in tears. Sometimes I'm just happy to be here...and a little concerned for my sanity. It's a fine line.

The speedometer breaks shortly after I entered Pennsylvania. Can't go over 62 miles per hour. That's not fast enough.

The labels...this is mania, this is depression, this is agitation...just make it more difficult to get out of the boxes they're slapped on.

Crossing the Susquehanna River near Gettysburg. Skirmishes breaking out all around me; the ghosts of Lee and Lincoln on my flanks. Caesar falling in the Forum...2052 years ago today.

Route 68. Rolling hills from 1200 to 2800 feet. Up and over, up and over. The VW slows to 50. That's not fast enough.

The sun sets oversize, full orange behind light haze as I come into Morgantown.

Maxwell's, 1 Wall Street, Morgantown, West Virginia. Dinner for $13.52. "Sinfully Nutty Tofu" for $8.50 or "Chicken Pie" for $9.50. Who in their *right* mind could make a decision like that?

The moon rises oversize, more pale-orange than yellow, above the Hotel Morgan as I climb the breathless steps up to the University. The view is stunning. The students are oblivious. I am invisible.

At some point you have to realize you can't blow on your own embers.

March 16, 2006: Morgantown, West Virginia to Morton's Gap, Kentucky. 556 Miles. Okay. Everyone who's been to Morton's Gap, Kentucky raise their hands.

Just as I thought.

After checking into a motel behind a truck stop, I go for an out-and-back bike ride. I prefer loops. Most bikers do. Especially guys. It's a corollary to the not-looking-at-maps thing. You only do an out-and-back when you're in the middle of nowhere, it's late in the day, and you realize that if you get lost you might be literally in the dark; or you find yourself in an area with lots of strange dogs (and perhaps even people) who aren't used to bikers and might consider you fair game.

Ordering Irish Whiskey in Kentucky is like saying the Sh'ma under your breath while everyone else says the Apostle's Creed. Which is something else I've done. Fortunately, tomorrow is St. Patrick's Day, so they take pity on me and find some Bushmills. I pass on the corned beef and cabbage.

The ~~mornings are the hardest. I always cry a little—not about anything; just something in the throat that flutter~~s. It's begun to feel natural, like brushing my teeth. Feel cleaner afterward. Should brush more often.

The evenings are best. Probably the whiskey and/or the exhausted relief at having survived another day…and/or the anticipation of sleep.

William Styron wrote:

> *The evening's relief for me—an incomplete but noticeable letup, like the change from a torrential downpour to a steady shower—came in the hours after dinnertime and before midnight, when the pain lifted a little and my mind would become lucid enough to focus on matters beyond the immediate upheaval convulsing my system. Naturally I looked forward to this period, for sometimes I felt close to being reasonably sane…*

Earlier today, past Lexington, Kentucky, I repeated, "I feel great" for ten minutes or so and had my first few calm moments of the day. I tried that same mantra an hour or so later. But this time my mind vehemently disagreed. It became like some kind of discordant bluegrass call-and-response.

March 17, 2006: Morton's Gap, Kentucky to El Reno, Oklahoma. 768 Miles. There's no legitimate reason to drive 768 miles by yourself in a VW Camper. Especially one with a reputation for blown gaskets, leaking fluids, failing fuel pumps, and countless other things that bump, grind, shriek or—worst of all—make no sound at all before stranding you in the middle of nowhere. A place that, perversely, can be very claustrophobic. Still, I keep going.

Between satellite radio coverage of a murder trial in Vermont of all places (I paid particular attention to how the wife allegedly drugged her husband with Ambien before killing him. Huh, maybe I should give it another try), a very good Michael Chabon resurrection of Sherlock Holmes, and occasional rock and roll—primarily an homage to St. Patrick's Day from U2, Van Morrison, and Sinead O'Connor—I keep going. Sometimes wondering what I'm doing. Other times wondering why I'm doing it.

I figure I'll spend the night close to Oklahoma City; see if I can pick up any illuminating vibes from one of America's many Ground Zeros of fear.

Under the circumstances, I've been paying a lot of attention to March Madness. Rooted for West Virginia last night, since I'd stayed at home court the night before. I feel like an honorary Mountaineer.

Turns out there's also an NCAA *wrestling* tournament going on...and it's going on in Oklahoma City. Who knew? On my fourth or fifth call looking for a room, the motel guy says unsympathetically, "Hey buddy, there aren't *any* rooms in Oklahoma City tonight."

"The NCAA?" I ask, now in the know.

"That and the big Farm Show."

(I didn't know about the big Farm Show.)

You'd think a guy who spent all that time and money buying a used VW camper would, upon learning this, cop to the fact that he's gotta stay in the back parking lot of some Walmart, open up the pop-top, and huddle in his sleeping bag as the temperature drops into the thirties, stumbling out at 3 A.M. to pee and see stars. Instead I keep driving. And calling motel after motel. Finally, thirty miles past Oklahoma City, this voice says, "You got a bed." It feels like I'm starring in a Motel 6 ad. After handing over the credit card, signing the form, and returning her cheery smile with a wan one of my own, I go to the room, turn on the TV and start writing. I keep thinking I have to be in some modicum of balance to write. But actually I don't. I can keep writing just like I keep driving.

March 18, 2006: El Reno, Oklahoma to Roswell, New Mexico. 468 Miles. Fifty three years, nine months, and three days after appearing on planet earth, I finally get to meet my people…in a place where humans make parodies of themselves in the process of trying to make parodies of "aliens."

I have many deep insights while walking around Roswell:

Humans make a lot of money off said aliens without paying any royalties—something which could have some pretty interesting unintended consequences.

It's perfectly clear who the real aliens are.

If they are here to possess our brains, they're in for quite an unpleasant surprise when they get a hold of mine.

On my way here, I drive past White Sands National Monument where they tested the first atomic bomb. And we're afraid of *them*?

While driving I continue to listen to Michael Chabon's *The Final Solution* in which he points out how the blitzkrieg would expose both the rats *and* the small treasures that were hidden in the bombed buildings. That's what cataclysm does. Hope he's right. About the treasures, that is.

March 19, 2006: Roswell, New Mexico to Lordsburg, New Mexico. 317 Miles. On the way out of Roswell, a friend calls and tells me that

Teddy Roosevelt line about the Black Care. I laugh and tell him that the Black Care seems to be having a pretty easy time outrunning a VW Camper.

I've tried to avoid any blatantly New Age perspectives, but sometimes it seems that everything is a manifestation of my inner state. Just after I hang up, I see an arch of dark clouds with the sun shining through in the center. Like I'm about to enter heaven. I'm not about to enter Heaven. I'm about to enter Las Cruces, New Mexico. But I do manage to find a decent lunch and latte there, although only after many quizzical looks and finger pointing from people who'd never met a dysphoric manic from Vermont. By later in the day, the cognitive dissonance returns with a vengeance and, for reasons I still don't understand, I check into a motel in Lordsburg, New Mexico—a town that's only one "u," one "e," and one half-decent restaurant away from being my salvation.

I'm staying here based on the twisted rationale of the road rather than common sense. I'm not due in Phoenix until tomorrow. And I don't have another 600+ mile day in me. Even restless agitation has limits.

So here I am, stranded at a Best Western in a dry, cold, windy, lifeless-on-Sunday town in southern New Mexico. After checking in, I go for a jog. I hate jogging, but think it might get the agitation out of my throat. It doesn't. So I come back to the motel, take a cold shower, and do a few muffled screams—keeping it down so I won't scare the family in the room next door.

I just had a shot of whiskey, a Valium, turned on the TV, and am now doing my best imitation of a post-modern existentialist. Who knew that Teddy Roosevelt was depressed?

March 20, 2006: Lordsburg, New Mexico to Phoenix, Arizona. 305 Miles. There are very few things from those two years that I really regret. Sure, some of the things I did were maniacally stupid. And I did cast a pall over certain events that deserved better.

But I do have some regrets from my visit to my godfather in the somewhat depressing Phoenix suburb of Sun City.

Larry was a youthful 94-years-old at the time, a well-respected,

old-school labor organizer who was still flying around giving rab-
ble-rousing speeches at Steelworker conventions. Faced with intolerance, insensitivity, and/or idiocy (usually real, but occasionally
perceived), he would get a guided-missile look in his eyes and start
verbally eviscerating the offender.

Still, he was among the most lovable and loving people I know.
I'm sure he didn't approve of my long hair in college, many of my
subsequent life choices, or even how I used a chain saw, but those
eyes just couldn't quite maintain that penetrating glare with me,
and his heart couldn't ever manage to get fully behind the criticism.
Being his godson forgave more sins than I care to remember.

During my visit, he told me his stories about organizing textile
workers in the 1930s, steelworkers throughout the 1940s into the
1970s, and even the ferry workers at Martha's Vineyard. This was a
guy who, as soon as he retired and moved to Arizona, started organizing retired union members, appalled by their inexorable political drift to the right.

I'd heard most of these stories before; many were full of brag-
gadocio and exaggeration; a few of his perspectives on people I
knew—including my father—were a little skewed; and, of course, I
could barely get a word in edge- or other-wise…which was a relief
under the circumstances. But, hey, that's the whole point of hanging out with people who've been around longer than you have…
especially when they have something to say that's still important
for you to hear.

So I regret that part of me was always wondering how much
longer I could sit in the chair across from him without jumping
up, moving my body somehow, screaming. I regret that part of
me was always wondering how I could come up with an insightful, coherent, or even relevant response when so much of my attention was always being wrestled back to earth by this weight I
was carrying.

I'm sure my mother had made some reference to my bafflingly
fragile state in one of their occasional phone calls. But I'm equally
sure that he would have considered it an affliction that, while troubling in someone you love, should simply be overcome—whether

through medication, hospitalization, or preferably, sheer will. Certainly, he had more to be depressed about than I did. Most of his comrades in arms had died. Most of the citrus trees that surrounded him and my godmother Lil when they moved there, had been replaced with developments.

That was, of course, the last time I saw him. I don't regret forgetting the stories. I'm terrible at remembering stories. I just regret not really being able to be there.

I know full well that this regret is more for myself than for him.

March 21, 2006: Phoenix, Arizona to Santa Monica, California. 402 Miles. The trouble with listening to books on CD is that if I miss a single sentence, I have to go back and play it again. And again. And again. Until I can keep my attention there for the entire five seconds it takes to comprehend it. A combination of obsession and a tenuous grasp on the literal.

Susan Orlean has traveled more and to stranger places than I ever will. And writes about them better:

> *There's nothing that has quite the dull thud of being by yourself in a place you don't know, surrounded by people you don't recognize and to whom you mean nothing. But that's what being a writer requires…I know where I'm heading. I'm heading home. But on the way there, I see so many corners to round and doors to open, so many encounters to chance upon, so many tiny moments to stumble into that tell huge stories that I remember exactly why I took this particular path.*

I hear that, burst into tears, pull into the next rest area, and look at the display maps of Arizona Highways, hoping that somehow they'll tell me where I've been and where I'm going.

Something in me just hasn't surrendered yet. There's too much to take in…too much to know. You can't know every little thing. You can't be aware of every little thing. I have a Talmudic brain and I'm trying to grasp instead of experiencing. I'm trying to remember things without even seeing them. I'm worrying my way across America, trying to parse out the lives of all the people I see…and mine. What are they doing? Why? What am I doing. Why?

Most of the time I don't know where I am. I don't know where I'm going to sleep. I don't know where I'm going to get a cup of decent coffee. I don't know the names of the plants. I don't know the names of the mountain ranges. The people in the cars passing and being passed feel so insubstantial.

It's a fool's errand. But who better?

March 22, 2006: Santa Monica, California. I emerge from the Arizona desert late in the afternoon, white-knuckle the van down various LA expressways at rush hour and find my way to my cousin's house in Santa Monica. The next morning we take a walk in the Santa Monica hills with her jet-black retriever.

Like most geographically-distant relatives, we rarely see each other, but are inexpressibly close. Once we get past the basics—in particular, what our kids are doing and how they should meet each other someday but probably never will—we get down to the serious business of our shared emotional gene pool. My father described it thirty years ago, in a welcome-to-the-world letter to her one-year-old son: "I guess what I'm trying to say, and I'm not saying it very well, is that this family is emotional, but tries to keep the fact a secret." (My dad treated all children as adults—he wasn't always so generous with actual adults.)

Secret isn't really the right word. We can be extremely sensitive and compassionate. We just don't wear our hearts on our sleeves and aren't all that fond of public displays of psychosis. More important, we're all committed to finding humor in virtually any situation, no matter how dark. So, while my cousin and I both have a vague idea of what the other has gone through over the years, neither of us is aware of the severity or how our respective families dealt (or are dealing) with it.

We also spend some time speculating about the degree to which our siblings, cousins, and children avoided that particular family gene (up to 100%) and trying to track it back through several generations.

"Remember how *he* used to sit there in that chair like he had never moved and never intended to...?"

"*Her*? She died before I was born, but I have this picture...she's standing with her hand on some kind of wrought iron gatepost holding flowers—so beautiful—but her head is tilted a little left and down, and those eyes...I know those eyes...I *have* those eyes."

"Now *that* guy...he was never depressed a day in his life! Probably adopted!"

"I used to wonder about *her*. But that wasn't depression. Or if it was, she channeled it into the fine art of loving intolerance."

"Now *he was* a drunk. No question..."

"Cut him some slack...he was married to *her*."

And so we laugh our way through our family tree.

We don't bother talking about the so-called Depression Gene (5-HTTLPR) which, allegedly, makes it easier to transform stress into major depression. Considering that some of these ancestors took considerable risks getting out of Lithuania and Romania during 19th c. pogroms, there was certainly plenty of stress going around.

But we know that nurture and nature are just two of *many* sides of a three-dimensional coin. And we've both paid our dues.

March 23, 2006 to March 26, 2006: Anaheim & Laguna Beach, California. You'd think that a Natural Foods Expo going on within a precious-crystal's throw of Daffy and Grumpy, wouldn't be the best place for a manic-depressive. But, actually, as outer events go, it goes pretty well.

First of all, things happen way faster than my brain can keep up with or run away from. So, I'm constantly distracted from the discomforting signals being sent by errant neurons.

Second, there are a lot of people selling products that use top-secret natural processes to extract top-secret vital components that contain top-secret energetic vibrations that, if taken in precisely

the correct top-secret dosages and sequences can help even a bla-
tant psychotic like myself. (While I don't have a chance to try everything, the free ice cream and chips cheer me up quite a bit.)

People constantly come up to our booth and ask deeply per-
plexing philosophical questions about the products my partner and
I are selling: "Is it all natural?" "Does it have _____?" (Fill in
blank with whatever natural ingredient some magazine just said
would either shorten or increase your lifespan.) "Is it cruelty-free?"

In spite of my beleaguered cranium, I feel compelled to inject
these repetitive conversations with some contrarian, albeit well-
meaning insights.

"Well, depends what you mean by all natural," I respond. "You
know...no artificial ingredients...stuff made from petrochemicals,"
they explain. "Petrochemicals come from way-ancient plants, you
know," I point out, feeling an uncommon solidarity with primor-
dial ooze.

"Ingredient X?" I respond thoughtfully. "It's hard to get it
out of the formula, because it's one of the primary ingredients
in water. Besides, what did oxidants ever do to you?" (It even
takes me a few seconds to understand what I mean by that.)
"Cruelty?" I ask with, I admit, a certain degree of indignation.
"Have you ever heard a flower scream when you pick it? Believe
me, it ain't pretty."

When the next person comes up, I switch gears and explain that
our products actually are all natural, cruelty free, and don't have
any of that nasty ingredient. I'm not trying to deceive anyone. I just
like entertaining different points of view—if you haven't noticed.

⁓

Just up from downtown Laguna Beach, California there's a long,
narrow oasis of calm in the midst of the touristy storm. It's called
Brown's Park. You'd think it was just an ordinary alley except for
the mosaic brickwork wall and the bronzed chairs, table, and book
at the entrance. The boardwalked alley leads to a low ironwork

railing that looks out over the Pacific. In the center is a poem that's written in wrought iron and set in a stained-glass frame:

> *In this fleeting moment*
> *what extravagant respite*
> *as booming surf speaks its*
> *mystical passage across*
> *the undreamed depths.*

I come upon this railing just before sunrise one morning in March 2006 during my jittery daily stroll. The poem...the view... the sounds of that surf...I know I should feel some fleeting extravagant respite. But I don't. It's like being given a gift you can't figure out how to unwrap. If anything, the experience just emphasizes the divide between the poem's spirit and my own.

I try, really I do. I take ten deep breaths with my eyes closed and then open them to the "booming surf." I do a few basic t'ai chi moves, with a yoga Salute to the Sun thrown in for good measure (even though the sun is in the opposite direction). Ultimately, all I can do is take a lot of pictures to try to at least capture the experience I seem incapable of having. If only I could focus on the outer scenery as ferociously as I do the inner.

March 27, 2006: Laguna Beach, California to Las Vegas, Nevada. 290 Miles. Las Vegas is a great place for an agitated depressive. Shaken, not stirred. Because the agitation you feel inside manifests all around you—that insistent drive for the next moment, born of intense dissatisfaction with this one. Just as the vibration in my solar plexus is on alert 24/7 to demand "just one last" gasp from my exhausted adrenals, so the town is always trigger-hair ready to demand just one last gasp from the slightest human fascination, compulsion, addiction, or obsession. The town truly never sleeps. Even at dawn, it tosses and turns. I feel right at home: The endless piped-in music. The insistent smell of fake flowers. The dazzling pumped-up colors of real ones. Guys polishing floors. Dealers polishing chips one by one.

Monuments to and from the past rise again—daring you to mock their pretensions. The Arc de Triomphe. Eiffel Tower. Caesar's Palace. Luxor Pyramid.

Bob Dylan is playing here soon. Waylon Jennings is playing here soon. Wayne Newton, Don Rickles, Barry Manilow and guys I've never heard of are playing here soon. What, no women? I walk into The Imperial and G-l-o-r-i-a is playing right now.

Revolving doors keep opening for you. Taxis keep waiting for you. Ramps and stairways keep appearing to shuttle you back and forth across the Strip.

Guys keep handing out cards with pictures of naked women. They'll come to you. Direct to your room. Totally nude. $49. Special. Anything you want.

Anything? What I lust for is a trick I doubt they've ever turned.

March 28, 2006: Las Vegas, Nevada to Zion National Park, Utah. 175 Miles. I love picking up hitchhikers. I know people think it's dangerous. But, most of the ones I pick up are in far more desperate physical and psychological straits than I am. We exchange the usual pleasantries: Where you going? Salt Lake City. I'm going over toward Zion. Just drop me at Route 9. Can I smoke? Sure. You want one? No, quit a while ago. But you go ahead.

He then lights up and dives in without further preamble:

Hitchhiker: This guy picked me up...I'd gone in to get a cup of coffee. And he says what's your game? And I said, I don't gamble. And he said, "Well you're going to gamble today." And he stuck a .45 in my ribs and pushed me out the passenger side door and they shot him to death...
Me: [shocked] Who shot who to death?
H: The security guards shot him to death. We parked out in the open parking lot. And he's got his gun.
D: So they saw his gun and shot him?
H: I rolled out of the car and yelled, hey this guy's got a gun and they shot him. Just unloaded on him.
D: Unbelievable.

H: I mean nothing personal but I've already been shot, I don't need to get shot again.

D: [laughing, thinking he's kidding] When were you shot?

H: He shot me an hour earlier right below the kneecap.

D: You mean you knew this guy?

H: Well, we'd been riding together since Salt Lake.

D: And why did he shoot you the first time?

H: We'd just got gas. I started to get out and wish to hell I would have. I wouldn't a got shot…He's twice the size of me, stronger than hell. But he's all hot, eating pills and smoking dope.

D: Oh I see [laughing nervously…]

H: And we didn't need no gas until he got to Caesars and he was almost empty. In the parking lot. Got to the door and I'm thinking yeah, I know these security guys. They just gunned him down. Son of a bitch. I got my leg taped up and glued. Cops said well we'll bag him and tag him. You know that dumb son of a bitch had $1200 in his wallet. He was just going down for the night. He had a room at the Tropicana, and he was going to stop at Caesars, the Pyramid, and the Tropicana and then he was going to leave early in the morning. He had a wake up call all ready at 5 or 6 in the morning.

D: Ended up dead.

H: Right. And this cop dug the .45 out of the corner of the car door… low velocity…the ballistic man's been here, and he's got all kinds of shell tricks. He's got chambers he puts in that barrel. I knew the guy had one gun. I didn't know he coulda had ten in a second. He had gun parts everywhere.

D: Jeez…so what were you doing in Las Vegas?

H: I spent the rest of the night there.

D: Yeah, but now???

H: Oh this time? I'm on my way home to Council Bluffs, Iowa.

D: What's in Council Bluffs?

H: I live there.

D: You have a place to live there?

H: I've lived under a bridge for almost 40 years.

D: Almost 40 years? Why'd you come all the way out here?

H: I had no winter clothes. Really. But now I'll just suffer through the winter.

D: 40 years? How old are you?

H: 80.

D: No...really? C'mon. Your life? You're not 80.

H: [changing subject] You can follow that dirt road all the way back to the town up there. I was crossing up there one time and an old black guy says, don't touch my pot! He's got a rifle and another guy's got a shotgun. Two kids got...You here to pick our pot? No I'm here to... shit.

D: Sounds like you run into some guns in your line of life.

H: You run into lots of idiots who carry guns. What are you doing out here from Vermont?

March 29, 2006: Zion National Park. It takes an impressively contrarian emotional life to feel claustrophobic about the idea of going to the Grand Canyon.

But I keep imagining my road-weary VW Camper being hemmed and heckled by loutish RVs, throngs of tourists jostling me dangerously close to the edge, and out-of-control scenic-ride planes strafing me on their way to the bottom of the Rio Grande.

Further proof that rational thought isn't my strong suit.

So, I've ended up at Zion—which may be more human-sized than the Grand Canyon, but still makes you feel like you just got unceremoniously shoved into the dispassionate face of God or a reasonable facsimile.

I've spent two cool, drizzly days here, wandering, biking, hiking, and uttering the occasional proforma soul-wrenching scream.

You can see how some native Americans would have been pretty impressed if someone had come along and said they'd been up-close-and-personal with the God who made all this stuff. No knock on Jesus, but it's still kind of hard for me to imagine an intermediary...you just want to worship the cliffs themselves.

March 30, 2006: Zion National Park, Utah to Sedona, Arizona. 303 Miles. I wouldn't say I have unreasonable expectations for my stay in Sedona. My thinking goes something like this:

This place is allegedly one of the earth's big-time power spots. Therefore, I shall be healed.

The true power of Sedona has been enshrouded in New Age babble. I am cynical about said babble and will be taught a valuable lesson in humility. Therefore, I shall be healed.

I've heard that viewing the sunset from the Sedona airport is a transforming experience, complete with Native American shamans banging on drums. And, while many tourists will be there, I will hear the beat of a different drummer. Therefore I shall be healed.

I will be able to escape the maddening crowds by waking up early and taking a solitary walk to Bell Rock, which is a famous energy vortex (that's a good thing, right?) Therefore, I shall be healed.

This morning, after my walk to Bell Rock, having checked off another box on my list of potential divine interventions, I hurry nervously back to the van and drive on.

March 31, 2006. Sedona, Arizona to Phoenix, Arizona. 142 Miles. For the last few days I've been at another trade show; this one at a "destination" resort outside of Phoenix, where I've re-rendezvoused with my business partner, close friend, and partner-in-crime (just two as I remember...crimes that is), along with his wife who's one of my oldest friends and mother of our goddaughter. In other words, we're family...and a fairly functional one at that. So I've been able to relax a bit, secure in the knowledge that they'll hustle me out of harm's way if I start staring catatonically, ranting deliriously, or both at the same time—no mean trick.

Like back in Anaheim, I realize that a trade show isn't all that bad a place for the borderline bipolar. Every few minutes you get to try out your latest imitation of a perfectly sane human being on someone new. If you screw up, you can just mumble an unintelligible but relatively inoffensive comment, and let someone else repair the commercial damage, if any. Next victim! Besides, everyone at this resort is clearly as deluded as I am. I mean the idea of vacationing at a place on the edge of the desert where, except when playing golf, you hunker down in air-conditioned comfort worrying about skin cancer, is easily as wondrously strange as anything that's ever gone on in my head. Every morning at sunrise, driven out of bed in my par-for-the-course morning frenzy, I find myself virtually alone on the trails under some seriously spectacular skies. Early Sunday morning I go for a bike ride. Phoenix looks like a pretty reasonable place to live at 6 A.M. The cars are sleeping.

Still, that ever-present waxing and waning shadow in the back of my throat remains as vivid as any of the colors of those dusty desert sunrises.

April 4, 2006: Phoenix, Arizona to Gallup, New Mexico (via Canyon de Chelly). 452 Miles. A lot of people have told me I have to visit Chaco Canyon in northwest New Mexico to get a sense of Anasazi history and culture and what the local hunter-gatherers were up to back in the B.C.s. They also said I'd be overwhelmed by its mysteries—both geological and human.

Unfortunately, I keep reading that you have to drive miles on hot, dry, rocky roads to get there—which conjures up images of me crawling, skeleton-like, in some ditch as my poor VW van goes up in flames behind me. I may be a poor man's Hunter Thompson, but I have no desire to pose for Ralph Steadman.

So I take the less-traveled road to Canyon de Chelly in Arizona—less spectacular perhaps, but still no slouch in the shock-and-awe department.

At various times during this trip the universe has conspired to give me privacy. Often, I've gone to relatively well-known tourist sites, and there'll be no one else in sight. But as soon as I leave, people appear. Same here. I'm alone, the only non-native at the bottom of the White House Trail, able to converse with the spirits in peace and quiet. But as I leave, at least a dozen people pass me, talking in loud voices, including a mother and father followed by two pouty teenage girls who also appear to be looking ferociously inside. Hearing an incongruously modern engine, I turn around to see a guide in an open-top jeep with another family, plowing through the stream, seemingly oblivious to the silence they're shattering. On the way out, I stop at "Mummy's Lookout." As soon as I arrive, two old women move off the rocks...I have no idea where they disappeared. Generations of Navajos haunt this valley.

April 5-6, 2006: Gallup, New Mexico to Albuquerque, New Mexico. 140 Miles. As a famous man once said, "One man's miracle is another man's matter of fact...and vice versa." So I tend to treat the ordinary as if it were extraordinary and the extraordinary as if it were ordinary. Some people think that all petroglyphs were drawn by ancient Native American tribes. Others think they were drawn by, or at the direction of, the kind of aliens that even Arizona can't deport. Some might be graffiti created by wild packs of drug-crazed teenagers sometime between 1000 A.D. and 1969. This morning, a friend with some serious shamanic chops takes me to see some petroglyphs that she's experienced as power spots, so I can dig down deep and see what I come up with.

Picture this: Two relatively normal looking 50-somethings, wearing hiking boots, jeans, and zip-up sweatshirts—no beads, sacred stones, amulets, or feathers in sight—strolling across and occasionally clambering up and down a rocky hillside. They're catching up, telling stories, laughing—doing what old friends do.

Every once in a while, she stops: "I know it's around here somewhere. Ah..." She proceeds to direct me to a rock that has a strange drawing on it. I walk over to said rock and instinctively start issuing your run-of-the-mill blood-curdling screams. After 30 seconds or so, I take a couple of deep breaths and follow her to the next one, continuing our conversation as if nothing's happened. Perhaps a casual comment: "That was a good one." We do this a half dozen times, until we're caught up on marriages, kids, and friends...and I'm spent. Then we go back to her house where I have a cup of coffee and talk to her husband about the stock market.

From my perspective, screaming with a friend in the desert isn't a whole lot different from going to some guy I never met, telling him all my problems, and having him give me a pill. Besides, back in the 1970s, a guy named Arthur Janov popularized "primal scream" therapy. And there are almost as many places where you can "rebirth" these days as there are maternity wards.

Still, it was quite a walk on the wild side. And while we spent a lot of the time laughing at ourselves, we were dealing with something that was bigger than the both of us.

It's true that none of the human figures I saw in those petroglyphs looked particularly sad to me. (Although it did feel that some of them seemed to be having a hard time expressing themselves...coulda been kids doodling for all I know.) Certainly people in other ancient cultures—Egypt, Hindu, Chinese, etc.—weren't strangers to depression. They suspected it was caused by everything from sorcery and bad humors to being forsaken by gods. One God in particular...Job was even a less happy camper than I am.

Back then, they tried the same kind of cures we do today—magical spells, hallucinogens, acupuncture, herbs, strange potions, and trepanation (that's the drilling into your brain thing).

So, who knows what subtle changes in my brain chemistry we effected or demons we exorcised?

April 6, 2006: Albuquerque, New Mexico to Pratt, Kansas. 552 Miles. I spend 200 miles on US Route 50, which is known as "America's Loneliest Road." Obviously, they haven't traveled my neural pathways. I left Vermont three weeks ago. And while I had various places to go and people to meet, and have passed through or stayed in ±20 states, my real destination wasn't on any map. It was a place where some Taos juju, Roswell alien, California healer, Las Vegas strangeness, or beatific vision of the Goddess of Sanity (*Beiwe*) appearing in a Toto-esque Kansas windstorm (or some combination of these) would inspire my neurons to do the job they were made for. Although my van is blown hither and yon in those vicious Kansas whirlwinds, my mind and heart stay stubbornly true to course. The hellish smell of sulfur fertilizer says it all. Purgatory would definitely be an improvement.

April 7th, 2006: Pratt, Kansas to Marion, Illinois. 659 Miles. A year before this trip, while driving in northern Michigan, I picked up a 24-year-old flashback of a 1960s hitchhiker. He was on his way to the annual Gathering of the Rainbow Family which describes itself as "the largest non-organization of non-members in the world." In the course of our conversation, he spoke glowingly of his base commune back in Cape Girardeau, Missouri.

I'd thought back on this conversation occasionally over the last year until—through the miracle of mad mental alchemy—this, to me, obscure town on the Mississippi had been transformed in my imagination into a cross between Cambridge, Berkeley and Lourdes; and was filled with people who combine the authenticity of Huck Finn with the wisdom of the Dalai Lama and the healing power of Mother Teresa.

Throughout this trip, I've been secretly plotting how to make an innocent detour to this Valhalla. By the time I leave Pratt, it has become an obsession. I'm certain I'll soon be surrounded by laid-back aging hippies and their young acolytes, dancing to live music, trailed by hints of marijuana and incense. I'm convinced that my enlightened spirit and tortured heart will prove irresistible to their every healing desire. I picture a comfortable futon. Maybe a massage. Cool, healing unguents (whatever they are) gently rubbed into my third eye. At the very least, some wine, tofu, and cute girls…or, as he put it, "righteous women."

All I know is that the ephemeral hitchhiker was clearly an incarnation of some powerful Native American medicine man, and my encounter with him was a sign that something magical will happen to me in Cape Girardeau.

Arriving on its outskirts, I blast through the commercial strip and soon reach the heart of the city where I begin slowly driving around looking for the countercultural hub of this heaven-on-earth.

But there's nothing going on. A huge mural blocks the Mississippi. The few people wandering around look as disappointed as I am. The only real action is at two huge billiard halls and an Italian restaurant where a troublingly well-behaved 50's-style wedding party is gathering on the street.

I check out a few hotels but can't imagine checking into any of them. I check out a few restaurants, but can't imagine eating in any of them.

I've already driven 12 hours and 615 miles. Some of which, by the way, is on the "Trail of Tears." Only to arrive in a town where the most illuminating sign claims that it was the birthplace of Rush Limbaugh.

This is the last straw. Clearly, I am now so disconnected from my intuition that I'm deludedly spinning profound portents out of simple encounters with stoned hitchhikers.

My disappointment is as palpable as it is irrational. I have to get out of Girardeau. And so I cross the river into Illinois where, after yet another hour of driving, I check into a nondescript hotel near the Marion Penitentiary, which is populated by about 50 death-row inmates as well as members of the Aryan Brotherhood, El Rukns, the Mexican Mafia, and D.C. Blacks.

I feel like I've escaped.

April 8th, 2006. Marion, Illinois to Somerset, Pennsylvania. 678 Miles. Over the course of 7,633 miles, you listen to a lot of music. When blended with a hair-trigger emotional life, this can easily lead to terminal indulgence in feelings that can only be considered maudlin, mushy, mawkish or way too many of the above. Because you inevitably end up thinking all those songs are about you. Which they're not. After all, if several million people feel exactly the way you do when you hear a song, you have to question just how special you are. That solidarity thing is one of the great things about rock concerts, but can be problematic in memoir since you're in serious danger of using phrases like, "soundtrack of my life"— at which point you might as well go find another line of work. While you'll probably never lose anyone's respect by saying you feel empowered by listening to *Beethoven's Fifth Symphony*—or even *Sympathy for the Devil* in a counter-intuitive way—the casual comment that *We Built This City on Rock & Roll* makes you feel the immensity and glory of creation is bound to raise an eyebrow. And, rightly so. At the same time, if you play your cards right, you can simultaneously experience the solidarity of those we-are-one emotions and your individual piece of the kaleidoscope. Which feels kind of good. Although, whether that excuses playing *The Rose* or *Pachabel Canon* at any more weddings is open to debate. I have to admit, however, that there's a song called *Long December* by Counting Crows that inevitably brings tears to my eyes. It begins with the singer, clearly a big-time depressive, hoping against hope that this year will be better than the last.

Three months into 2006, it's increasingly hard for me to keep that hope alive.

The song comes on just as I'm leaving Marion, Illinois on another section of the "Trail of Tears."

April 9th, 2006. Somerset, Pennsylvania to Dummerston, Vermont. 561 Miles. I arrive in Somerset, Pennsylvania well after dark, and check into the Budget Host Inn, where, to my dismay, I discover that not all shabby hotel rooms are alike. Some are even shabbier than others. After finding an ice machine deep in the catacombs—you have to take a big ice pick, both to defend yourself and to chop off pieces—I briefly calm my 14-hours-on-the-road nerves with a Jameson's before staggering out like some refugee from a Sartre novel in search of comfort food. I find it at The Summit Diner: scrambled eggs and home fries, served by a waitress who's overweight, pierced, tattooed, and savvy. It only takes her a couple of minutes to know everything she needs to know about me—just leave the guy alone, call him "honey"—more kindly than usual—and go give the other customers a hard time. The dinner's $4.50. I leave a $2 tip.

Now I'm driving off into the sunrise on Route 219 toward Johnstown, and then cutting over toward Altoona which I can see in the valley off Route 99. Another town. Another world. Another universe I'll never explore. Later, as I drive along Route 220, barely avoiding Penn State, I'm confronted by a series of signs that give me pause: "Beware of Aggressive Drivers." "Beware of

Tailgating." "Keep two dots apart." (Don't ask.) Culminating in: "Attention Drivers: High Crash Area." They have no idea.

After 230 miles, I stop at the Turkey Hill Convenience Store in Wilkes-Barre, Pennsylvania to get gas. My last stop. Just over 200 miles to Vermont. I fill the van, check the oil and transmission fluid one last time, and go into the store to buy a protein bar, Smart-Food, and a bottle of Starbucks coffee with a big cup of ice (the only alternative when you can't find the local coffee shop).

I come back out, get into the van, take a big bite of the protein bar, open the popcorn, and turn the key. The van doesn't start.

I try to stay calm. Maybe I'm not in "Park." Yes I am in "Park." Try again. The van doesn't start. Try neutral. Nothing.

I remember how we used to crawl under our old 1970 Volvo and tap the starter with a hammer. I find the crowbar and work my way under the van. Can't find the starter. Check the manual. It doesn't know where the starter is either. Call my repair guy back home. He tells me it's pretty hard to get at the starter without pulling out the engine or transmission or something equally intimidating.

I get back in the van and turn the key. Nothing. I take three deep breaths. Nothing. I try ten breaths. Nothing. I get out and start walking toward the store. Turn around and try again. Nothing.

I tell myself not to panic. That it's okay. What's one more day after three weeks? I don't believe myself for a minute. This is apocalypse now. I go in and ask the cashier if there's a repair shop nearby. She points to a tire place just a few doors down, which I'd managed not to notice.

I go back and try to start the car again. Nothing.

Reluctantly, I go over to the shop and point at the van. They say they can probably tow it over and take a look later in the day. "Later in the day???" They say not to worry…if it needs a starter, they can definitely get one tomorrow. "Tomorrow???"

I hand him the key.

I decide that I should go for a bike ride to calm my nerves. Odd-ly, there's a bike shop two doors down from the tire place. I stop in to see if they have a bike map. They don't, but give me precise directions for getting to an area where the biking is good. Unfortunately, I can't pay attention. I'm on the verge of hyperventilating.

I go back to the van. Realize I have a spare key in my backpack. What the heck. Put the key in the ignition. Visualize all manner of positive things. Nothing.

Call Wendy. Tell her I guess I won't be back that night. She's disappointed, but seems a lot more concerned with how I'm taking it than how she's taking it. If I were her, I'd be relieved that I had one more day of peace before my deranged spouse walked in the door. To her credit, I don't hear that in her voice.

I go into the store to apologize for the fact that my car will be stuck there until they tow it. They tell me no problem. (No problem for them maybe.) Go back to the van. Try to start it. Nothing.

I decide to go for a walk before biking. That way I can keep an eye on the van in case it suddenly decides to start itself up and drive over to pick me up and go home. I start walking up a steep hill in a prototypical working-class neighborhood. No one is around—everyone is at work.

At the top, I can see the whole town. Doesn't look like good biking to me. A few blocks ahead I notice a young man talking with an elderly woman. Jehovah's Witness…no question. My first impulse is, of course, to turn in the other direction. But the lady looks so helpless. So I keep walking toward them, watching the drama unfold. She cleverly shakes him off by suddenly turning a corner just as he's about to step off a curb. He hesitates, briefly tripped up by this act of God, whose ways we will never fully understand, until he looks up and sees me—a miracle if he's ever seen one.

By now, I've surrendered any resistance I have left to whatever the universe has decided to throw at me. As he talks, I nod my head and respond with genuine enthusiasm (what happens in a parallel reality, stays in a parallel reality): "Jesus? Sure I've heard of him. Amazing guy. Son of God? No question. Really? Jesus says that? Sounds like good news to me. Huh? Of course I love him. What's not to love? The money changers? Great story. He sure showed them. And the thing with the fishes?…it doesn't get any better than that. Yeah. I know. Me too. Yes. Absolutely…of course. Thank you.

I'll definitely read that brochure. And that one. And, sure, that one. Yes, that one, too. Thank you. Thank you so much. Yes, I'll take a good look. I'm so glad we met. Thank you."

Satisfied he's filled his convert quota for the day, he gives me a big smile and walks away. I turn around and say out loud, quite clearly, so my intention cannot possibly be misunderstood, "Okay Jesus, start the f-ing car."

As I walk down the hill, I invoke the names of several other saints, perfect masters, gods incarnate, and shamans of my acquaintance. I create a universe in which the entire notion of my van not starting doesn't exist. It'd be like anti-matter or something.

I get back to the Turkey Hill Convenience Store, put my backpack on the ground next to the van. Dig calmly around until I find the spare key again. Open the door, get in, toss the backpack on the passenger seat, put the key in the ignition and turn it. No deep breaths or anything. Just turn the key.

God damn if it doesn't start.

∽

Having successfully called upon the intercession of Jesus, Buddha, Isaiah, Dale Carnegie, and Okomfo Anokye (a seventeenth-century shaman) to perform the minor miracle of starting my car, I figured it was only a matter of time before they realized I had bigger fish to fry—and would really welcome their help.

A few weeks after my road trip, I decided to dig up a rock that had been harassing my lawn tractor for years. I approached this borderline boulder with a long iron pry bar, pickaxe, two boards, two shovels, two hands, and equal parts determination and wariness. Slowly, methodically, I began to work my way around it, stopping every few minutes to re-evaluate its emerging size, contour, and depth. Each time, it returned my gaze rather sheepishly. As if it would like to help but, having been stuck there for the last 10,000 years, didn't have the slightest idea how to begin.

Naturally, the rock was bigger and heavier than I'd imagined.

A lot bigger and a lot heavier. But I kept at it, slowly working the edges, finding a ray of hope every time I was able to release one of the many smaller rocks that were wedged up against it; rocks that I could then use as fulcrums to release others. Eventually, I began to get a little wiggle room. Something the rock seemed to kind of enjoy.

I enjoyed it too. A rare balance of body and mind. First one straining, then the other. Instead of one taking charge and beating the other one to a pulp.

Once I got some serious purchase on the rock, I started sliding boards underneath. More purchase. More leverage. More boards. Slowly—to our mutual surprise—the rock began to rise from the earth. And kept rising. Except that, every once in a while, no matter how carefully I levered and pried, it would shift slightly off one of my precarious supports and fall back into place with, seemingly, more determination than before.

Diagnosis

To name an illness is a literary act before it becomes a medical one.

—Siddhartha Mukherjee

౷

YOU KNOW WHAT'S REALLY HARD about writing this book? It's certainly not sitting in a cabin in Vermont watching the snow come down, drinking my version of a café mocha, and listening to rock & roll. That's not hard at all.

It's not trying to transform years worth of erratic journaling, essays, emails, and medical records into one more-or-less coherent whole without sucking all the juice out. That's what writers sign up for every time they pick up a pen or open up the laptop.

Occasionally, it *is* hard to maximize the creative waves that ebb and flow during the day. But by juggling food, research, working out, paperwork, conversations, and coffee, I can usually put in a good day's work.

It's hard, of course, to avoid getting distracted and procrastinated by email and the Internet. But, for me, that's just part of the process. In the old days, I'd light another cigarette or pace the floor.

No. The hardest thing about writing this book is that there's no single word that I can use for what ailed me.

౷

If you have a heart attack, you have a heart attack. If you have cancer, you have cancer. If you have diabetes, you have diabetes. These diseases, horrific as they may be, have names. In general, medical professionals can give you a pretty good description of what's going on inside you, and which medicines or procedures (or both) may help.

What we call "depression" has many names. And—despite all the talk of serotonin, norepinephrine, dopamine…SSRIs, MAO blockers, and tricyclics…cognitive therapy, shock therapy, and alternative therapies—diagnosing and treating it is a crapshoot. As far as I'm concerned, the most trustworthy healers, whether western or eastern, traditional or alternative, are those who have the wisdom to admit they don't really know *what* it really is, but do have the knowledge, experience, and sensitivity to have some idea what might help.

William Styron, whose *Darkness Visible* describes his version of depression with more excruciating exactness than any diagnostic manual ever could, wrote that "brainstorm" is a more accurate term…"a howling tempest in the brain."

I've been called all kinds of things over the years. My official diagnosis is currently Major Depressive Disorder, Recurrent, in Partial Remission. That sounds kind of tame, although during one particularly difficult phase, I earned the term "Severe," which is a little more impressive. I've also been "accused" of having a severe Cyclothymic Disorder . That's a little technical for my taste, although its definition as a "persistent instability of mood" is something to which many people would testify—going back to my childhood when my parents and brother found those unstable moods alternately amusing and annoying.

Agitated Depression, "a state of clinical depression in which the person exhibits irritability or restlessness," is a pretty accurate descriptive term, as are Overlapping Cyclothymia or Double Depression.

As a writer, I'm partial to Dysphoric Mania. It sounds noble, in an early-twentieth century kind of way. The Merck Manual describes it as "prominent depressive symptoms superimposed on manic psychosis." Even better is Melancholia Agitata, which makes me picture myself, hand on forehead, swooning onto a Victorian fainting couch, and twitching uncontrollably until I collapse ignominiously onto the floor.

In Dante's day, I would have been labeled as having *acedia*. That word is unfortunately usually translated as sloth. This may be how it seems from the outside, but it's a far cry—actually many far cries—from how it feels.

I definitely think I deserve a little credit for surviving *akathisia*— the inability to sit still—and *anhedonia*—the loss of capacity to experience pleasure. One time my doctor asked me if I was having any fun. I looked at him as if he were from another planet. Fun? Fun? To me, that was like asking a homeless person if they'd eaten at any good restaurants lately.

This was not fun.

There seems to be some disagreement as to whether I was or am bipolar or not. I know from my reading that in cases of extreme Bipolar I, the highs are way out-of-control higher than anything I've experienced…except perhaps many years ago on hallucinogens…bordering on and occasionally crossing the line into delusion. And the lows are virtually catatonic. While there were times I displayed symptoms of Bipolar II (the lesser of the two evils), my manic phases usually weren't sufficiently psychotic and didn't last long enough to qualify. Besides, my mania was dysphoric; that is, the opposite of, and not as much fun as euphoric. Instead of swinging wildly from low to high, my moods would swing from depressed to intensely, agitatedly depressed.

But if I had to choose my favorite diagnosis, I'd say Melancholic Depression–Severe with Hypomanic Episodes. Just seems like a nice blend of literary and technical, with intense visual undertones—a dark brooding figure in a medieval Doré woodcut next to some shrieking Ruben-esque figure on a nonstop train to Hell.

౷

Big-time depression is way more than extreme sadness. Every psychiatrist, textbook, and pharmaceutical company may draw the line in a slightly different place. But for us case studies, there's no question when you've crossed it.

To use a biking analogy, sadness is like finding yourself at the bottom of a steep hill that you know well. You may be discouraged when you realize you have to climb this hill again, but you just had your bike tuned up, the road's in good condition, you know which gears to use, and are confident you *will* eventually reach the top.

Depression, however, is like finding yourself at the bottom of a real steep hill you've never climbed before. You don't know the road or how steep it gets. Turns out it's not even paved. You have your road bike instead of your mountain bike. The shifting's screwed up so you can't get into the lowest gears. The tires are worn smooth and you don't have any replacement tubes. Or a pump. Oh yeah, I forgot: a bunch of drunk kids drove up the road the night before and threw empty beer bottles out the window, shattering glass all over the place. You have serious doubts you'll ever get to the top.

For me, the line between sadness and major depression can't be drawn based on the quality or quantity of sad *thoughts*. In both cases, they ooze around all the time—appearing in a wide range of inner conversations about things that worry, frustrate, and upset me. In both cases, outer circumstances can fuel or calm these thoughts. Still, specific thoughts aren't the hallmark of the experience.

Nor do I experience the distinction between sadness and depression based on the quality or quantity of my sad *feelings*. In both cases, I can feel hopeless, despairing, and overwhelmed. In both cases, outer circumstances can make these feelings better or worse. Still, specific feelings aren't the hallmark of the experience.

For me, the hallmarks of big-time depression are *physical...visceral*. More than the classic heaviness of sadness, it's a scrim that coats my insides—a swath of sensation that runs from behind my eyes, through my tear ducts, down into the deep base of my throat, through my chest cavity, and into the formless abyss of my gut.

ᡣ

Big-time agitation is way more than a bad case of the nerves. More than a little vibration caused by something that triggers your garden-variety adrenaline rush. It's a high-frequency wave that radiates out from the base of your throat and throughout your whole body, pulsing a new charge every few seconds, with little relevance to or concern for what's going on at the time. ("Oh my God, I don't know whether to get a burrito or taco and the waitress is waiting!!!")

Everybody has phobias. There are certainly enough to go around: ±600 of them—most of which, I'm happy to report, I've never had. For example, I've never been afraid of paper (*papryophobia*), progress (*prosophobia*), or puppets (*pupaphobia*)—although, as a child, Pinocchio was pretty frightening. I'd also prefer not to be in the presence of certain popes (*papaphobia*) or politicians (*politicophobia*), but neither would make me break out in a cold sweat. Remarkably, no one lists a writer's worst phobia (*typophobia*), which rears its frenetic head anytime you realize there's a typo in an email you already sent or a book that's already been publised. (See what I mean?)

I don't think the dosage of my inner adrenaline shots were any stronger than the kind anyone with a serious phobia experiences. The real difference is that, when you're in the throes of agitated depression, you can have paralyzing phobic reactions to just about *anything*—or even the thought of anything...especially anything that can't be remedied *immediately*. And, underlying all those phobias is the fear that someone around you might realize how dysfunctional you really are.

At their worst, the attacks feel like your whole body is under siege, the ramparts constantly assaulted by forces that cannot be denied. When it's over, whether for a moment or an hour, you're in a kind of shock, gasping for breath, relieved, but wary of what the next moment might bring.

∽

True "mixed-states" are more than mood swings. When I'm manic, it's like my brain is weightless. Ideas rise and soar out of it virtually untethered—zipping around my consciousness (and often out my mouth) as if they're tripping across a high-wire. Ideas that roll over each other in exhilarating succession, multiple connections elaborating themselves in waves, often faster than words can identify them.

The subsequent crash, which can come a few hours, sometimes a day later, is a depression like that described above, only cranked up, or actually down, a few notches. When people talk about mood swings, it sounds like a kind of emotional pendulum. To get the full picture you'd also have to knock that pendulum's base around once in a while so those swings remained unpredictable in frequency, duration, and intensity.

I wasn't delusional—well, depends who you ask. And I was rarely catatonic. I couldn't sit still long enough. Rather, I was somewhere in between...and not anywhere for long.

∽

The first step in getting an official diagnosis is to fill out the dreaded "Patient Questionnaire." Instead of pacing the waiting room floor...instead of gazing longingly at the drug company salesperson with his briefcase full of free samples...instead of just slumping in that metal chair with your head in your hands, so disassociated you can't even get interested in *People Magazine* (what *did* happen to Lindsay Lohan?), you have to answer 132 personal questions on a scale from **0** (Not True) to **5** (Very True). Looking back, I seem to have seamlessly careened from painful honesty to shameless denial:

Question #10: Do you ever feel life isn't worth living—that you have a hopeless outlook?

My answer? 5. (Very True.) Fair enough.

Questions #48 / #53: Are you a worrier? Have you ever been bothered by persistent, unwelcome thoughts or images such as…that you would be responsible for things going wrong?
My answer? 1. Not true? Are you kidding me? C'mon, David, you've spent your whole life worried that you would be responsible for things going wrong. From the car not starting to the universe coming to a screeching halt.

Question #126: Do you tend to drive yourself pretty hard, like you need to do just a little more?
My answer? 5. That's more like it.

Question #91 (Everyone's favorite): In the past 12 months, have you had 3 or more drinks of alcohol within a 3-hour period on 3 or more occasions?
My answer? 1. 1??? This isn't a job application, Dave. You're trying to get help. I know it usually takes you four hours…even five, instead of three. But have you seen the sizes of those drinks?

Fortunately, my doctor based his diagnosis on a lot more than this highly suspect information. Here are some choice nuggets from one of my Psychiatric Evaluations:

- Identifying Data: *54Ymarwm; m28, 27y ♀*. No, he didn't suspect me of having a sex-change operation at 28. He was referring to our, at the time, 28-year marriage and 27-year-old daughter.

- History of Present Mental Illness: *Treated for depression for years, but not for mania. Historically: Either off/on; high-energy guy—but "loves my sleep." Ups—few days. Downs—Few hours to days. Currently: Severe Major Depressive Disorder.*

- Substance Abuse History: The notes indicate that he had suspicions of alcoholism but was withholding judgment. I told him that pot was never really my drug of choice. (True.) I admitted that I'd done a respectable amount of cocaine in the 1980s. I told him I had particularly liked it because it gave me *"clarity of thought and vision."* I had a similar fondness for Ecstasy, which, as I remember, gave me that and a whole lot more. For some reason there's nothing about the LSD I took in college, which must have had *some* effect on how my synapses were behaving. But either I was shy about those experiences or he'd run out of room on the page.

- Appearance and Behavior: *Slight build, disheveled, unhappy, poor eye contact, restless, listless, somatic, poor coping skills.* Wendy would probably have added that I needed a haircut.

- Speech: *Soft spoken, flat.*

- Mood and Affect: *Dysphoric, despondent.*

- Thought Process and Thought Content: *WNY (within normal limits).* I'm a little disappointed with myself there.

- Mini Mental Status Exam: *Alert and Oriented.*

- Potential for Destructiveness: *[re suicide]* I told him, *"I wouldn't...I'd just rather be dead than continue like this."* I'm happy to say, however, that I categorically denied having any interest in homicide.

- Strengths: *Likable, intelligent.* Don't worry, they got drugs— or at least side-effects—for that too.

Which brings us to the final part of a psychiatric evaluation: the "Diagnostic Impression." This is an entire category, all its own. To even begin to understand it, we have to go boldly forth where few laypeople have gone forth before: to the infamous *Diagnostic and Statistical Manual of Mental Illness* (DSM.)

The American Psychiatric Association publishes the DSM in a well-intentioned attempt to provide a linear classification system for our multidimensional minds. It's 886 pages long, lists 297 disorders, and sits on most psychiatrists' desks...or over on the bookshelf—

even if she or he just uses the online version. It's as important for establishing their credibility as those diplomas on the wall.

The Manual is based on extensive—one could say OCD—collaborations between psychiatric professionals all over the country. They analyze countless research reports, clinical trials, and various subjective criteria in order to assign labels to what ails us.

While those of us on the other side of the looking glass may rebel against the restraints of these labels, the criteria do at least give psychiatrists some kind of common language for discussing our behavior.

DSM-I was published in 1952, the year I was born. Which I consider prescient and timely, even though I wasn't officially diagnosed until 47 years later. Based on an ever-evolving understanding of how our minds work (or don't), they add, subtract, and merge diagnoses with each edition. If nothing else, this wreaks havoc with computers throughout the healthcare system.

As of this writing, DSM-V is about to be released. While some popular diagnoses may be eliminated or, more likely, lumped together, there will also be more total diagnoses. Many people consider this a plot by the so-called "Medical Establishment" and "Big Pharma" to sell more drugs. But, clearly, they're just suffering from Paranoid Personality Disorder (300.1).

There's a lot of understandable disagreement about what should be included. Like Paraphilia NOS (302.9). While a bad case of paraphilia could easily interfere with your everyday functioning, being sexually obsessed with specific acts or objects seems technically okay as long as nobody and/or no-thing gets hurt. But Paraphilic Rape isn't included, because if you call it a mental illness, then people convicted of it could plead insanity.

While on the subject, I'd like to bring up the issue of hypersexuality. All in favor raise their hands...or something. It's sure a more polite term than what you'd hear in some bars or on talk radio to describe women whose interest in sex exceeds our society's shifting and often self-serving norms. Plus, don't guys also deserve a more polite way of being accused of thinking with our balls instead of our brains? Are they suggesting we should get our Viagra with a side order of Valium? And who was the hypersexual psychiatric clown who decided Hypoactive [low] Sexual Desire Disorder (302.71) and Sexual Aversion Disorder (302.79) *do* earn labels? After all, they say up to 10% of people are simply not interested in having sex. Of course, that doesn't necessarily mean they don't qualify for *Voyeurism* (302.82).

As much fun as it is to poke fun at the DSM, doing so is clearly a sign of Oppositional Defiant Disorder (313.81). More important, it's another reflection of the challenge of treating us. If we're going to talk about this stuff, we have to have a language to do so, and the DSM is a worthy attempt to create that language out of shimmering synaptic whole cloth. And, frankly, the terms are way more specific than *nutty as a fruitcake, retard, head case, loony, mong,* and *bonkers.*

NOTE: The most important thing about the DSM is that it gives doctors a code to put down when they're billing your insurance company. No code...no reimbursement. (And don't forget to check whether your prescriptions need pre-approval.) But I digress. See Avoidant Personality Disorder (301.82).

The key diagnostic tool within the DSM is a five-axis system. For perspective, or because I'm a little too narcissistic (301.81) for comfort, I've included some of the "ratings" I've earned over the years. (Note: R/O = "Rule Out.")

Axis 1 describes the stuff that needs immediate attention: *Major Depression; R/O Bipolar and ADHD.* It seems I was able to stay on just this side of ADHD as well as alcoholism.

Axis 2 offers 10 possible personality disorders, such as paranoid, schizoid, histrionic, narcissistic, obsessive compulsive: *Defer but R/O Panic Disorder and NOS* (Not Otherwise Specified). There was really no reason to rule out Panic Disorder. I think the doctor was just being polite.

Axis 3 labels any general medical conditions that might be affecting your mental health. That's where he mentioned the fact I'd lost 25 pounds.

Axis 4 specifies "psychosocial and environmental problems." At my worst, he wrote: *Severe; wearing on marriage.* It did bend, but it didn't break.

Axis 5 is a "Global Assessment of Functioning Scale," an overall rating of a person's ability to cope with normal life. My worst score was 35. That was depressing for two reasons: (1) I never got less than a B on any test in my life and, more troubling, (2) it was accurate: *Some impairment in reality testing OR impairment in speech and communication OR serious impairment in several of the following: occupational or school functioning, interpersonal relationships, judgment, thinking, or mood.*

Impairment is a pretty word for it.

For those who want to do a little self-evaluation, you can find the complete rating scale on the Internet. Suffice it to say that if you score 100: *Person has no problems OR has superior functioning in several areas OR is admired and sought after by others due to positive qualities,* there's a good chance that, secretly, nobody really likes you.

Whereas if you score 1: *Persistent danger of harming self or others OR persistent inability to maintain personal hygiene OR person has made a serious attempt at suicide,* I pray you or the person nearest you picks up the phone and calls 1-800-273-8255 or 911.

Meanwhile, the rest of us will continue to muddle along somewhere between those two extremes.

∽

Throughout history, people have been wrestling with how to categorize the causes and manifestations of mental illness. Nontraditional diagnoses may not meet the criteria of the DSM, but at least they capture the thing in flight, and give it names that reflect its fluid nature as much as its thing-ness. And they can be as descriptive as traditional diagnoses:

The Egyptians, for example, were suspicious of the influence of the planet Saturn on depression.

Folks like Hippocrates, Galen, and Aristotle would have said my black bile was totally out of whack, and my balance of yellow bile wasn't anything to brag about either.

An "energetic" shiatsu massage therapist explained it in terms of *kundalini* energy:

What's happening with the kundalini…it just gets all the hormones. It travels through the endocrine system. It travels through the central nervous system. So it feels like everything is just moving, moving, moving and there's no place for you to put your feet.

A tarot reader also put it in more occult terms:

The first card we're looking at here is the manifestation of your Crown Chakra area. The head centers. Pituitary, pineal glands. It'll give us a picture of your connection to the Divine right now. [Turns card over] Oh boy…the Hangman.

Which certainly hit the nail on the noose, and was one of few things I found funny at the time.

Mystical and Jungian folks, along with Dante, chalk the experience up to a dark night of the soul—a process of inner transformation.

People who believe that all emotional problems are caused by toxins in our systems brought on by self-destructive lifestyles and poisonous diets, might suggest I'd been asking for trouble…and was continuing to ask for it.

Fire and brimstone aficionados would undoubtedly see me as someone with a demon that needed to be cast out (especially if they found out I gave credence to tarot readings). Sometimes, it did feel like being possessed. Although, ultimately, I was able to make this friend of the devil a friend of mine.

I don't try to diagnose other people, but usually I can see it in their eyes. At first, it's just the way they look in more than out. As the depression goes on longer or gets more serious, it invades the edges: drawing squint lines that resemble the "crinkles" of a smile and expose hints of skeletal structure. Eventually, you can gauge its severity just by standing near them.

One time I was at a workshop with a bunch of people, all of

whom were very supportive of this haunted figure walking among them. There was a similarly afflicted woman there whom I'd known for years. I saw it in her eyes. She saw it in mine. There was nothing to say. But it made us both feel a little better. Like, if she can take it, I can take it. If I can take it, she can take it.

Then, there's a picture I took of myself alone, in the middle of an Arizona canyon. In the middle of nowhere. All I see are the eyes. Looking through them, I can still hear my thoughts as they raced back and forth from "I'm still here" to "I'm okay" to "Oh, God, when will this end?"

But, of all the non-traditional diagnoses I received, the most accurate was, of all things, astrological.

The "fault," dear Dave lies not in you, but in the stars. By July, 2006, "How long is this going to last, oh Lord?" had tied, "What's should I try next, oh Lord?" and was threatening to overtake, "If you got something to say, why don't you say it, oh Lord?" on my list of top 10 existential questions.

Which, from a theological point of view, represented at least some kind of progress for a lapsed Jew. So, when someone suggested I visit her favorite astrologer, I was more than happy to do so.

I like serious astrologers. As much for their descriptive as predictive powers—both of which have little relation to the mass-produced newspaper, magazine, and short-form web variety.

In other words, I'm not talking about the, "your partner has different ideas how to spend money," kind of description. (Wendy and I both know *that*.) I'm talking: "Pluto is coming opposite your ascendant, and will soon start moving toward your descendant… it's kind of like a death and rebirth. And all you can do is surrender and align with the meaning."

Even in a therapeutic context, I'll take that kind of talk any day over: "What I hear you saying…" I *know* what you heard me saying. I just heard me saying it. But I never heard me saying that my problems were caused by Pluto. Besides, the experience *did* feel a whole lot like a death and, hopefully, rebirth.

She went on to explain that the purpose of this time in my life

wouldn't, "always be clear at the moment. So," she continued omi-
nously, "all your knowing is not useful here."

That's tough love for someone who prides himself on being
able to scale tall cognitive dissonances in a single leap of logic. Still,
in some small way, it put my mind at ease. At least *it* wasn't going
to have to take *all* the heat for this thing.

But, at the time, what mattered most to me was that she gave
me a chronological timeline to cling to:

> *So you're absolutely experiencing this Pluto transit now. There it
> is [she points to a place on my chart], opposing your Venus back in
> September 2005, then your rising sign and sun between October and
> December. It's influencing them all last fall...this is long...and going
> all through December of this year [2006]. Looks like it's moving off
> there...even when it comes back, it doesn't come all the way back.
> So, as of the end of December, it's moving away. Through this year,
> it's going to be at its most intense. Meanwhile, Saturn is coming up
> to conjunct this natal Pluto from the end of August through early
> October, and it's going to come back in March 2007 through June
> 2007. Then it's gone.*

Gobbledy-gook, you say? Well, in March 2007 I indeed went
through my final major crisis. And, by June 2007, the storm was,
indeed, well on its way out to sea. Power of suggestion? Mental
placebo? Fine. Bring it on.

∽

Maybe the only reliable diagnosis is the treatment. Maybe we
should give up trying to label all the different flavors of mental
weirdness. Doesn't the fact that there are so many diagnoses suggest that it's an effort in futility? Especially since a whole lot of
them are *NOS* (Not Otherwise Specified). C'mon. That's clearly a
cop-out.

Why not, instead, diagnose people based on whatever ever-
changing formulation of prescription drugs, alternative remedies

and therapies, random symptoms, psychological/spiritual practices, everyday functioning, and self-medication that's getting them through the day? (Or failing to do so.)

There are as many variations on depression, obsession, agitation, mania, attention deficit and combinations thereof as there are patients. But I'm currently the only guy I know who's a fairly highly functioning, Lamictal-Cymbalta-Klonopin taking, alternative-medicine-trusting, wood-splitting, road-biking, single-malt drinking, melancholic, hypomanic writer in remission.

...Who, during the 1980s and 1990s was an extremely unpredictable, cigarette-smoking, whiskey-drinking, racquetball playing, business-owning, vitamin-taking, garden-variety (and vegetable-gardening), self-medicating depressive with hypomanic spells.

...Who, after surviving his first big-time breakdown in 1999, became a fairly high-functioning Celexa, Wellbutrin, acupuncture-ing, freelance writing, squash-playing, moderate major (or major moderate) depressive in remission.

...Who, one fateful day in 2005 became, for the next two years, a barely functioning, try-just-about-anything, desperately self-medicating, exercising-like-crazy, anxiety-ridden and occasionally screaming major depressive with a touch of hypomania.

To provide a "precise" diagnosis of anyone, you'd have to add details about their gender, weight, genetics, hours of sleep, diet, the number of close friends...the list is endless.

The disease is that personal.

The treatment is that elusive.

♋

When I told a friend I'd had a nervous break*down,* he suggested, with a slightly maniacal if transcendent grin, that maybe I'd actually had a break*up.* With a single preposition, he changed the entire way I understood my experience.

Things break *down*—bicycles, laptops, nuclear power plants, etc. You want them to work the way they did before. Even if it means buying a few new, identical parts.

Relationships break *up*—teenage romances, marriages, negotiations, etc. In those cases you usually *don't* want things to work the way they did before. You want to use the opportunity to try something new.

Mental illness rides the line between them.

During what I called my break*down*, I thought I wanted my mind to work the way it did before. During remissions, I'd say: "I think I'm back."

At the same time, my relationship with and perspective on myself and the world had completely broken *up* and there *was* no going back—any more than there had been after I got stoned for the first time, lost my virginity, got married, watched our daughter being born, or buried my father.

Our brains are *things*. Physical objects in which cells divide, cerebral spinal fluid flows, and neurons exchange molecules. When those parts break *down*, we want to get them working *physically* the way they did before. Or, better yet, like they did when we were younger!

But each of us—the whole package—is an ever-changing, seemingly limitless, network of complex *relationships* between the physical and the distinctly (albeit mysteriously) ineffable.

And so, while in many ways I yearned desperately for a brain that I could relate to as I did before—a brain that didn't keep sending fight-flight signals to my adrenals; that had internal circuitry which tickled some pleasure points once in a while; a brain where millions of tiny synaptic electrical signals created the occasional wave of calm; a brain that could convince itself that this too would pass—I also sincerely hoped and believed the experience would be transformative…one way or another.

Perhaps even a break*through*.

PURGATORY

NOW I'LL SING OF THAT SECOND KINGDOM
WHERE THE HUMAN SPIRIT CAN BE PURGED OF SIN
AND BECOME WORTHY TO ASCEND TO HEAVEN.

~ *Purgatory, Canto 1 (4-6)*

B ACK IN HELL, DANTE ACTED LIKE A TOURIST. HEY, IT wasn't his fault he was down there. It was part of a research project. Beatrice wanted him to learn as much as he could about the structure of the universe. And, as part of his final presentation, he was able to make sure all his enemies got what they deserved. Talk about poetic justice!

But now Dante's entering Purgatory. Which is an entirely different scene. He's been on the road—circling round and round Florence—long enough to begin realizing that those damn clerics and politicians don't have a monopoly on sin…*he's* no angel either (yet).

As he walks through the Gates of Purgatory, a *real* angel carves seven Ps on his forehead—representing the seven deadly sins. Every time he successfully works his way around and up another terrace of Purgatory Mountain, one of those Ps is brushed away.

But it takes work. He walks along the First Terrace bent over with the prideful (as well he should), all of whom carry massive weights on their back. On the Third Terrace, he walks with the wrathful through black smoke.

The key scene takes place when it's time for Dante to cleanse himself of the final deadly sin: lust. To do so, he has to walk through flames. He hesitates. Virgil pushes and prods. Dante resists. Virgil tells him not to worry…nobody dies here, so to speak. It's only when Virgil promises Dante that Beatrice is on the other side, does he manage to screw up the courage to do it.

Isn't it kind of ironic that he needs lust to transform lust?

By now, even Dante must be thinking that the whole sin thing is getting kind of old. Throughout history, it's been such a moving and often self-serving target. In order to make sure they're in the right, people's definitions have ranged from outer rules so strict that there's little margin for error to inner disciplines that are supposed to cultivate qualities of wisdom and judgment in and of themselves. Doesn't make much difference: regardless of beliefs or philosophy, people find ways to justify the most outrageous behaviors.

While the seven deadly sins can definitely get you into a lot of trouble, they aren't really deadly. Even more heretically, they're not even sins *per se*. They're the other side of the story. Pride is part and parcel of courage. Envy, aspiration. Wrath, energy. Sloth, contemplativeness. Greed, hunger. Gluttony, completion. And lust? Lust? Lust is passion.

There's a famous Zen story about some monks going to their Master to complain about one of their fellow monks—a real screw-up. The guy coughs, sneezes, and makes even less-pleasant bodily sounds during meditation. When it's his turn to serve dinner, he trips and spills hot soup on the Master's lap.

One day they're all out working in the woods and this guy fells a tree so close to the group that a branch whacks the Master on the side of his head and knocks him out. That's the last straw.

"We gotta get rid of this guy," the monks say to the Master, who's finally come back to (enlightened) consciousness. He's lying in a hospital bed, sipping chai tea through a bendable straw, his head held rigidly in place by one of those contraptions that holds your head rigidly in place.

The Master hears them out and thinks (or no-thinks) about it deeply for a while. So deeply and for so long that they think he's fallen asleep, is resting in *satori*, or both. Finally the Master speaks: "Okay. We'll send him away."

The monks are surprised, but very relieved. At last, they can get back to the serious business of stillness—without worrying about what that crazy monk is going to do next. But, as they begin to file out, the Master calls them back into the hospital room. Even with bandages covering half his head, the monks can tell the Master is still pondering the issue. They wait expectantly. The Master sighs.

They wait expectantly. The Master looks up at them quizzically—
as if he's been working on a koan of his very own:
    "But who will we replace him with?" he asks.
    Without lust—okay, passion—how would we get anywhere?
    Of course, without love, how would we survive the flames?

Hard Turns and False Tops

Nobody realizes that some people expend tremendous energy
merely to be normal.

—ALBERT CAMUS

⁌

THERE'S A LEGEND among road bikers in Vermont that back in the 1700s when they first cut roads in the Green Mountains, they'd eyeball the height and start working their way up—at, say, a 6%–8% incline. But, they inevitably miscalculated a little, so toward the top, rather than bother with another full switchback, they'd take one more hard turn and head straight up at a 12%+ pitch.

More than one good biker has rounded that last corner only to realize he's got no more gears on his bike or strength in his quads.

The other bane of a climber's existence is the false top. Glimpses of treetops on surrounding hills make you think you can tell how much elevation remains, only to find out that, thanks to some unseen dips, you still have several steep climbs to go. (Or, as they say, the problem with downhills in Vermont is that they're mostly up.)

⁌

My most vivid memories of returning home from my trip out west in spring 2006 are of the calmingly familiar smells, sounds, and textures of early spring in Vermont. While I certainly wasn't out of the woods, the comforts of home did keep the vibrations in my chest and throat down to a dull roar.

Spring came particularly early for me that year, because I'd followed it all the way from Missouri, daring the dogwood to keep up with me on my mad dash north.

By the time I arrived at our home, the forsythia were in full bloom, the maple buds were swelling, and the sweet smell of manure (it's an acquired taste) was in the air. I did my best to join in this riotous celebration of renewal. Instead of relying on divine intervention, I found a down-to-earth mechanic to replace my VW's starter. I successfully poured some of my restless energy into regular squash games and bike rides. I transformed the stories of my hellish weeks on the road into a collection of humorous *shticks*. I acted relatively normal during a three-day visit from mom. I even had a crown made—the tooth kind—and, while I may have gagged on that clay stuff they use to make the cast, I refrained from bolting out of the chair, uttering unearthly screams, ripping the dental bib off, and running out the door.

Most impressively, one day I had a flat tire a few miles from home and fixed it calmly, actually smiling as I imagined all the far worse places (mostly in Kansas) where it could have happened.

Throughout the spring of 2006, I told myself and anyone who asked that the hard periods weren't quite so hard, and the okay periods were a bit more okay. But, in reality, I didn't really feel all that different from when I'd left. Occasionally, in the privacy of my own solitude, I dropped the thin veneer of optimism. One day, I made these notes "for future reference."

Wake most mornings 4:30 with what feels like a vibration or "racing" in my heart or throat chakra, or occasionally solar plexus. Can't go back to sleep, but feel exhausted and can't focus enough to get up and write. Wish I could sleep for a million years and wake up refreshed. No real suicidal thoughts, but I appreciate how people do it. Appreciate? Weird word.

Occasional bursts of sunshine, optimism, and normalcy. Sometimes focusing on a project helps. Sometimes doing anything seems like a burden. Total debilitating breakdown every week or so. Utter hopelessness; crying jags; how can I spend another 20–30 years like this? When that happens, Valium is the only relief.

Stopped virtually all caffeine. Just a little to clear my head once in a while. Clear my head? Yeah, right, Dave, just have a cup of coffee and clear your head.

Speaking of Valium, among my more vivid memories is the look on my doctor's face when I confessed that once or twice I'd taken up to 30 mg of Valium between about 4 A.M. and 8 A.M. as I desperately tried to avoid facing the day.

He managed to retain his calm, clinical tone while explaining that he didn't mind prescribing that much for someone who arrived at the ER just one un-restrain-able thrash short of a straitjacket. In that case, they usually gave an injection. Fortunately, the idea of self-injection never appealed to me, or else he would have been giving the wrong person the wrong idea at the wrong time. I mean it's not like I was overdosing per se: 30 mg–40 mg is, as far as I can tell, the maximum daily prescribed dose. It was probably the 4-hour time period that troubled him. And the fact I was down to 125 pounds. And the fact that I wasn't eating much. The shot of Jameson's the evening before may have also helped visions of rehab dance in his head. It wasn't like I was taking that much every night, either, I reassured him. Often I took as little as 5 mg–10 mg.

I'd been hoping my trip, some spring sunshine, and warm weather would cook the madness out of my system. Instead, I continued negotiating hard turns and false tops on a daily, weekly, and monthly basis. Trying to catch my breath on the occasional downhill.

᪶

Just act normal. Those three words are the legendary mantra of all who've ever been drunk, stoned, or more seriously inebriated in public. They are also the moment-by-moment mantra of the mentally incapacitated.

As the spring of 2006 went on, I got a lot of practice.

There was the trip to Burlington with a close friend to see our daughters who both happened to be living there. A calming drive through the familiar Vermont hills. A fascinating conversation that ranged from farming to writing to politics to education to God. Followed by a wonderful brunch with all four of us, before each of us wandered off to catch up on the life and times of our respective daughters. Yet, what I remember most is trying to act normal; trying to act normal; trying to act normal. My friend and my daughter were both as aware as they could be of what was going on inside me, but I wanted to do whatever I could to make it normal for them, too. Regardless, when that perfect day was over I heaved a sigh of relief.

There was the trip to New York to do some presentations, during which I frantically dug around in my deep store of small talk so I wouldn't suddenly burst into tears and freak out the young, enthusiastic PR person who was guiding me through the day.

There were all those lunches and dinners and midday coffees with friends and acquaintances, during which I managed to provide reasonably good color commentary about what I going through, while trying to mask the fact that I was actually doing play-by-play. My friends weren't totally oblivious, but they had little choice but to play along.

All these experiences reflect the endless internal tug-of-war of agitated depression or mixed states. You want to be alone—away from the pressure to "act normal." You want to be with people—away from the prison of your own experience. You want to sit still and relax. You have to keep moving or you'll explode. You desperately want to do something. You desperately want to rest.

Like an actor struggling to remember his lines, you present a slightly frazzled, but usually reasonable facsimile of who you were before, while trying to restrain the crazed director from dragging you off the stage. And so you walk through life—the two of you—side by side.

The Wit and Wisdom
of Neurotransmitters

*A thing is mysterious if you don't know what or how to feel about it
and wish you did. Mystery is a lack not of information but of meaning.
Indeed, greater knowledge of certain subjects can intensify rather than
soothe emotional itchiness about them.*

— Peter Schjedahl

૭

I'VE NEVER TAKEN A CHEMISTRY CLASS. So, when I was prescribed 40 mg of $C_{20}H_{22}BrFN_2O$ (a.k.a. Celexa) back in 1999, I just rolled my eyes, rolled the dice, and swallowed.

But, the more I've explored the deep dark recesses of libraries and the Internet, the more curious I've become about what's going on in that twisted bundle of ganglia on top of my neck.

I certainly don't want to belittle the efforts of anyone who's spent countless years and dollars trying to master the jargon and formulae of modern biochemistry. But, neither do I want to belittle the intelligence of any of us who take the drugs they prescribe.

I figure if doctors insist that the best patient is a well-informed patient, we might as well give them a run for their money.

Admittedly, the fact that I spent a couple of hours trying to figure out how many molecules are in a 100 mg tablet of Lamictal may be more a reflection of my OCD than my thirst for knowledge. Fortunately, I gave up and asked my favorite Physics Ph.D., who told me 100 mg of Lamictal has 24.5 hundred billion tera molecules. A tera being a thousand billion. That's a lot of zeroes. (See the Chapter Notes for his entire email. Good luck!)

With the caveat that professionals might quarrel with some of the following, or even the fact that a guy who's never taken a chemistry class is trying to explain it in the first place, I'll try to describe the neurotransmitter theory of depression in terms we ordinary mortals can understand.

This explanation is based on many hours staring at illustrations in a lot of books and on a lot of websites. So, if you really want to follow along, you might want to look up one of those pictures for reference. If, however, this explanation is already giving you headaches, dizziness, palpitations, or, God forbid, sexual dysfunction, I encourage you to move right along to the next chapter.

In other words, "Abandon all hope, ye who enter here."

∽

It's all in your mind. Sure, but what exactly "it" is, what causes "it," how to fix "it," what "fix" even means under the circumstances, and whether it really is "*all*"…well, there are a whole lot of angels dancing on the heads of those pins and, if you're going to write about the science of depression, you're going to have to dance with quite a few of them.

About fifteen years ago, I came across an article in *Scientific American* (June 1998) entitled, "The Neurobiology of Depression." After reading it, I convinced myself and many unsuspecting friends that I understood how antidepressants worked. My spiel went something like this:

> *Basically, your neurotransmitters (whatever those are) aren't doing a very good job of getting your brain cells to communicate (synapse) with each other. To remedy this sorry state of affairs, there are: Tricyclics which keep all kinds of neurotransmitters from being sucked back (re-uptaken) too soon from whence they came; "Selective" reuptake inhibitors (SRIs) which target the reuptake of specific neurotransmitters, and MAO blockers which forcibly restrain the enzymes that are trying to devour those same well-meaning neurotransmitters before they've done their jobs.*

Since then, researchers have learned a lot more about these processes. And, although it's not a bad overview, I've learned a *lot* more about how *little* I know.

Brain cells (a.k.a. neurons) can't stop talking. Even after you're dead, they keep talking. For a day or more. Until the last one realizes there's no one left to talk to, gets bored, and sends its molecules off to greener pastures.

What with there being ±100 billion neurons up there, you'd think they could just communicate by rubbing up against each other. Unfortunately, they're not allowed to touch. It's against the rules. Instead, each one is separated by a "great" divide called a *synapse*. Synapses are 20–40 billionth of a meter across. That might not sound like very much to you and me, but for a little neuron, it's quite a leap.

Fortunately, neurons know how to make molecules that can leap across that great divide. Those molecules are called *neurotransmitters*, because they *transmit* information between *neurons*.

If you've seen one neurotransmitter, you definitely *haven't* seen them all. Depending on who's counting, there are more than a hundred different kinds, and each one is a slightly different size and shape. However, in terms of whether you are optimistic, pessimistic, paranoid, confident, compulsive, or laid back, there are only a few we need to worry about. Actually, there's no reason to worry. Although, if your neurotransmitters are a little off-kilter, you might not have a lot of choice.

As far as depression goes, the most famous and prolific neurotransmitter is *serotonin*. *Norepinephrine* and *dopamine* also get a lot of play. A little *GABA* and *glutamate* come in handy. And then there's *acetylcholine*, which, for some reason, you don't hear about as much—probably 'cause it's even harder to pronounce than the others.

Neurons shoot these and other neurotransmitting molecules out of hairs at the end of an umbilical-like cable called an *axon*.

The rest of the neuron is covered with little receptive filaments called *dendrites*. You'd think dendrites would be the end of the line, size-wise. But each one features even tinier *receptors*. They also come in a variety of sizes and shapes, which bear a suspicious similarity to the different sizes and shapes of the neurotransmitters. This ensures that only certain kinds of neurotransmitters can hook up with certain kinds of receptors to transmit certain kinds of signals.

There are, for example, about 13 or 14 subtypes of receptors for serotonin alone. The scientists can't seem to decide. And each one is part of a specific neural pathway that's responsible for relaying certain types of messages. That's why the activity of a single neurotransmitter or type of receptor can affect so many different aspects of your life. And, in turn, why everyone responds a little differently to meds that increase synaptic levels.

Once a neurotransmitter finds a compatible receptor, it settles in for a quickie, and gives the "target" cell a charge. Some scientists call this neurotransmitter-receptor relationship a lock-and-key kind of thing. Seems more like kamikaze speed-dating to me. Especially since, as soon as an individual neurotransmitting molecule has made its point, it skedaddles. Which it quickly lives to regret because (like drone bees who mate with the queen), once it's done, it gets eaten up by an *enzyme* which breaks it into smaller molecules. They, in turn, become the raw materials for more neurotransmitters. Elegant, huh?

This complex dance doesn't happen one synapse at a time. Every axon of every neuron has ±1000 synaptic endings spewing out neurotransmitters like there's no tomorrow; as well as ±1000 of those dendrites which are receiving those messenger molecules from other neurons. Axons can be up to 12 feet long, so we're not exactly talking a bucket brigade. More like a switching station that would blow even Bill Gates' mind. Fortunately, most of those axons and dendrites know what they're doing. So, with minimal, if any, conscious help from you, they usually do a good job of helping you digest your food, type on your laptop, or try to explain something inexplicable.

Put a few of those puppies together, do a little algebra, and you realize that one little neuron can share synapses with tens of thousands of other neurons. Move on up to Algebra II, add all those billion or so brain cells, and we're talking like a quadrillion synapses in all—give or take a trillion every second (or less). What a racket! Pretty amazing when you think of it. Which, hopefully, you can, even if one of those neural pathways is slow on the uptake.

What's even more amazing is that your brain is able to assemble this unceasing barrage of synapses into experiences and thoughts such as: "I'm happy." "I'm sad." "I'm starving." "I'm full." "I want a beer." "I'm freaked out." "I can't wait to get to work." "I can't wake up." "Ouch, that hurts." "Mmmm, that feels good." "I need to buy 1,000 copies of this book and give it to all my friends."

When you feel "off" in any which way, one or more of the following things is probably happening:

1. Your axons aren't shooting enough neurotransmitters out into the wide open synaptic space. It's enough to make you want to sleep all day.
2. A bunch of shy or lazy neurotransmitters have been sneaking back into the neuron they came from. That is, they don't bother sticking around in the synaptic space long enough to see if they can find a willing receptor.
3. A voracious MAO enzyme eats them up before they can hook up with a receptor. (MAO stands for *monoamineoxidase*. Aren't you glad you asked?)
4. Too many neurotransmitters are flooding the synapses because the neurons just can't keep them under control. It's enough to make you crazy!
5. The neurotransmitter keys don't fit so good. Or more likely, some of the receptors are hard to open.

You might be wondering why, instead of taking little pills, we don't just flash flood our brains with neurotransmitting molecules and hope for the best—i.e., take a pill filled with a balanced combination of neurotransmitters themselves instead of something that inhibits their reuptake or their ultimate demise. Unfortunately, in the "How-to-Make-a-Human" manual, they put in something called the "blood-brain" barrier. Only neurons have the right stuff to make neurotransmitters. We can eat or drink more of the ingredients they need to make them. But *they* have to do the work.

Dealing with the blood-brain barrier is the *raison d'être* for a lot of natural/dietary treatments for depression. Supplements like tryptophan, SAM-e, and 5-HTP *can* get through the blood-brain barrier. And they're just what a productive neuron needs to make more neurotransmitters. Although even supplements with the best of intentions might get detoured into some other job on their way to your brain, or throw something else out of balance.

Things like alcohol, nicotine, and heroin are *really* good at messing around with receptors and encouraging your neurons to release more neurotransmitters. This can make neurons kind of lazy, because they figure it's only a matter of time before you give them another hit. That's one reason withdrawal can really suck.

One of the latest theories for why it can take a while for meds to work is that they're actually not directly affecting the synaptic success rate of neurotransmitters, they're actually cajoling your brain into making more neurons. Either theory implies a third: that antidepressants cause significant changes in your brain's electro-vibrational frequency. I never had electro-shock treatment, but that clearly affects the connections between neurons, and definitely helps some people. Ditto for, say, acupuncture. And, perhaps, even homeopathy.

All these theories don't matter a whole lot as far as we head-cases are concerned, except as a reminder that most know-it-alls don't.

☞

Let's not forget about hormones. In the midst of my *extremis*, a friend who was in the process of setting the world record for hot flashes, wrote: "Have you thought about how your mental state might have a relationship to your hormones?" This was and is a really good question. Particularly when discussing a 53-year-old guy having a nervous breakdown...not to mention a mother dealing with postpartum depression, an anorexic teenager, or hyperactive child.

I wasn't exactly thrilled with the idea that my fragile mental states were being exacerbated by a virulent case of rapidly vanishing testosterone, but I figured I might as well man up and do more research.

Both hormonal and neurotransmitting molecules pass messages between cells. The difference is that, instead of being created in neurons and leaping across a synaptic divide like neurotransmitters, hormones are created in glands and *travel through your bloodstream* in search of receptive cells.

Norepinephrine, for example, tends to be attracted to cells that deal with stress. So, if your neurons do a better job of making norepinephrines, and give them a good swift kick across the synapse, they might help you get out of that catatonic funk. However, norepinephrine is also synthesized in the adrenals and travels through your bloodstream, in which case it's considered a hormone. *Those* norepinephrine molecules know how to spread the word that you need to increase your heart rate and blood flow. This helps you leap into action whenever you feel threatened: like when a car is heading right at you or—if you're in the state I was in—you can't find the top to the yogurt container.

This hormonal/neurotransmitter connection explains why adolescence and menopause in particular can trigger big-time mood changes in both men and women. It also makes you wonder how people could question the diagnosis of "postpartum depression." Telling a new mother—whose hormonal system is thinking, "What the heck just happened?"—that she'll get over it seems remarkably insensitive considering that "it" can last months or years. Just as with any depression, there are numerous options for treating it—although paying attention to the warnings and caveats would seem particularly important in that case, especially if you're nursing.

Bottom line: It's a real good idea to tell your psychiatrist if you just had your first period, are starting to grow your first beard, are pregnant, nursing, showing signs of male or female menopause, or are in the middle of a sex change procedure.

Prescription Medicines

If you do need to take medication the math is really simple:
which sucks less?
Taking an imperfect medication that controls the symptoms of a condition
that puts your life somewhere in the spectrum of "barely tolerable"
to "dear God please kill me now;"
or trying to get through life with that same condition...
which will keep getting worse the longer you go without treating it?

—JEROD POORE

ɔຈ

YOU'VE DECIDED to take the plunge. Actually, you've already taken the plunge and you're in way over your head.

So you've finally gone to see someone with an M.D. or N.P. tacked on their name who, thankfully, appears to have heard most of it before. And, more important, appears to have a reasonable idea how to deal with it. They've taken their notes. They've handed you Kleenex. They've looked in their big books to check on potential interactions. And then...then...they get out the pad and start scribbling. Yes!

They hand you the piece of paper with an expression that combines concern and optimism: "This should work. Remember, you *might* feel something right away, but it could take a couple of weeks. Don't worry. We'll figure this out. Make an appointment for next Wednesday. Try to get some rest."

"Rest?" You say with a pitiful choking sigh.

And then...then...they get out the pad and start scribbling again! Yes!

You walk out and go back to the receptionist's window. He or she sees folks like you all day, and struggles between sympathy and professionalism, with a hint of job fatigue. You make the appointment. A reminder card? Well, sure. But there ain't no way you're going to forget *this* appointment. For the next week, it's going to be a faint lighthouse of hope. On the way from the doctor's office to downtown, you clutch those two pieces of paper like lottery tickets with a winning number.

You take the first pill as soon as you leave the drugstore—unless you are dissuaded by those warnings that say not to drive until you see if you have side effects. In that case, you rush home. Or to the office if you *have* to go back there. Get some water. And swallow. Full stomach. Empty stomach. Whatever.

And then, in spite of all the warnings that it could take weeks for the drug to be effective, you sit down and wait to "get off." The same way you'd wait, and expect, an ibuprofen to take away pain.

After a while, you accept that it's really not going to work right away, and reluctantly go about doing whatever it is you do. Later that evening, you tell your spouse, partner, or friends what happened at your appointment and what drug(s) you're taking. There's a good chance you go online and read everything you possibly can about those drugs.

At the end of the day, you get into bed and reach for the other bottle (remember that second slip of paper?) and take one. With any luck, you get some sleep.

∽

As a one-man clinical trial, I'm often asked about specific meds. After trying to answer those questions for a while, I realized that while I could toss around acronyms like SSRI, NDRI, TCA, MAO, AED, and CNS with the best of them, there was something about the way that antidepressants are classified that didn't make sense.

All those years I thought I'd been trying to understand the difference between apples and apples, it turns out I was actually dealing with apples and oranges—with a few fish and fowl thrown in for good measure. As best I can tell, this is how it breaks down:

Drugs classified based on what they do in the brain. Anything with an RI (that doesn't refer to the state where I was born) acts on the brain by Inhibiting the Reuptake of neurotransmitters. Those are the various Selective Reuptake Inhibitors (SRIs).

MAOIs (Monoamine Oxidase Inhibitors) are also named based on what they do in the brain. They inhibit the enzymes that are waiting to chow down some nice juicy used-up neurotransmitters.

In both cases, the goal is to have more synaptic connections.

Drugs classified based on the condition they treat. Or, in many cases, the condition they were originally designed to treat. An AED, for example, is an Anti-Epileptic Drug. However, I, and many other people who have never had an epileptic fit, take them as mood stabilizers. They're also prescribed for bipolar. Still they're called AEDs.

Drugs classified based on their chemical structure. For example, the "tricyclics." This is the classification that's the most annoying. The researchers should be ashamed of themselves. Tricyclics are Reuptake Inhibitors too. They're just not as selective. They're named for what they *are*, not what they *do*. Their molecules have three (tri) rings of atoms—whatever that means. The cyclic part comes from the citric-acid *cycle* which is made up of seven chemical reactions, or maybe it's nine. I can't remember. Regardless, what goes around comes around. It's also known as the tricarboxylic acid cycle (TCA) or the Krebs cycle—and I don't think they mean Maynard G! Bottom line: tricyclics should be called PRIs: Promiscuous Reuptake Inhibitors.

Neither fish nor fowl. The notorious "Atypicals." This is almost as much of a scientific cop-out as the diagnosis NOS (Not Otherwise Specified). Atypical antidepressants and antipsychotics are called atypical because, at one time, they were different from the typical ones prescribed for a certain purpose. Although now they are often now prescribed more typically for that and other purposes.

To make matters worse, doctors often use brand and generic names interchangeably. And prescribe them for both FDA-approved and off-label conditions. So, for example, you might be taking a drug named sertaline, which is the generic version of Zoloft. It boosts serotonin levels by blocking reuptake and makes certain serotonin receptors more or less receptive. While it's selective for serotonin (i.e., an SSRI), it also blocks more dopamine reuptake than the other SSRIs. So you *could* call it an SDRI. Maybe that's why it seems to cause fewer problems with sexuality and weight gain. And why it's sometimes prescribed "off-label" for eating disorders, fibromyalgia, hot flashes, and migraines.

See? It's hard enough to figure out what's what and why without having to figure out what the heck it's supposed to do. So, if you're curious why your doctor prescribed what he or she prescribed for what ails you...ask. And keep asking. I mean, it's *your* mind. Even though it occasionally feels like someone else's.

Drug companies put a lot of effort into coming up with names. They need something with an obtuseness only a doctor could love (and prescribe). At the same time, they want to give patients at least a subliminal message of encouragement. Typically, they spend more than a million dollars to achieve these goals.

In retrospect, the name Prozac doesn't seem to fit that bill. Allegedly, it's just a mishmash of positive sounds. (I get the "pro" part. But "zac"?) Doesn't matter. The word has become so much a part of the lexicon that we don't question it anymore. The names Zoloft and Paxil are more calming and uplifting. Effexor certainly sounds effective. Wellbutrin suggests it may actually tame the beast. And, for some reason, Cymbalta has a relaxing ring, even though the image of crashing cymbals isn't exactly soothing. The name BuSpar seems unpleasantly Germanic, but does imply it'll put up a good fight. Abilify sounds like a performance-enhancing drug trying to pass as a mild-mannered pick-me-up.

Like Prozac, the brand named Valium has become so ingrained in our vocabulary that it makes most folks feel faintly drowsy just hearing the word. At least it's a whole lot less sexist than "mother's little helper." (Which included Librium and Quaaludes as well as Valium.)

"What are you taking?" Once you've identified someone as a fellow traveler, that's how you usually break the ice. Before you ask what they do for a living, whether they're in a committed relationship, have children, or root for the Red Sox or Yankees (correct answer revealed later), you want to know what drugs they're on. It's a bonding thing.

Once they answer, the proper response is a thoughtful, "Huh..." followed by a few pleasant stories about anyone you know who has ever taken that drug *successfully*.

There are *some* people who respond by telling stories of people they know who took that drug and broke out in hives, had brain-crushing headaches, and/or ended up in an Inpatient Psychiatric Unit.

I consider this to be in extremely bad form.

Despite my uncertainty, if not total ignorance, about these things, when I used to hear what drug someone was taking, I thought I had something useful to contribute to the discussion. After all, I did much better with Lamictal than Depakote. Celexa made me crazy (literally) this time around after working for years. Wellbutrin helped even out my moods in the late 1990s; this time, it did little more than blunt the occasional edge—just enough so that when I told folks I felt a little better, I didn't feel I was perjuring myself. Seroquel left me uncomfortably numb. When combined with Depakote I felt drugged (a delineation that might seem meaningless in my case). Lorazepam made me feel just weird. Buspirone has a short half life and allegedly doesn't cause cognitive or memory impairment. I took it two or three times a day and it made me feel stupid. Valium was addictive for me. But, for whatever reason, I can take Klonopin on and off with no problem.

The point is that my experience is irrelevant. All my opinions and attitudes are based on the assumption (delusion) that how something affected me might affect you.

⚭

I'm not trying to show off here. (Well I am, kind of.) It's just that understanding the dysfunctional categorizing and fairly irrelevant nomenclature of drugs helps me understand what the ones I take are supposed to do, how they relate to each other, and how they relate to other ones I've taken in the past. Call it idle curiosity. Call it an obsessive thirst for knowledge. Call it empowering. When I learn this stuff, it makes me feel better.

For example, I've always wondered why there are so many different SSRIs. Seemed to me that a drug inhibits serotonin reuptake or it doesn't. It turns out that there are a whole lot of different molecules that can inhibit serotonin uptake. And they all do it a little differently. In particular, they all influence different combinations of receptors and metabolize at different speeds.

The speed of metabolism is particularly important for anyone who wants to understand what's happening in their brain when they take a psychotropic medication. Because it explains a drug's average "half-life." (Average because of everyone's different size, shape, metabolism, etc.) A half-life defines how long it takes for half of the drug to get out of your system. Which helps explain:

- Why you might be told to take one drug, say, three times a and another once per day;
- Why they make ER (extended release) and/or SR (sustained release) versions for some drugs and not others;
- Why it takes different lengths of time to get up to a therapeutic dose...in other words, for all those overlapping half-lives to stabilize into a fairly steady amount in your bloodstream;
- Why they usually tell you not to double-up after missing a dose;

- Why some drugs are more addictive than others;
- And why, since we all metabolize drugs differently, you should tell your psychiatrist everything you can about your health history and daily habits. She or he might not be pleased that you smoke, drink, and never exercise, but it's better to fess up, rather than be given the wrong amount of the wrong drug.

You can have a basic understanding of *all* these things just from knowing the half-life of the drug you're taking. Because, unlike the Strontium 90 they just found in the soil near my friendly neighborhood nuclear plant—which has a half-life of about 30 years—the half-life of most medications can be measured in minutes, hours, or days. Obviously, the longer the half-life, the less problematic it is to miss one dose. Again, we're talking *average* half-lives. And none of us is average.

Here's a case in point. One morning, well after I'd stabilized, I realized I was running out of Lamictal. I called for a refill, but, having no other excuse to go downtown, I decided to split my two doses that day (i.e., 50 mg twice a day instead of 100 mg twice day).

The next morning, I took a whole 100 mg pill because I was *sure* I'd get downtown sometime that day. But I didn't. Maybe it was snowing or something. So, I took 50 mg that night and 50 mg the next morning. I can't remember why I didn't go to the pharmacy *that* day. In any event, I took my last 50 mg that night. I knew had had to go downtown the next morning. No matter what.

The writers of those tiny-type prescription inserts whip themselves into a frenzy about how you can break into weird rashes, send your blood pressure soaring, and/or die if you lose at medication roulette. But, at least with the antidepressants I've taken, they're rather la-di-da about missing *one* dose: don't double up, just take your next regular dose and get on with your life.

They do *not*, unfortunately, include the warning, "Hey, Dave… yeah you, the guy in Vermont…we're assuming you're not an idiot.

In other words, that you'll go downtown and get a refill ASAP after you realize you're out."

The half-life of Lamictal is particularly variable, ±25 hours seems to be the accepted average for someone taking it on a regular basis. So, on the day after a given dose, you have about 50% of *that* dose left in your system; 25% the next; 12.5% the next, and so on. Since, in this case, over the previous three days I'd taken about half as much as usual...well, you do the math. (I get really confused when I try.) Bottom line, I was reducing my blood levels way faster than I would have if going off intentionally.

As I said, half-lives depend on a lot of subjective factors, e.g., how much you weigh, other drugs you're taking, and whether your kidneys and/or liver are operating at full power. For example, if you're also taking valproate acid (Depakote), the half life of Lamictal is considerably longer; i.e., you need significantly less. That's why, when I segued from Depakote to Lamictal, my psychiatrist gave me a special pack that dispensed exactly the correct amount to take of each, every day over a five-week period.

Statistics aside, when I woke up around 6 a.m. the fourth morning, I was seriously agitated. But the pharmacy wouldn't open for a few hours. I took a Klonopin, which calmed my mind a little but didn't do much for the shakes. By the time I was in the car, my heart was racing, I was beginning to cold-sweat, and it took all my powers of persuasion to convince myself I wasn't having a heart attack. At one point, I almost pulled over and called 911.

I got downtown and managed to feign some measure of calm while picking up my prescription. I started sucking on one before I was even out the door. I felt better almost immediately—maybe a placebo effect, although Lamictal is absorbed pretty quickly (reaching peak concentration in 1.4–4.8 hours). Most of my symptoms were gone within an hour, leaving me with that feeling of shaky relief you have after narrowly escaping a car crash.

When you first go *on* a medication, you *might* feel shaky, lose your appetite, get headaches and/or nausea, and/or dizziness, and/or insomnia—the list goes on and on...even in 8 point type.

You also *might* get more depressed, more anxious, more manic, and even more suicidal. All of which could also happen if you *don't* take the drug.

Going *off* a med can be just as risky. And, with many of them, doing it suddenly can be downright dangerous. In fact, one of the best arguments for universal healthcare is that some patients stop taking medications too quickly because they can no longer afford them…sometimes with tragic results.

I always considered myself to be a well-informed patient but, reading the literature now, I'm amazed at how little research I did back then about specific drugs. Although, in the midst of this kind of experience, it's hard to know whether a little knowledge is a good or a dangerous thing.

♈

Drugs can cause headaches, stomachaches, heart aches, flu-like symptoms, incontinence, impotence, indigestion, dizziness, blurriness, bloatedness, and any other malaise you can imagine. Of course, so can everyday life. But, if you happen to be taking a drug when one of these symptoms arise, there might be a cause-and-effect thing going on.

When you start taking an SSRI, it can take a little time for your body to adapt to having so many more successful serotonin synapses. And since, as I mentioned before, 90% of the serotonin in your body is in your gut, stomach problems are a common side effect. In extreme cases, it can feel like you just swallowed a vibrator—which was one of the symptoms of my "Serotonin Syndrome" episode in October 2005.

So if you feel extreme agitation in your stomach, it's time to call your doctor. And make sure you tell him or her if you're taking any supplement or herb that might also be affecting your serotonin levels.

While side effects like this usually occur when you *start* taking the drug, in some cases they appear down the road. Troubling as

104

that may be, it's a relief to know that your blurriness is probably due to medication and not brain cancer. Usually it'll go away after you and your doctor change the dosage or wean you off that one and work you onto another. But, don't let that stop you from dialing 911 if you get into a real panic.

⁓

The package inserts have a lot to say about side effects, but most of us only care about a few things:

Will I gain weight? Since I lost 25 pounds during my breakdown, this was not a huge concern for me. In fact, I've considered writing a book called, *Psychotics Guide to Weight Loss & Lower Cholesterol.* (The latter dropped about 50 points.) But it is a concern for many people and certain meds *are* more likely to cause weight gain than others.

Is it okay to drive? Since driving a car is kind of difficult if you feel groggy, have a splitting headache, and/or are throwing up, it's a pretty good idea to be careful when you start taking a med or raising a dose. Feel weird? Pull over. Whoever's waiting for you… they can wait.

Can I drink? I've never seen a pill bottle with a warning that says: "For maximum effectiveness, get smashed daily while taking this drug." Pharmaceutical companies and most medical professionals err on the side of caution and often say outright that you should not drink. Others will use the famously subjective: "in moderation" phrase. There's also the argument that, since alcohol is a depressant, you're kind of defeating the purpose to drink while taking an antidepressant. (Although, they're actually depressing different systems.) You can work those fine points out with your doctor.

However, I hasten to point out that, as hopefully everyone knows, combining alcohol with anti-anxiety drugs that *depress* your system (like Valium or Lorazepam) is a seriously high-risk behavior.

Can I have sex? If you and your partner are consenting adults, why not? Sure, you may find you're not as interested, or might not be able to, uh, perform to your, uh, satisfaction, if at all. And, that might throw your partner for a loop—although she or he might cut you some slack since she or he is so relieved that you're not curled up on the floor with a blanket over your head. That's not particularly sexy. There are also, in some cases, changes in weight and body image that, let's face it, can affect both partners.

On the other hand, you might find your orgasms last longer and are more intense. Or, if your drug-taking partner is a guy, maybe he'll last longer—if he gets there in the first place...which can't hurt—within reason. And, like sex itself, it's certainly different for men and women and from person to person, couple to couple, and I imagine—but only imagine—threesome to threesome.

Plus, different antidepressants affect your sex life differently. So, if it's an issue for you, your doctor may be able to prescribe a different med or a performance-enhancing drug (the legal kind) that can be safely taken in combination with your antidepressant. If you're in a relatively committed relationship, it might help for you and your partner to see a therapist. After all, your depression is affecting both of you and it can alleviate some stress to get your sexual concerns out on the table.

I am way oversimplifying this issue. In particular, the fact that depression can greatly exaggerate a whole lot of other issues in a relationship besides sex. Fortunately, most therapists are very aware of these dynamics, and in many cases can help.

To be crude, my advice would be, if possible, to get sane first and get laid second. And to trust that the two aren't mutually exclusive.

Taking psychiatric medications is a commitment. Sometimes, you may have to try more than one. Sometimes, you might need some big-time psychotherapy at the same time. Sometimes, yes, you may get worse before you get a lot better. There frequently are side effects. You have to remember to take them every day and, in many cases, never stop suddenly unless so ordered.

But, if your moods have reduced you to a dysfunctional blob, remember: It's about you, not some point on an indecipherable graph. It's about you, not friends who think you should just think positively or should try this or that "natural" cure or do yoga or t'ai chi. It's about you, not some drug company that says you'll live happily ever after if you take their drug. It's about you, not some researcher who says drug companies are getting rich by duplicitously marketing antidepressants to people who don't need them.

It's about you, not some guy who's writing this book!

Talking to a doctor about antidepressants is not a sign of weakness. There's no reason to be embarrassed. In fact, when you're juggling your own personal blend of high anxiety and deep depression, it can take a lot of courage.

One time, at the end of a recent six-month check-up, my psychiatrist suggested that we increase my meds for the winter. I knew, intuitively, that he was right. The signs were all too present: the bottom falling out for a few hours every day or two instead of every month or two; periods of agitation that made me want to get away from everyone in sight...including myself. Few if any outer triggers for either.

"The sadness..." he asked, "on a scale of 1–10?"

I didn't want to lie...or tell the truth. I compromised: "Uh, 7 or so."

"And right now?" he asked.

I tried not to look down: "Uh, 6." (He doesn't accept 5 as an answer...he considers it a cop-out.)

He understood the question behind the question behind the statement...and he had the answer ready: it's time to get ahead of this thing. We did. I was significantly better in three days.

Some might say: "Oh, too bad you needed to up your meds." Whereas they would never say, "Oh, too bad, you had to up your B vitamins."

Even though I've claimed that perspective is a contraindicated prejudice—particularly in my generation—I confess to sharing it.

Something in me *would* like to find a long-lasting, more "natural" solution than having to take .03 grams of a mysterious compound called duloxetine HCl (Cymbalta).

I'm not trying to disparage anyone's choices. I just think it's healthy to be aware of the underlying cultural assumptions that lead some people to feel that they've failed when they "resort" to Western medicine; as well as the dismissiveness or even scorn other patients face when they try an "unproven" complementary treatment. I've learned the hard way that it's best *for me* not to be swayed or limited by *any* philosophical ideology.

∽

Purgatory isn't as different from Hell as you might think. For example, in Hell, the Gluttonous lie in putrid mud. In Purgatory, they lie stretched out, face down, bound hand and foot. In Hell, the Wrathful continually tear each other limb from limb, whereas in Purgatory they have to walk through smoke darker than night. In other words, you're damned if you do and not purged if you don't. And both are worlds of hurt.

There are three particularly purgatorial times in a psychiatric patient's life: (1) When you're prescribed a med and are waiting to see if it works, especially since you might feel worse before you feel better; (2) When (if) a medication stops working. Which can make you feel like you've reached the promised land only to be thrown unceremoniously back in the lion's den; and (3) When you're trying to find a new med that does work. Because it often takes a couple of seemingly endless weeks to wean yourself off the first drug and then another couple of endless weeks to work your way up to a therapeutic dose of the new one—which, itself, may or may not might work. (By the way: in the case of many meds, this transition can be done simultaneously.)

Recently, I emerged from a bad day or two. Maybe it was a three-week flu that kind of exhausted me. Maybe it was some stress here and there—nothing to write home about. In any event, it happened. I could tell it wasn't *that* bad…that I was still several giant steps back from the edge. I managed not to panic. I didn't push myself to write. I *did* do my workouts. I made sure I took some extra vitamins and a smidge more Cymbalta. By now, I have a lot of experience with these dips. For the most part, they're just like the way most people feel when they've had a "bad day." But I totally understand why patients who've been doing really well can get totally freaked out when this happens. You've survived Hell. You may still be in Purgatory, but you're making progress and figure you're heading in the right direction (up). The idea of going back down can be unbearable.

∽

But what about me? What should *I* do? I've done my damnedest to explain just how hard it is to diagnose mental illness, give it a name, understand the different types of drugs available, and why they may or may not work for some of the people some of the time.

So, if you're able to get out of that funk by working out every day, eating less sugar, taking some vitamins, getting more sunshine, and/or meeting with a therapist every week, you might consider holding off on the meds.

But, if you have been depressed, intractably depressed for months—so much so that you have trouble getting up in the morning and feel like you have to fight your way through a thick curtain of sadness just to do a simple task—medications may not only make you feel a whole lot better, but could save your job, relationships, and make it far easier to parent and parent well. (Since you may have already passed the DNA along, it'd be nice if you could spare your kids some of the more troubling emotional displays— especially of the more violent type.)

And/or if you are so agitated you can't sit still, every thought sends an adrenaline rush through your body, and the smallest life challenge can paralyze you...

And/or if you're so manic that you can't sleep, have racing thoughts, feel what is politely called hypersexual, and are one blink short of hallucinating, only to crash a few days later so badly you can't leave the house...

...It's time to consider *anything* you think might help—from radical lifestyle changes to antidepressants and antipsychotics. Frankly, if you're suffering that much, I'd start with the drugs. But I'll keep to my pledge of not taking sides...

Except to say that if you are entertaining thoughts of suicide, it's important to know that there are medications that can keep those thoughts at bay and make you pretty glad you didn't go through with it. If you don't believe me, at least call 1-800-273-8255 because there's a good chance they can convince you.

∞

Yes, let's all take a deep breath...it's time to talk about suicide. In most cultures, suicide is the ultimate taboo. But how can something almost a million people a year do (including 30,000 Americans) be, as the *Encyclopedia Britannica* so indelicately puts it, "too accursed for ordinary individuals to undertake, under threat of supernatural punishment"? That's a lot of supernatural punishment to go around.

Dante isn't any help. Back in Hell, he consigned suicides to the Seventh Circle, where they're transformed into stunted, twisted trees that are continuously pecked upon by harpies.

I have the feeling he protesteth too much. Surely, those many years of exile, unsure whether anyone will ever truly understand his masterpiece, could make a guy wonder if it's all worth it. Interestingly, he did have a soft spot for Cato, a pre-Christian era Roman consul. Dante let him out of Hell so he could guard the gates of Purgatory, allegedly because he chose to commit suicide instead of submitting to tyranny.

Maybe the taboo shouldn't be committing suicide...the taboo should be not making the effort to understand the tyranny that people feel *within* themselves that can drive them to do it.

I could write a book about suicide. Fortunately, I don't have to. Because Kay Jamison already has (*Darkness Falls Fast*). Her lifelong study of bipolar and suicidal urges—in herself and others—puts her in another league. It might not be the best birthday present for a depressive, but it's a must-read for anyone involved in suicide prevention.

Suicide is often an impulsive act. Even if someone has planned it for a long time, the final decision is often impulsive. We cannot stop all suicides. But we can try not to be inadvertent accessories-before-the-fact which, as Jamison puts it, means doing whatever we can to keep the tools of self-destruction from being readily available...and making sure that resources to help severely depressed and agitated people *are* readily available.

A suicide is not a wasted life. As she points out when discussing the controversy over the probable suicide of Meriwether Lewis (of Lewis and Clark fame), he "should be allowed to keep such a disinterred peace as he might have. He has earned his rest and in me and for all of us, it is his life that remains."

I smile (wryly) when people say someone who committed suicide had so much to live for. Or they ask how she or he could have done this to his family. Yes, suicide is an unfathomable tragedy for family and friends. But, it may not be for the person who commits it. I can't speak for that person, but I'm fairly certain the reason he or she could do it is because the unremitting chemical processes in his brain made any other option seem impossible. He carried out suicide because he couldn't imagine carrying on any other way.

So, when I hear that someone committed suicide, my response is never "how awful." Instead, I instinctively but gently set my jaw, purse my lips, nod my head, and think, "Hmmm..." the way you'd think about someone who went exploring, perhaps recklessly, to a distant and dangerous land and never returned. Who am I to say that what was probably the most important decision of that person's life was wrong?

Janis Joplin, Jimi Hendrix, Phil Ochs, Jim Morrison, Brian Jones, Sid Vicious, Rory Storm, Del Shannon, Richard Farina, Keith Moon, Richard Manuel, Kurt Cobain...I had a really good time at the Rock & Roll Hall of Fame in Cleveland when I visited it in July 2006 with my brother and nephew—even though it was a rather odd choice of venues for a mentally-tentative relative. Particularly considering that all of the above died of suicide or overdose (or both).

Tentative though I may have been when I walked in the door, I was soon overwhelmed by the shameless outpouring of creativity in every single acoustically shielded exhibit. I walked out after about an hour, still gasping at the synesthetic connections that had taken me back 35 years faster than a speeding bullet (poor choice of metaphor there).

The specter of suicide and drug overdose floats gently through the place: the childhood drawing of a flock of sheep by Jimi Hendrix (with one black lamb off to the side), Kurt Cobain's electric guitar, Brian Jones's dulcimer, Keith Moon's velvet outfit trimmed in white squiggly fringe, Janis Joplin's '65 Porsche, Jim Morrison's baby book...

I don't glorify their suicides...I doubt many people in my generation do. But I certainly don't blame those people for what they did. Or think it lessens in any way how potent a role their music plays in my generational DNA.

Indeed, Neil Young, who is going straight to rock & roll heaven if, by any chance, he actually dies, has written several lines about suicide/drug overdose, including the iconic (and ironic) suggestion that for some of his fellow famous musicians, it may truly have been better to burn out than fade away...

☙

Extensive studies have been done on whether antidepressants increase the risk of suicidal thoughts and behaviors. And the subsequent headlines, like those based on many such studies, have generated a whole lot more fear than insight.

Just as chemotherapy can make some patients feel worse, and ultimately, even shorten their lives, so antidepressants can make some patients feel worse and, sadly, be a contributing factor in suicides.

These are strong drugs. But the underlying diseases are pretty virulent to begin with—which makes the attempt to draw direct causes-and-effects seem a bit simplistic. Is it fair to say that trying an unproven chemotherapy drug is brave (which it is!) even though it may "hasten" death, while, at the same time, saying that taking an antidepressant is foolhardy because it can "cause" suicide?

While the link between taking antidepressants and suicidal thoughts is somewhat tenuous—albeit enough to require careful monitoring of anyone taking them—the link between hopelessness and suicide isn't.

So to imply that medications "cause" suicide feels like a disservice to all of those who are or might be helped by them. And even a disservice to the unique individuality of those who, having tried everything, feel there's simply no more hope.

Ultimately, we're all part of a clinical trial. And the results may never be in. Without discounting the possibility of sudden, miraculous out-of-nowhere cures, it can take a long time and some serious help to recover your balance. We're talking months. In my case, almost two years. In some cases, it's the work of a lifetime. While that may make our lives a little more scary, it can also make them a little more sacred.

Alternative Medicine

The fact is that those who are enslaved to their sects are not merely devoid
of all sound knowledge, but they will not even stop to learn.

—GALEN

∽

WESTERN = Eastern = Alternative = Traditional = Complementary = Conventional = Holistic = Integrative. I have
extraordinary respect for both modern medications and alternative
therapies. While we may or may not be over-medicated, we're certainly under-cured. But that's not for lack of trying.

The much maligned drug companies are trying to help. Over-
worked psychiatrists, doctors, and nurses are trying to help.
Supplement companies are trying to help. Non-traditional practitioners, nutritionists, and alternative healers are trying to help.
Sure, these people and companies all have a vested interest in
wanting *their* cures to be the ones that work. But to cast asper-
sions on a whole class of businesses or professionals seems unfair.
About twenty years ago, practitioners of "alternative" medicine
started referring to their practices as "complementary." By then,
they'd seen enough patients who'd benefited from combining their
treatments with Western medicine that there was no longer any
reason to draw lines in the sand. Fortunately, Western medical professionals were seeing the same thing.

More recently, the phrases "holistic" and "integrative" have become popular—honorable attempts to acknowledge that practitioners should do *everything* they can to learn *all* about their patients
and find the best combination of *all* possible treatments. This ap-

proach is not new. Centuries before Dr. Andrew Weil (who, I must admit, never seems to age), holistic medicine was recommended by healers from Hippocrates, the "father of modern medicine," to Paracelsus, the great alchemist of the Middle Ages.

This mutual medical peace accord continues to progress in fits and starts. While there's still some shoulder shrugging, eye rolling, equivocating, and outright cynicism on both ends of the health-care spectrum, those of us on the receiving end no longer feel that we're caught in middle...except by the insurance companies who feel *they're* caught in the middle and spend a lot of time number crunching trying to figure out how to make sure we stay in there with them. (A Chinese-finger puzzle of socio-political complexity that strains even my commitment to neutrality.)

I like the phrase "continuum of care." No boundaries, no either/ or. *Your* complementary medicine is *my* traditional medicine. And vice versa. Professionals can call it whatever they want. All we patients care about is moving toward greater health any way we can.

ෆ

One of the tenets of complementary medicine is that it treats the whole person, not just the symptoms. This is quite a claim, considering we're talking 11 systems, 22 internal organs, 206 bones, 600 muscles, 60,000 miles of arteries, veins, and capillaries; 100,000 hairs (on a good day); and 100 trillion cells of which a billion are replaced every hour; *plus* individual combinations of genetics, lifestyles, environment, and astrological influences; *plus* individual mental, emotional, physical, sexual, and spiritual capacities and/ or experiences. As I've said before, under the circumstances, it's amazing that any two individuals can ever be cured with similar medications or "modalities."

Mental illness is not just a disease of the mind. It puts down roots throughout your body, emotions, and spirit—implicating every organ and system. Sometimes your thoughts weigh on you; other times your heart is heavy, your throat is wired, and/or you sense that life has no meaning. At its worst, all of the above.

The fact that depression can be a contributing factor to heart disease is now scientific knowledge as well as common wisdom. And a dermatologist once told me, only in part tongue-in-cheek, that she can see mental illness written all over the faces of her patients.

The mind-body connection is real. And it goes every which way. Constantly.

The idea that every part of you is implicated in your mental illness is humbling, but empowering. Because while it explains why there's no panacea, in the process it restores *your own* intuition to its rightful place as the ultimate arbiter of your own care.

Say you have weak adrenals, thanks or no thanks to something that happened to mom during her pregnancy. Over the course of your life, your adrenals have become increasingly stressed by environment, diet, life circumstances, and/or other factors until by now they're thoroughly compromised. If those weak adrenals are one of the proximate causes of your anxiety, you may be helped by anything from bodywork to taking licorice root. If, however, some childhood trauma is constantly pumping out traumatic childhood memory vibes into your whole system, no amount of bodywork or licorice root is going to provide a long-term cure.

On the other hand, if your adrenals are totally shot, maybe you need to heal them *while* you're doing the therapy you need to do to release those childhood traumas. And, if you're binge drinking you may have to go to Alcoholics Anonymous to get a handle on *that* first or else you'll keep missing your therapy appointments. And, maybe you can't deal with *any* of this until you find a medication that lowers your cortisol levels or raises your dopamine levels.

In other words, the issue isn't necessarily figuring out what's going to work, it's making your best determination of the most effective way to begin untangling this tangled web.

Some people with mental illness might be helped by a prescription drug; others, a drug and a therapist; others, an herb and acupuncture; others, blood-pressure medication and a two week vacation; others, a regular meditation practice; and others, the spiritual/karmic purging of their choice. Or any of many combinations of the above.

The important thing is that there's a wide range of places where you can introduce some healing. There's no absolute right way. Rest assured that in some way—no matter how inscrutably personal or even karmic—you are doing exactly the right thing for you. There's no need to suffer the truly debilitating anxiety that can come from thinking you might be doing the wrong thing.

There are times, of course, if you pose a threat to yourself or to others, that others may intervene. Hamlet, for example, felt the only cure for his misery was karmic intervention—which involved killing his two-timing Uncle Claudius and committing suicide. I'm not sure either licorice root, Valium, or family therapy could have helped, but who knows?

To add convolution to complexity, different treatments work at different speeds. So, while as little as .25 mg of Klonopin could calm you down pretty quickly, it might take 300 mg of valerian root a couple of hours for a similar affect. Of course, if your anxiety is genetic, you might have to wait for the latest breakthrough in gene therapy in order to get to its roots. And that past life when you had a stake driven through your heart? Jeez. It's amazing you even make it through the day.

I know there were probably times I would have felt better faster if I'd done what some person, book, or website told me; and other times when I took advice that increased the suffering. But, ultimately, I'd rather follow my own intuition and own innate intelligence—informed by any knowledge I can garner, advice I can get, and any experience I've had—than live chained to the idea that someone else always knows what's best for me. To return to the wisdom of Paracelsus: "If you're not your own man, you're someone else's." That was his motto. And he was a doctor.

∞

My 2006 calendar is cluttered with appointments with alternative therapists. Including a homeopath, an acupuncturist, a Rolfer, a

Craniosacral practitioner, and a Shiatsu therapist. I also spent a lot of time standing indecisively in front of the supplement section at our health food store. You could say this demonstrates an unwavering commitment to restoring my mental health, a heroic Dantean journey through various alternative purgatories, or simply indiscriminate flailing.

Regardless, I can't remember a single "treatment" that *didn't* help at least a little. To me, the issue was how long it held. A few hours were a relief. A day was even better. A few days...unlikely. In fact, at one point I realized that there was a good chance that if I had gone to the acupuncturist every day, I might have muddled along fairly well. Or, if I could have daily blood tests so I could fine-tune my supplements with a really experienced naturopath, I'd have been able to stay closer to fine. It's as if alternative therapies also have "half-lives" that are, unfortunately, even more unpredictable than medications:

June 4, 2006 [email]
A couple of days ago I took a bunch of magnesium and it really calmed the flutter in my throat. For the next 24 hours, I had energy and enthusiasm for all kinds of different projects and ideas. But the next day and now, after two days of rain here, my head/heart balance is all jumbled again. The "coarser" outside elements (amount of sunshine, balancing certain nutritional elements, and exercise) seem to be the only things that make a noticeable difference in how I feel. But they don't last. I've tried just about everything: Chinese herbs, amino acids (SAM-e seemed to help for a while but then not—the others seem to just make me more jazzed), B vitamins, Bach Flower remedies, avoiding caffeine, cutting out sugar, etc. etc. etc. They all seem to help and then not. My system can't get any traction.

Within alternative medicine, there are four types of overlapping complementary therapies. These categories are not cast in stone. In fact, I made them up. But they're useful for discussion purposes.

- Diet/Supplements
- Bodywork
- Energetic Treatments
- Meditation/Positive Thinking

My first attempt to "heal" myself through diet was in the summer of 1971. I had heard somewhere that it was a good idea to do a one-day "rice fast" every few weeks. On the self-designated day, I skipped breakfast, and when I went out for my lunch break, I walked with profound esoteric seriousness to the local Chinese restaurant where I bought a container of rice and walked back to the village green to eat it.

I vividly remember the feeling of those tasteless globs of white rice, which I managed to chew and swallow with ascetic determination.

We didn't really know about diet back then. (I didn't even know about brown rice back then!) Diet was something you did if you wanted to lose weight or, maybe, pump yourself up for sports... but not as a form of healing.

Bread & Circus, the forerunner of Whole Foods in New England, had just opened. Celestial Seasonings had just introduced their first herb teas (*Red Zinger* and *Sleepytime*). And the only supplement anyone knew about was One-a-Day. Oh, there were vague notions of calories and sugar and fatty foods. But adusting or supplementing our diets certainly wasn't our first line of defense against illness.

That changed pretty quickly. Between 1976 and 1986, I didn't even go to a traditional western doctor. Rather, I lived in a subculture where people paid a lot of attention to how different foods affected them. I was still willing to "pay the price" for "too much" sugar, caffeine, and carbs, but I became increasingly aware of what that price was.

I know that, in terms of mood, more complex carbs and proteins (for me, particularly red meat) are stabilizing. Whereas, no surprise, caffeine, alcohol, and sugar can be destabilizing. Nicotine, oddly, can be both. My knowledge is not theoretical. I have gone days without eating any sugar, weeks without caffeine, months without red meat, and years without alcohol. And I've had fewer than ten cigarettes in the last 25 years.

During my breakdown I did modulate all of the above with varying degrees of success. I have friends who insist that if I had immediately taken up a certain diet—macrobiotic, ayurvedic, raw food, or others—I would have healed far faster. Proponents of such diets will also usually suggest you add certain supplements to your diet because, when you're sick, it's difficult to get everything you need from a regimented diet alone.

About 50% of Americans take some form of supplement. Primarily vitamins and minerals but also amino acids, tinctures, essences, herbs, and those strange extracts from the glands of cows and pigs that gave their lives so we could feel better.

I'd venture to guess that depressives are right up there with heart and cancer patients in terms of exploring every possible way to supplement their diet and whatever other therapies they're receiving.

Our choices are informed by books, blogs, websites, suggestions from herbalists, naturopaths, acupuncturists, friends, and detailed (albeit caveat-laden) explanations from people at the supplement section of the natural-foods store. Some folks use a crystal on the end of a pendulum or kinesiology to leverage their innate intuitive powers. Don't knock it 'til you've tried it.

Most of these therapies are based on the premise that your body, given the right tools, can do a better job at figuring out how to heal itself than a doctor can through direct intervention with powerful medications. This makes a certain amount of sense since your body, until this current episode, has presumably done a pretty good job.

Feeding your body with supplements to cure depression, however, is like feeding your soil with nutrients to grow better tomatoes. It can be a slow process and needs to be fine-tuned on a regular basis, making the process even more individual than taking meds. If possible, you want to work with a practitioner who has extensive experience putting custom combinations together and will monitor you as closely as a good psychiatrist would monitor someone taking an antidepressant.

The most famous book on healing depression with supplements is by Dr. Patricia Slagle. It's called *The Way Up From Down* and has the subtitle: *Rid Yourself of Low Moods and Depression with This Easy-to-Follow Drug-Free Program of B Vitamins and Amino Acids.*

This book combines a brilliant explanation of how depression works with why and how certain supplements can treat it as well as pharmaceuticals. It also has (at least in our edition) 306 pages, a 34-page bibliography, and six appendices. Which makes it many things, but not "easy-to-follow." She does have a fairly straightforward "basic program" on page 56 that can help a lot of people, but she spends the other 272 pages giving you information to help you understand and treat your specific condition. While I'm convinced that her programs can work, I would no more start slugging down amino acids and B vitamins based simply on reading her book than I would pop Cymbalta and Lamictal without a doctor's prescription and oversight. That is, if I had managed to see Dr. Slagle (or some other *experienced* expert in nutritional treatments for depression) and knew how to reach her in an emergency, I would have been more likely to consider that approach.

Again, we're talking about major depression. If you're just going through a sad period—maybe a little seasonal depression—there's no reason not to experiment with supplements. But, without contradicting that self-empowerment pep talk I gave a few pages ago, if you're in crisis mode, you might consider trying to find someone with a little experience whom you trust to hang in there with you.

∽

I saw various bodyworkers during my sickness. I still do when I'm really wired, my muscles are really sore, and/or I'm feeling rich.

There is something immensely powerful and soothing about any kind of "laying on of hands." It does way more than relax your muscles. It's like respite care for a restless soul.

I always looked forward to these appointments. Knowing I could count on experiencing at least some calm at a specific day and time helped keep me going from week to week. I vividly remember the hopeful anticipation; the sense of release that came from lying on a table while one of my friends—as I considered all these practitioners—surrounded me with their own particular brand of kindness; the lightness I'd feel afterwards for a few minutes, maybe hours.

No matter how hard my bodyworkers tried, however—one went so far as to come to our house and do a two-hour session at 6 A.M.—those treatments didn't "hold" either.

August 2, 2006 [email]
A couple of days ago I went for a Craniosacral treatment from a woman who's as nuts as I am. Actually more so. She's been even further down many of the roads I've been traveling (and taken many of the same meds!), plus she sees energy lines so, well, I guess, I just sort of trust her, eh?

Well, I walked out of the session and was myself...for like a few hours. Went to a business meeting and was smart and funny! (Hard to believe, eh?). Had dinner with some friends and was outgoing... and funny. Came home and was, like, interested in being alive. Next morning, the terror started to creep back, but not completely. And I've been back and forth since then...into the darkness and out...overall a relief. Sometimes it just seems I'm out of practice, you know?

႙

Acupuncture is the most well-known "energetic" treatment. It's done a lot to break down the barriers between traditional and complementary medicine. Millions of people use it without thinking it's all that weird. The FDA approves acupuncture needles as a medical device. And insurance companies are beginning to offer coverage.

Of all the various "whole-body" paradigms, I think acupuncture is the most elegant and intuitively comprehensible. Maybe it's because most acupuncturists have a cool chart on the wall that shows a prototypical Leonardo human with elaborate networks of meridian lines going from point to point, crisscrossing and circulating energy throughout his various glands and organs. Anyone who's ever tingled all over has a sense of why sticking a needle into BL17 on your mid-back might help your headache go away.

Acupuncture—along with chewing on nuts, leaves, roots, and berries—is also the most time-tested medicine. Its roots stretch back to before recorded time. They must be doing something right.

It's actually never been my alternative treatment of choice. On the one hand, I'm a little too sensitive to needles (even though they really don't hurt) and, on the other hand, the effect is a little too subtle for a fast-moving worldly guy like me to appreciate. But, I have friends who've used it to manage all kinds of conditions, including chronic ones that have resisted other treatments.

The sessions did help some, however, and gave some insight into my condition and how to deal with it:

A: In Chinese medicine there's the concept of mucous obstructing the heart. It's like a veil that seems to be acting as a buffer. Sometimes that veil can become thicker and thicker like a curtain and in extreme cases it can become quite brick-like. So we're trying to soften that veil...get that circulation moving so your heart can communicate better, from the inside out and the outside in.

D: That corresponds with what I'm feeling somehow.

A: Your arm...you're also manifesting this big clog of stagnant blood.

D: You can see that?

A: When I picture you exercising hard, I wonder how much you're able to release because your ch'i is so congested. You're unable to throw it out, so it's like these lightning bolts inside, and where does it go? It recirculates back up.

D: A lot of what I do...writing, biking, puts a lot of energy into that part of the arms. That's why I throw my racquet in squash. Let go of it...Crying is a release but, for me, it can also be a pathway into darkness. Like a road that goes in two directions...

A: It's important to see the depression as being almost a wound, so we need to be gentle with it. If you need to have "stitches" you

123

want those stitches, or the fabric of the scar tissue, to eventually get incorporated, supple.

Depression can be a very rich experience that holds you in the moment; that slows the moments down; but at the same time it can become so painful because it is like a tearing that exposes a very vulnerable part of yourself. And that's why when you have congested ch'i surfacing around that wound, it makes that energetic tissue much more vulnerable. By circulating the ch'i, it recreates that energetic tissue. That's also what the antidepressant can do.

That last sentence, which implies that a prescription antidepressant can cure the cause as well as the symptoms, is an admirable and remarkable statement for an alternative practitioner to make.

Several months later, as she put the needles in, her words were like a free-verse Chinese Mother Goose rhyme, complete with commentary:

These points are to boost your immune system.
These are for the blood to settle it down.
These are for the heart to give it some cover
So it will stop bleeding memories.
As people get older, those who are yin
Can get brittle...
We need to soften, smooth the yin
So those connections can be made.
Others who are more yang are
Like a swollen bog that needs to be drained.
The anxiety can be both protective
And make you more vulnerable.

If you were a Victorian gentleman
You'd just relax in your rose garden.

Great image. Although I have no idea how that Victorian guy was able to relax.

Researchers have proven that there's absolutely no proof that homeopathy works. Still, in America, millions of people take homeopathic remedies. In some European countries, as many as 50% of physicians—yes, M.D.s—prescribe them.

Even if all those people are victims of a network of shameless quacks (which, of course, psychiatrists have also been accused of being), you gotta figure that if homeopathy can't be proven scientifically, the remedies must be the most fabulous placebos ever invented or homeopathic practitioners are actually big-time shamans with seriously good juju, for whom the power of suggestion is child's play.

Either of which would be good enough for me.

The basic operating principle of homeopathy is that "like cures like." In overly simplistic terms, if you have poison ivy, a homeopathic dose of poison ivy might help alleviate the symptoms. I think of it as kind of an "energetic" immunization. Although I'm not sure most homeopaths would be comfortable with that description.

When I talk about homeopathic remedies here, however, I am primarily talking about what they call "constitutionals," as opposed to the more symptom-specific remedies in little bottles and tubes that people buy to deal with aching muscles, insect bites, teething babies, and this year's version of the plague, a.k.a. the flu.

The right constitutional isn't designed to cure any one thing. Rather, it gets so deep into the fundamental energetic causes of everything that ails you, that it can bring about a pretty radical transformation in your physical, mental, and/or emotional well-being.

I think of it like this: Some have an affinity for a particular animal or insect or plant. Some feel good when they hold a specific gem or are in a room painted a certain color. All these different substances vibrate at different levels, so maybe if you are in contact with the right one it can help you get vibrationally aligned back with yourself.

When a constitutional works…okay, fine, when someone *thinks* a constitutional has worked…it feels like a true panacea. That magic bullet.

This isn't as strange as it seems. In spite of all the relatively modern focus on observable and/or measurable phenomena—such as germs, cellular aberrations, and heredity—there's a certain undefinable something that seems to determine how, why, and when each of us gets sick in our own individual ways…an undefinable something that underlies not only how rambunctious the germs inside us are able to get but even our positive or negative thoughts, our ability to love and be loved, or what we eat.

Homeopaths look for that certain something.

A lot of people walk into their offices complaining of a chronic headache, back problem, a cough that won't stop, or manic depression so bad they didn't have any idea who was actually going to show up for the appointment. But from the homeopath's perspective, each of those symptoms is just one of a myriad of ways that you are "presenting" what really ails you.

He or she wants to know what time you wake up in the morning; if you have a history of knee problems; where it hurts; where it itches; if, how, and when your private parts have been working; your thought patterns at different times of the day; everything you can remember about your dreams; and way more than you'd like to tell anybody about your phlegm, sweat, snot, and bathroom habits. In fact, during the first appointment—which can last a couple of hours—you may wonder whether the guy is more voyeur than physician.

Based on one or more of these in-depth examinations, a homeopath gives you a few tiny sugar-based pills (or an extract) that contain some essence of an animal, vegetable, or mineral substance *that's been diluted so much that scientists often can't find a single molecular trace of it left*. This makes traditional M.D.s throw up their hands in disbelief.

While I'd had some success with homeopathic remedies for various ailments in the past, I never found an effective remedy this time around. Still, I spent a lot of time feeling that there must be something out there—something to hold, to sit with, to do, that would provide relief. I confess to hugging the occasional tree, usually quaking aspen…you know, the like cures like thing.

Back when I was walking in the Santa Monica hills with my cousin, she suggested I stop by a large homeopathic pharmacy in Santa Monica and see if they had any ideas for me.

There, I had a very serious conversation with a very serious Germanic woman, appropriately named Greta. She listened empathically to my symptoms and asked if I'd tried any flower essences. I knew about flower essences. A German doctor named Edward Bach developed these mild plant-based tinctures back in the 1930s in order to treat emotional and mental imbalances (of which I had plenty to choose from). The most famous one is called Rescue Remedy. Lots of people take Rescue Remedy to chill out. Including my mom, who took it along with her blood pressure and thyroid medications. She even went to an acupuncturist. See what happens when you combine an open mind with a touch of hypochondria? And, she lived to be 90!

I told Greta that I'd indeed tried Rescue Remedy, as well as a more specialized Bach Flower remedy called Aspen (as in *Quaking Aspen*.) She explained that, contrary to my assumption, these remedies don't really work on the homeopathic like-cures-like principle. So, even though Aspen is indeed recommended for "vague unknown fears…that something awful is going to happen even though it is unclear what exactly," she suggested I would benefit more from Oak because it gives you strong roots. Plus, she recommended White Chestnut for some reason I don't remember—although I hope it wasn't because she thought I was too prickly…or, worse, about to become extinct.

The next morning I wrote:

I bought the White Chestnut and Oak and did what she said. By the time I got to the airport to pick up my partner an hour later, I was hungry for the first time in days. Last night I still woke up at 3:30, but

I didn't mind lying there because my thought patterns weren't frantic.
Finally took a little Valium because I needed to sleep. Woke up at 5:30,
measurably better than usual. And the flutter in my solar plexus (it
moves from my throat chakra to my solar plexus) was much milder.

That particular feeling of well-being lasted only a day or two. So
I decided to follow up on Greta's other suggestion…something
called gemmotherapy. Even though I'm a walking encyclopedia
of counter-cultural cures, I had never heard of this one. She had
explained that it's sort of a cross between homeopathy and flower
essences. Unfortunately, they didn't have any in stock. Fortunately, I was in LA for that Natural Foods Expo. I figured that if you
couldn't find this gemmotherapy stuff there you couldn't find it
anywhere. I couldn't find it there.

The best I could do was a long conversation with a beautiful
Lebanese homeopath who knew all about gemmotherapy but refused to suggest a remedy unless she and her father (an even more
experienced homeopath) were able to perform the official two-
hour homeopathic examination of my entire physical, mental, and
emotional existence. Unfortunately, I was leaving for Las Vegas the
next day. After I begged a little more, she admitted that she had
a sense that my remedy might be "neon," which is a very noble,
albeit unstable element. Like cures like! Unfortunately, neon's not
the easiest thing to get your hands on—especially the homeopathic
kind. A few days after I met her, however, I stepped out on the bal-
cony of my hotel room in Gallup, New Mexico, and found myself
a foot away from the hotel's 1950s-style neon sign. Happy to grasp
at yet another straw, I sat next to it for almost an hour. Nice color.
Nice energy. Nice try, Dave.

∽

Meditation is another way to bring some balance to your frac-
tured body, emotions, mind, and/or spirit. There's no need to
limit yourself to traditional forms of "meditation." As far as I'm
concerned, anything that calms any part of you down is a medi-

tation. If you're too agitated to hold a yoga posture, you can always do some aerobics or take a fast walk in the woods. If you find it a wee bit difficult to open your heart to accept all that is—which is understandable under the circumstances—watching "stupid" TV sitcoms is an excellent alternative. In fact, *anything* that helps you laugh is a meditation.

Most teachers of mind-stilling meditations believe that those techniques can help reduce or eliminate the need for medications. Even the Dalai Lama, who tends to look at all phenomena with phenomenal equanimity, has said, "Those emotions that disturb our peaceful mind must be eliminated. In times of great distress, our best friend is inside the heart...it is our compassion." While he and others usually make exceptions in the case of severe depression or bipolar, I'm not sure whose criteria they use to decide if you qualify. I *am* sure that words like "must be eliminated" can be *extremely* agitating, especially for someone who has, for many years, put his "faith" in meditation and finds that stillness is currently the last thing from his mind. Several times I've heard of long-term depressed meditators whose teacher and fellow students are convinced that meditation is the "true" way out. Which seems kind of, well, closed-minded for an open-minded practice.

By the way, if you do manage to achieve some stillness from meditation, when you get up from your cushion, look out! Because the demons may just be biding their time. Talk about mixed states!

Sex is also a great meditation—no special technique required. It can give you a sense of balance and help you feel connected to something other than that black cloud swirling inside you. It helps to have a patient and understanding partner—the last thing you need is performance anxiety, on top of everything else. At the risk of seeming *schmaltzy*, a long heartfelt hug can be remarkably soothing. If even *that* feels intimidating, you can always hug a tree. Maybe you can even find someone to hug it with you.

Positive thinking, chanting, and other kinds of affirmations are safe and low-cost treatments for depression. Once in a while, I would repeat the words, "I feel great," over and over. Just for a minute or two. I took my measure. Any time I vowed to say it for a lot longer, I risked feeling guilty for forgetting. Maybe if I had more discipline and had kept it as my anchoring mantra, it might have made a more serious dent in my state—or, rather pulled some of the dents out.

As it was, I have no idea whether, over time, it had any effect on my cerebral wiring. But, there was something empowering about doing it. Like I'd at least taken a swing.

When all else fails, or even if it doesn't, there's the popular Coffee-Drinking Meditation. (Make it decaf.) There were days when the refuge of sleep was no longer possible, but the thought of another day brought such a wave of mental anguish—such a nausea of the mind—that I was too exhausted to even get it together to go outside and walk. On those days, if the agitation wasn't too bad, I could occasionally just get up and sit in front of the sun, or even one of those full-spectrum lights, with a cup of coffee. If I managed to wait patiently, after maybe a half hour, a thought or two of some bearable human activity might arise. Nothing too strenuous. Maybe trimming a tree. Raking some leaves.

Obviously, there's nothing wrong with encouraging someone to meditate if they're depressed. Just remember: asking a serious anxiety-riddled depressive to quiet his mind, get over it, and/or not be so attached to his/her state can be like asking someone who's color-blind to see red.

Self-Medication

COOKIES!!! UMM-NUM-NUM-NUM-NUM

—Cookie Monster

☙

W E ALL "SELF-MEDICATE." We started doing so the moment we realized that we felt better after eating a chocolate bar, which affects the action of serotonin, dopamine, endorphins, and opioids. Or that we felt kinda nice and drowsy after having a spoonful or two of cherry-flavored cough syrup, which can *really* do a number on your histamine and serotonin receptors.

Considering that Coke, Mountain Dew, and that sweet, milky, Swee-Touch-Nee tea my aunt used to give me all have plenty of caffeine (which affects dopamine and glutamine) I unwittingly developed a limited but fairly high-powered neurotransmitter pharmacopoeia by the time I was in elementary school. To paraphrase Bob Dylan: I started out on mother's milk, but soon hit the harder stuff.

Between 1969 and 1999, alcohol, caffeine, sugar, cigarettes, and the occasional illegal drug were, for me, part of a well-balanced emotional life. The first three still are. I gave up cigarettes when I was 36. I did all my LSD before age 21. And it's been many years since I've done any other illegal drugs. (Okay, fine, I have developed a fondness for marijuana tincture, but I only do it on very special occasions. Medicinal grade, of course...)

Until I started writing this book, I didn't know that alcohol affects serotonin, dopamine, and GABA. I did know that it could help

131

me relax and, in the right measure, let my creativity flow a little more easily. I didn't know that cigarettes are powerful regulators of acetylcholine and dopamine. I did know that they picked me up and helped me focus. I didn't know that marijuana increases serotonin levels and activates cannabinoid receptors. I did know that it could turn a relaxing evening into a *really* relaxing *and/or* erotic evening. I didn't know that the LSD molecule bears a remarkably close resemblance to the serotonin molecule. I did know that it took me to the outer limits of mania, depression, and insight.

1969 to 1999. That's thirty years during which I never saw a psychiatrist. Thirty years during which I never took a prescription antidepressant. Thirty years during which I was never hospitalized (for anything!). Thirty years during which I never physically harmed myself or anyone else. Thirty years during which I got married, had a child, and ran a successful business. Thirty years is a long time. At what point is effective long-term "self-medication" as good as a traditional cure?

To give credit where credit is due, I should mention that my dad, like many in his generation, set a great example of successful "self-medication" with alcohol or cigarettes. I don't even like using the term…it was how he lived. I mean at some point, if your "steady state" is having a couple of drinks every night, where's the harm? In your liver, perhaps. But given the choice of relentless depression and a challenged liver, I'd take the latter. He never took antidepressants until the last months of his life when his doctor prescribed a tiny dose of Prozac with his morning orange juice to ward off any morbid melancholy. While my dad did enjoy listening to Wendy read him Wordsworth "Intimations of Immortality" during his last days (and was able to recite along from memory) it wasn't the Prozac as much as his well-practiced professorial bemusement that took the edge off any melodramatic angst.

You don't have to read reports by the Surgeon General to know how these substances in excess (an ever-moving target) can cause long-term damage to various parts of your body, other people, and even society at large…at least financially.

You also don't have to read lurid memoirs to know that addiction sucks. I never did heroin, but cigarette withdrawal was hard enough for my taste. And, although at various times I've gone years without drinking, I still have an emotional reliance on alcohol. Dependency? Depends on your definition.

You don't have to walk down more than one big-city block to realize that virtually *everyone* is doing *something* to manage their moods…in many cases, making life more challenging for various parts of their bodies and society, in the process. Can I offer you a double-latte? How 'bout a burger and fries? Hi, kids! Would you like a 32-ounce soda?

In the name of full disclosure, here's the complete list of things that I've taken to regulate my moods over the last 50 years or so:

Everyday: (not *every* day, mind you) Sugar, coffee, black tea, green tea, herb tea, and various other over-the-counter drugs including aspirin, ibuprofen, acetaminophen (and their nighttime versions), naproxen sodium, and various cold remedies.

"Alternative": Vitamins, minerals, run-of-the-mill herbs, Chinese herbs, homeopathic remedies, and those mysterious glandular supplements whose source I never really liked thinking about.

Controlled: Cigarettes, wine, beer, and hard liquor of all kinds, including long-term relationships with cognac, bourbon, and Irish whiskey (fortunately, not at the same time). You'll be happy to know I gave up cigarettes in 1988.

Illegal: Marijuana—including brownies and tincture—hashish, mescaline, LSD, mushrooms (although, as I remember, I didn't get off), MDA and its more famous bastard child Ecstasy, cocaine, and the very occasional amphetamine. No needles.

Prescription: BuSpar, Celexa, Klonopin, Cymbalta, Depakote, Effexor, Lamictal, Lexapro, Lorazepam, Lunesta, Ambien, Seroquel, Valium, Wellbutrin. And let's not forget Versed (the best reason to have a colonoscopy) and nitrous oxide (the best reason to have a root canal).

I provide this shockingly extensive (even to me) list in order to explain why I will not be running for president and to remind us that, whether consciously or not, we all try to fine-tune our synapses. On the one hand, it's kind of sobering. Shouldn't we be satisfied with the simple gift of being alive? On the other hand, isn't it amazing how willing we are to explore new ways to feel, think, and be all we can be?

Regardless, if the extensiveness of this list makes you feel I "deserved" to be depressed, that's fine. If it makes you feel I'm lucky I'm not dead, well, I'm not sure how much luck had to do with it. If it makes you think I should have my own talk show, maybe you should think again.

It'd probably be best if my grandchildren or yours don't read this until they're grown up…if ever…but, before you cast the first stone about what anyone else ingests or inhales, you might want to see how many words you can check off above.

To quote Paracelsus, "No thing is without poison. The dosages make it either a poison or a remedy." Whether we praise, judge, ostracize, or jail people for ingesting one of these substances is based largely on current societal norms.

Admittedly, safety is an important issue. But let's not forget that cocaine used to be in coca cola, ibuprofen used to be only available by prescription, vitamin D therapy is now mainstream, prescription drug overdoses are now the leading cause of accidental death, marijuana is being legalized, and a few people have almost died through an overdose of ḥikram (hot yoga).

For some people, self-medication, particularly with cigarettes and alcohol—plus generous amounts of sugar, caffeine, and chocolate—may lead to longer, more enjoyable lives; lives in which their depression is at least manageable. For others, the same things may lead to deeper sadness, addiction, and even death.

I'll never know whether all these different forms of self-medication precipitated my breakdown or, on the contrary, delayed it for many years. Certainly, I exhibited depressed and hypomanic symptoms back in elementary school—well before I'd even heard of most of the stuff on this list.

We all have the ability (and, I daresay, right) to try to feel better—however we experience that. It's one of the things that make us human. And the way we use that ability is an essential part of our individuality…for better or worse, in sickness and in health, 'til death do us part.

Understanding and regulating our moods isn't rocket science. It's way, way, way more complex than rocket science.

Who Knows?

It seems that I am wiser than he is to this small extent,
that I do not think I know what I do not know.

—SOCRATES

༄

HELL IS OTHER PEOPLE'S OPINIONS. Dante was pretty
lucky. Except for that sign telling him to abandon all hope, he
only had two people giving him advice—Virgil and Beatrice—with
a little *kibbitzing* from a few other folks they introduced him to
along the way. Since no other *living* person had ever been in those
realms before—and the Internet hadn't been invented yet—if Virgil told him that the way through Purgatory was to walk stooped
over, find his way through thick black smoke, or stroll through a
wall of flames, he couldn't exactly get a second opinion.

I was lucky too. With very few exceptions (actually, none I can
think of at the moment), my family and friends didn't second-guess
the various paths I chose to negotiate my personal purgatory. They
shared their ideas, made appropriate suggestions, and only gave
opinions or advice when I asked for them.

But many people aren't so lucky. They're continually dealing
with the opinions of family, friends, and casual acquaintances.

There's always someone who's just read something in a magazine or book about how there's a new medication that works better than all the previous ones combined; or that placebos actually
work even better; or that the right combination of herbs or amino
acids or both will definitely make you feel better "without any side
effects"; or that if you'd just give up sugar, alcohol, coffee, and/or
sex, you'd be fine in no time at all.

They'll tell you about some psychic or energy healer who cured someone they know in three seconds flat. Or worse, tell you that someone they know saw the healer *you're* seeing and got way worse. They'll say you should just snap out of it. They'll say you should take a vacation. They'll say you should read this book or that book, listen to this music or that music, go to this self-help group or that self-help group. Oh, and by the way, depression is genetic so you better keep an eye on your children.

Maybe it was better when people were in denial. When everybody wished that whatever was bothering you would just go away. At least then, you could suffer in peace. Just kidding. Kind of.

The hardest opinions to deal with are those of so-called "experts" on TV, radio, newspapers, magazines, and most of all, these days, the Internet. (Even I wasn't totally immune to those.) With 43 million search results and counting, finding your specific solution under "How to Cure Depression" takes on trappings of the quest for the Holy Grail.

Most of these sources of information are well-meaning. Some are well paid. Many acknowledge that in *some* cases of *major* mania or depression, you can throw their theories out the window...although you can always tell they're including that caveat with a certain reluctance, as if it were fine print. (You gotta say one thing for drug companies. They spend a lot of time and money telling you the ways their cures might *not* work. Of course, "We the People" had to pass laws to make them do it, but sometimes it seems that they go overboard.)

All "cures for depression" work some of the time. A few work a lot of the time. None work all of the time. Having people second-guess you just increases the sense of self-consciousness, self-criticism, and terminal anxiety about doing the "wrong" thing that nips at depressives' heels all day. Nothing wrong with gentle suggestions. Gentle. Non judgmental. Given with explicit or implicit permission.

Maybe the fine print on every article about depression should be the Socrates quote above.

I'm always surprised—and, of course, occasionally astounded or annoyed—when people have the *chutpah*, *hubris*, or clinical narcissism to believe that their perspective on mental illness represents any kind of ultimate truth.

My perspective, of course, *does* represent the ultimate truth! I think everybody who writes about depression should start their article, book, or blog with the following:

> WARNING: I don't pretend to know the best way for you to deal with your depression. I'm writing this because [select one or more]:

1. I'm under the delusion I do know.

2. I'm fascinated by the subject and think maybe I can help you understand it a little better.

3. I had (or am in the midst of) a paralyzing depressive episode and I need to write about it because, well, I need to write about it.

4. I'm working on a Ph.D. or trying to get tenure.

5. I make my living by selling some product or service related to depression and:

   a. I'm under the delusion that it helps all of the people all of the time.

   b. I need money real bad.

   c. I've found it helps some of the people some of the time and believe it's worth a try.

6. I've treated a whole lot of patients with all kinds of psychological conditions by using all kinds of prescription and/or alternative medications. I've also read a whole lot of books and survived some professional meetings and workshops. So I believe that I might have enough knowledge and experience to help you. But I have a lot of respect for the fact that the mind is a strange and wondrous thing.

These are all legitimate reasons to write about mental illness—although several are somewhat suspect. I'm a Category #2 and #3 kind of guy myself. More important, the health professionals I've trusted have implicitly fit into Category #6.

༄

Many people have serious objections to the use of prescription drugs. And yet, for each, there is a balancing point of view:

Spending on antidepressants is bankrupting our healthcare system.
What isn't bankrupting our healthcare system? Mental illness represents about 7% of our total healthcare costs. Undoubtedly many people could deal with their mental health problems in less costly ways. (Ditto, by the way, for many physical illnesses.) The federal per diem *base rate* for *inpatient* psychiatric care is about $700. The *per diem* cost for even three *brand-label* psychiatric meds would rarely be more than $40...and often *way* less. A savings of $660 per day if those meds manage to keep you out of inpatient psych. This book is about people, including myself, who have major depressive episodes that severely impact(ed) their ability to function. People who could, if things got worse, end up hospitalized. In our cases, meds are a bargain—in more ways than one.

Different drugs are popular during different decades (e.g., tranquilizers in the 1950s and 1960s). So, clearly a lot of diagnosing and prescribing is based on what's trendy.
What's wrong with being trendy? Attaching electrodes to a patient's brain...a treatment that was trendy for a while and then considered, uh, shocking, has become far more sophisticated lately and is now being used again with reasonably good results. Eventually, prescribing meds will *not* be considered trendy...probably soon. Something else will come along. I can't wait to try it. But, I won't be first in line.

Prescription medicines may help one disease, but throw other things off balance.

That's true of all "interventions," natural or pharmaceutical. Of course, by the same token, those interventions can bring a lot of other things *into balance*. The body does seem to try to maintain some kind of homeostasis and will use all the help it can get.

We are overmedicating our children and it's going to have catastrophic results.
Throughout history, cultures have tried all sorts of ways to "deal with" kids—from potentially catastrophic tribal rituals to potentially catastrophic 16-hour work days to potentially catastrophic medications to potentially catastrophic denial. Children are always pushing the envelope of consciousness. That's their job! How we encourage and guide that energy is the most critical creative challenge faced by parents, society, and humanity at large. But, most of all, it's a challenge for every child. And nothing is going to stop a child from pushing his or her personal envelope.

The body has its own wisdom and can, ultimately, heal itself.
In many cases, that's true. In many cases, it's a judgment call. In all cases, it depends on the person, the illness or injury, and many other factors.

It's important to treat the whole person, not just the symptoms.
You mean you're going to treat all ±trillion of my cells all at once? Cool.

Antidepressants are actually placebos.
Great! Where can I buy more?

Incidences of mental illness have actually increased since antidepressants were invented.
This is an interesting argument popularized by a recent book called *Anatomy of an Epidemic: Magic Bullets, Psychiatric Drugs, and the Astonishing Rise of Mental Illness in America.* And Robert Whitaker, the author, does an excellent job of making his case, based on one way of evaluating clinical-trial and epidemiological data. But who

knows whether the relationship between diseases, drugs, environment, and culture is co-dependent, independent, or coincident? My guess would be all three. Certainly, most people would agree that societal and environmental stresses have increased *significantly* since antidepressants were invented.

ᴄᴂ

Many people have serious objections to the way pharmaceutical companies do business. They refer to them collectively as "Big Pharma," and say all they care about is making money. But consider this:

Hundreds of thousands of people work for pharmaceutical companies. Undoubtedly, some of them just want to sell as many of their drugs to as many people as possible. They might as well be selling widgets. But most of them would sincerely like to help cure what ails us. Plus, they have bills to pay and kids to put through college. So they hope their drugs prove more effective than other treatments—whether traditional or complementary. They enthusiastically advertise any scientific or anecdotal report that says so. To medical professionals as well as individuals.

By the same token, hundreds of thousands of people work in the egg industry. Undoubtedly, some of them just want to sell as many eggs as possible. They might as well be selling potato chips. But most of them really think eggs should be part of our diet. Plus, they also have bills to pay and kids to put through college. So they hope their eggs prove to be as good a source of protein as any other food. They enthusiastically advertise any scientific or anecdotal report that says so. To professional nutritionists as well as individuals.

Ditto for people at companies who manufacture nutritional supplements, gluten-free products and (shocking as it may seem) even the family growing organic vegetables down the road. Undoubtedly, some of them just want to sell as many pills, and rice cakes, and organic carrots as possible. They might as well be selling, well, prescription drugs! But most of them really want us to feel good. Plus, they also have bills to pay and kids to put through college. So they hope their products make us feel better than the competition's and even taste better! They enthusiastically advertise any scientific or anecdotal report that says so. To professionals in complementary therapies as well as to individuals.

Ditto for people working at manufacturers of cars, computers, beer, and so on. Some might as well be selling snake oil. But most of them sincerely want you to enjoy life more, and believe their products might help you do that. They advertise to that effect.

Same with books. Undoubtedly, some writers just want to sell as many of their books as possible. They'd say anything as long someone paid them to say it. But, like most authors, I really hope my book helps you understand more, and/or feel better, and/or just pass a few pleasant hours. Plus, while our daughter graduated from college years ago, we still have bills to pay. So I hope this book does as good a job of talking about mental illness as other similar books…if not better. I will enthusiastically put any reviews that say so in the next edition!

There's a word for this vast conspiracy. It's called capitalism. Whenever two or more people are gathered in its name, some people feel better, others feel worse. Some make money, others lose money. Some feel manipulated, others feel empowered.

I have no opinion about capitalism. I do know that no one has ever put a gun to my head and made me take a drug; eat an egg; swallow a multivitamin; bite into an organic carrot; or buy a computer, car, or six-pack of beer.

There's certainly nothing wrong with letting people know your feelings and opinions about the motives and behavior of pharmaceutical companies, egg producers, organic gardeners, computer makers, and authors of books on mental illness. In fact, let's get as many perspectives on the table as possible.

But do we really have to demonize each other so much in the process?

Many people also have serious objections to relying on alternative medicine to treat depression. And yet again, for each objection there is a balancing point of view:

It's hard to design reliable clinical trials for supplements—particularly because the purity of nutritional supplements and amino acids can't be guaranteed.
There are also variances in the molecular structure of generic drugs versus the original brand names. Some patients notice a significant difference in their effectiveness.

If you feel better from taking herbs or supplements, it's probably just a placebo effect.
Same deal as with prescription drugs: if they work, all I want to know is, "where can I get more of them placebos?"

The idea that we have some kind of "energetic body" around our physical one is downright weird.
I know, but it's sure a good explanation for all kinds of other "weird" stuff.

The very idea of Craniosacral therapy is preposterous. It's a biological impossibility.
Ever had one? Maybe you'd be more open!

Homeopathic remedies are so diluted, there's no there there.
Millions of people—and thousands of doctors—rely on them more than prescription drugs.

You believe in astrology? Are you crazy?
Well, I think we've established that fact. But, remember, it was an astrologer who gave me the most accurate timeline of how my breakdown would progress and, eventually, end.

Throughout history, there's an interesting kind of synergy between humans and their cures. I wouldn't be surprised if the notion of treating depression by screwing around with neurotransmitters, receptors, and synapses is eventually considered as archaic as black bile and bloodletting. In the meantime, it seems that anything that proves helpful to anyone is worthy of our consideration and respect.

∞

One clinical trial is a proof. Two clinical trials is half a proof. And three clinical trials are no proof at all. I'm paraphrasing one of the great philosophers of the twentieth century. Well, he was actually the beloved seventh generation Yankee who owned the orchards that surround my home. That's how he described managing the teenage boys he hired to pick apples: "One boy is a boy. Two boys is half a boy. And three boys is no boy at all."

There are articles, dissertations, complex research reports, and entire books—all with countless caveats and footnotes—written about whether antidepressants work. We're not talking your basic incoherent academic dispute. This has turned into one giant medical cluster f—.

Many experts use clinical trials to prove convincingly that mind medications *are* effective. According to their studies, meds work about 60% the first time around, with the likelihood of success rising for those who can keep it together enough to try another one or two if necessary.

Others use clinical trials—and often the same ones!—to prove equally convincingly that clinical trials have proved beyond a shadow of a doubt that placebos work just as well as antidepressants.

Even more impressive, there's now some evidence that the exact same experiments, following exactly the same rules of scientific protocol, can yield significantly different results over time. Makes you want to take two aspirin and call Hippocrates in the morning.

Then there's the quantum issue. Oh yeah, the quantum issue. The one that says you can't ever really measure anything because the act of measuring changes the thing being measured. Can we just agree not to mention the quantum issue?

One thing everyone does seem to agree on—although some rather begrudgingly—is that the controversy primarily involves people with mild to moderate depression. Once they see you sobbing uncontrollably in the waiting room, they're usually willing to let you give drugs a try.

I accept that the occasional scientist will fiddle with results—consciously or subconsciously—based on who's paying for the research. More important, you don't have to be Einstein (or Heidegger to be imprecise) to realize that researchers' conclusions are inevitably influenced to some extent by their own assumptions and conventional wisdom.

William Blake, a guy who knew a thing or two about mental illness, wrote, "What is now proved was once only imagined." I would add that what many now consider imaginary may one day be proved.

Academic disputes aside, there are several questions that every self-respecting gobbler of antidepressants, antipsychotics, and anti-all-kinds-of-other things will eventually wonder: Why are clinical studies such unreliable predictors of which treatment(s) will help me? Why can a drug/remedy that was perfectly effective for me for many years suddenly stop working? Why can it have an entirely different effect when I start taking it again after stopping for a while? Why should I worry about having an erection for four hours when I can barely get up in the morning?

They are excellent questions. And, since the scientific answers are all over the place, I'll stick with the philosophical and the commonsensical:

Humans evolve. All the time. Individually. And as a species. So does all of nature. So does the entire universe. Every "subject" in those clinical trials is a swirling mass of energies in constant flux, whose individual complexity can make a mockery of any particular data point.

As I've said, we admire the determined fight of someone with cancer who insists on breaking down doors to get into the latest clinical trial, even though the treatment could be more fatal than the disease. Why don't we equally admire people who will try an antidepressant even if it hasn't been clinically proven and may also prove to be more fatal than the disease? Why don't we talk about how *they*, too, fought a courageous battle with their illness, and tried everything they could in an attempt to ward off an inevitability they felt they couldn't avoid?

Just askin'.

⁓

The real problem is that there's no quantifiable way to measure depression. Which makes life kind of difficult for traditional data-driven researchers. A psychiatrist can make his own before-and-after observations. And he can ask you the same questions before and after you start or stop a medication. Scientists are also beginning to be able to measure the amount of certain chemicals in your brain that may indicate neurotransmitter level and functioning.

It's just not the same as with other drugs.

We know what will *probably* happen if we take an aspirin, smoke tobacco or marijuana, have a glass of wine, or a cup of double espresso. However, we don't know with anywhere near 100% certainty whether a specific prescription mind med will alleviate our symptoms; fix what ails us; have significant side effects (including death); or work for a day, month, year, or lifetime. There's an overload of facts, figures, and anecdotal evidence out there.

You can measure whether a blood pressure medication is lowering your blood pressure. You can measure whether a cholesterol medication is lowering your cholesterol levels. You can even measure whether a cancer treatment is reducing a tumor or the number of cancer cells in your blood.

Even with other immeasurable or "subjective" medications there are at least some reasonably reliable indicators. Inhalers do or don't help you breathe better. Sleep medications either put you to sleep or they don't. Pain medications either relieve the pain or they don't. There may be questions about the placebo effect even with these drugs. But, tell that to anyone who's gasping for breath until they take a shot of their inhaler.

146

∽

Whatever you decide to do, it is really helpful to have one or more professionals go along for the ride. Maybe if your depression is situational, your psychological immune system can manage to remain intact—the exposed inner "skin" slowly scarring over while your neurons and/or esoteric energetic patterns find other ways to get the job done. As your life improves or at least evens out over time, your moods may improve or even out accordingly.

In cases of clinical mental illness, however, the neural patterns are usually so out of kilter that changes in external circumstances have minimal effect. That's when it's probably time to call a professional.

By professional, I mean anyone who has a lot of experience working closely with people suffering from big-time depression or mania. It could be a psychiatrist, psychologist, chiropractor, homeopath…even a psychic or priest. Or any combination of the above. As long as they are open to discussing any possible treatment you're curious about without making you feel like an idiot; as long as they answer your phone calls when you're desperate, or at least call you the next morning; and as long as you feel that they are truly committed to your healing…partners, I daresay, in the process.

Fortunately, everyone's become a little more open-minded. Nobody ever told me that prescription meds were the devil's work. A few people suggested that natural remedies were better, but even my most rabid vegan, natural-remedy-adherent therapists and friends acknowledged that sometimes medications might be necessary…at least temporarily. By the same token, no conventional medical professional ever gave me a hard time about having some needles stuck in me from time to time.

Still, it can feel weird to tell your psychiatrist that you're also taking mega B vitamins, SAM-e, tryptophan, and doing full-spectrum light therapy. It can make you squirm to tell your homeopath that you've decided to go back on your meds, just when she or he is convinced they finally figured out the right remedy for you.

I'm a big fan of putting your cards on the table. Their opinions and prejudices aren't your problem. By the same token, they don't have to agree with what you're doing. They just need to do their best to understand where you're coming from and explain the potential risks and rewards as best they can. And you owe it to them to provide as much information as you can before they prescribe anything, natural or otherwise.

I don't know, for example, if combining acupuncture, herbs, deep tissue massage, and prescription drugs helped trigger my breakdown. For all I know, the combination kept it from being more severe. I have no regrets. But I know that, at times, by not coming clean, I missed an opportunity to work more openly and closely with my psychiatrist, in a way that might have been helpful to both of us.

The important point is that most professionals—conventional or alternative—don't have a whole lot of experience in how *other* therapies might interact with theirs. An herb or pressure point over here is likely to affect a gland or neurotransmitter over there. And vice versa. Same is true for massage, meditation, prayer, illegal drugs, and SSRIs. We're still in uncharted waters here…and it's best if we admit it.

Bottom line: It's a miracle that any one treatment can help more than one person. We're dealing with more synapses in our brains than we can imagine. Our thoughts, feelings, words, actions, and biology emerge from our distinctly individual history, physiology, genetics, environment, culture, race, color, and creed, as well as our astrological sign, karma, past lives, energetic body, and a host of other factors that aren't quite so apparent to the naked eye. (You may not believe in those last few. That's fine. I think that means you're an empiricist.)

That's why so many different people are convinced there are so many different "best" ways to treat major depression.

Some people insist natural remedies are better. Others say only pharmaceuticals have been proven effective.

Some people think alternative treatments are weird. Others think that electrical stimulation of deep areas in your brain is weird.

Some people think you'll get fired if your boss finds out. Others figure your boss will get sued if she or he fires you.

Some people think seeing a psychiatrist is a sign of weakness. Others think it takes courage.

Some people think medications are too expensive. Others think it's worth begging and borrowing if you have to.

And, just when you think you've found a treatment that works, winter comes…there's less sun…so you start producing less vitamin D which somehow affects your serotonin levels. So maybe you take a vitamin D supplement and feel a little better. And then you have a massage and feel a lot better. And then you wake up with your mind racing down roads that are best left untaken, so you roll over and take a .5 mg tablet of Klonopin and doze off for an hour, but when you wake up an hour later you're still agitated, so you do an intense workout to calm down. Which leads, after breakfast, to a surprisingly pleasant early-morning nap, only to wake up wired again, so you take a little calcium-magnesium and call your psychiatrist who suggests that instead of taking 60 mg of Cymbalta every day, you do 60 mg one day and 30 mg the next.

And then, just when you think you've got things in balance again, you get fired or divorced or start to have unrelated angina, or break a leg so you can't work out, which confuses your neurotransmitter systems in a whole different way.

That fictional scenario might make you question the possibility of *ever* stringing together more than a few blessed moments of sanity. But, lest I scare anybody who is currently on a similar roller coaster, I've been good—really good—for *years* with only a very few very brief relapses.

There are countless treatments for this disease, many of which I have had the pleasure of experiencing. I'm as tempted as the next "expert" to offer an opinion on what someone is doing or taking. But, I know that what helped me could have an equal and opposite effect for someone else…or even for me the next time.

Fixed opinions are luxuries that I, and I daresay most depressives, can ill afford. We may ask you what you know about depression and meds. We may want to hear about your experiences or those of your friends. We may ask for your suggestions. But ultimately, what we really need is as much support as possible, regardless of our choices.

Visible Means of Support

It's often just enough to be with someone. I don't need to touch them.
Not even talk. A feeling passes between you both.
You're not alone...

—MARILYN MONROE

႒

EVERY MOMENT of intimacy is its own little miracle. Whether with casual strangers, long-term friends, or family. Whether it manifests as a random act of kindness, simple acceptance, gentle humor, light touch, heartfelt hug, or passionate romance, love has a kind of energy that accepts no substitutes. Even if there were no prescription drugs, no supplements, no acupuncture needles, no homeopathic remedies, and no meditation practices, the most powerful remedy of all is still swirling around. Unfortunately, when you're that involuted, it usually feels just out of reach... even in the midst of orgasm, which releases more than enough serotonin, dopamine, acetylcholine, and norepinephrine to perk up most human brains.

I recently heard a story about a doctor who uses sophisticated brain scans to diagnose and treat illness. Early in his career, a friend of his who had just fallen "madly" in love stopped by his clinic for a visit. Curious, the doctor did a scan and, when he read it, it looked exactly like the brain of someone on cocaine...

From the epicenter of my personal psychotic universe, I was surrounded by many people who—knowingly or not—provided some form of support. I see them radiating out in Dantean spheres from an inner one that only Wendy could occupy to outer orbits of those who saw me so infrequently that I figured they never suspected there was anything wrong. Wrong.

Masking the symptoms of mental instability—or making them seem like not such a big deal—is the depressive's version of an Olympic event. It takes an extraordinary amount of energy to manufacture manifestations that will seem relatively normal to the people around you. I figured I usually earned at least a bronze medal. But it appears even in that I may have been deluded. A few years later after "outing" myself in a local paper, I received a letter— a real, handwritten letter—from someone I've known for almost thirty years but, except for the occasional party or chance meeting downtown, rarely saw. She wrote:

> In our small community we are all intertwined and tangled and not much goes unnoticed. I would be fibbing if I said I didn't suspect at times that you were not feeling well. Sharing your writing is a beautiful way to break the silence and get folks talking, engaged and moving toward, if nothing else, supporting one another.

She's right. We are all connected. But...but...but...what do you say when you see someone who's clearly fallen into an emotional sinkhole? You want to help, but how? Everything you say seems to disappear into a bottomless pit. Trying to cheer him up seems somehow insensitive. Too much empathy can make you pretty damn sad yourself...which can, in turn, make him feel even worse. After all, if you feel someone's pain, that's twice as much pain, right?

You wait for an opening—maybe a few good hours here or there—so you can do something together that resembles fun as you formerly knew it. But you still feel like you're walking on egg-shells—one innocuous comment and he'll start talking in mono-syllables again...if he talks at all.

Depending on how well you know him, you can ignore his behavior (or lack thereof), shrug it off, share ironic jokes about it, or get really worried and upset. Regardless, you know the deal. He knows the deal. And there ain't a helluva lot either of you can do.

Maybe he'll still work out with you. Show some faint interest in business. Plan a road trip that you both know he won't take. (Or, worse, will.) Maybe go for a walk. Watch a game. If you're lucky, he might even go out for a drink. Or briefly engage in relatively normal conversation, before looking skittishly around and saying he has to go somewhere. Anywhere.

Every time you see him, you take a quick look…to see if maybe Dave is Dave again. Once in a while you see hopeful signs: he actually laughs wholeheartedly; his wit doesn't seem slashed in half. But it doesn't last. The center does not hold. You should know, however, that even if we look down, turn away, change the subject, and/or try to act like this moment does not exist, we appreciate how hard it is for you. We don't enjoy casting a shadow over your life. Far better that you keep enjoying your own good humor, rather than letting us drag you down. Just being able to let down our guard is helpful.

As I began to recover, the first thing I wanted to do was reach out…call people…interact. So be patient. If you can. We've gone on a long voyage. But we'll be back.

Probably the best thing you can do is acknowledge/accept deeply depressed people as the not-exactly-happy-go-lucky people we/they are; and remain as happy and loving as you possibly can. I better stop before I appear too New Age, but, if we don't look too ornery, you can even give us a hug.

☞

It's really hard to see inside the world of a friend who's going through a breakdown.

After a visit in the winter of 2006, I asked a friend to write what it was like:

> *I thought the winter setting reflected your personal space—blanketed, not quite smothered but clearly weighted down by a heavy force and yet still showing evidence of life inside/below—accessible but muted.*

The analogy that comes to mind is one of an astronaut on a space mission. It is a mission that the astronaut has in some way signed on for. From space the earth and all its precious beauty is visible but not tangible. There is a clear understanding that this is a mission and it will end, but the astronaut does not believe himself to be the director of this mission. He knows he will return, he knows he will embrace the earth again, but he does not know when. And this not knowing is the most difficult part and it creates a void that has its own enchantment for an active mind.

It's even harder to know what to say. But people found ways. Often I'd get little notes from friends…just letting me know they were there…and so was I.

Just wanted to say hi, and rather than bug you by calling you each day, I'll check in via email and send my love this way.

In the department of clichés department vis a vis you and your states in re my availability: 24/7. 'Nuff said.

[From a friend who drove by and saw me on a street corner]:
So amazing…through the rain I see…that's david…from the distance of the road you seemed somehow one step removed from this world… here yes…but…stay here, david…there are more adventures!!!!

No more breakdowns for either of us—or energy that wraps around one's heart and fucks you up. I find a lot of it comes down to loving myself. Hope your wailing and moaning is swept away with the rain.

David, it's time to release now. And it won't be enormous. It will be like the bee flying away and leaving its stinger behind.

By the way, being depressed does not necessarily mean you've lost your sense of humor. One day, I got an email from one of the funniest people on the planet who's known Wendy as long as me, and loves her almost as much. He wrote:

And as for nervous breakdowns…dude, you've been living with her for umpteen years. There's no mystery here. You're in line for the frickin' Distinguished Service Cross. If I was you I would have downed a quart of Liquid Plumber years ago and been done with it.

⌀

I was reluctant to talk about it. The very question: "How are you doing today?" made me claustrophobic. One of my best friends, however, did perfect the art of just glancing briefly and/or putting his hand lightly on my shoulder and asking, "How ya doing, buddy?" in a way that made it clear no answer was required, while acknowledging that if there happened to be anything he could do, he was more than willing.

I was also horrified by the notion that people would pray for me. I mean, I appreciated the thought, but it felt like an invasion of privacy. I didn't want the attention. That's just me. Prayer is probably really helpful. In fact, I'm happy to pray for anybody anytime. Just ask.

But the hardest question to bear was: "Have you tried…?" No matter how well-meaning, I'd experience the question as another person's opinion/expectation I'd have to add to the invisible Sisyphean load of indecision I was dealing with.

If you really, really believe something will help, consider taking the matter in your own hands: For example,

- Show up at his house with your bike and tell him you're going for a long ride together. Note: Be prepared to fix the flat tire he's been staring at for two days because he's so sure he'll do it wrong and doesn't want to take it to the bike shop because he's embarrassed he can't do it himself.

- Show up with two tickets to a Rolling Stones concert. (Trust me…he'll go no matter what state he's in.)

- Say in no uncertain terms: "I'm making an appointment for

you to have (a complete checkup, Craniosacral treatment, frontal lobotomy, etc.) and I'm driving you there."

☙

I did try to reach out sometimes…often in emails. To read them today gives new meaning to the phrase "mixed states." One minute I'd be writing an email about how I was definitely getting better, even though less than a half hour before, I'd had a blanket over my head and having the dry heaves, and sobbing. Later that day, I'd be writing another one that described the experience in excruciatingly objective detail.

Why did I write so differently to different people? To control the message, of course, Because, ironically, the more out of control you feel, the more urgency you feel to control how people relate to you. While it was helpful to have a good excuse for missing a meeting, dinner, party, or other seemingly intimidating social situation, I didn't want it to be *so* good I'd never be invited to another one. I did have a few "special correspondents." People I knew would read my words with a certain kind of understanding that—through some strange alchemy of communication—would make me feel better just by writing.

☙

Realizing it wasn't a great idea for me to be home alone every day that Wendy was working, I made arrangements with an artist we know to work in her studio on Wednesdays.

Our friend is so guileless you wish there was a better word for it. Finding an iota of deception or manipulativeness in her is harder than catching a glimpse of the famously rare Vermont catamount.

Being at her studio finessed two big issues for me of being around people: space versus confinement and wanting to be alone versus needing to be around people.

It was a big studio…maybe 30 feet x 30 feet. A little kitchenette to make tea. A fire escape to walk out on. She spent almost all of

156

her time painting flowers or a model, while I pushed around parts of a novel. Every once in a while, she'd come over and sit down to share the table and tea and talk with me. While she was well aware of my condition—and had gone through something similar 20 years before—she wouldn't have considered wanting it to be otherwise. Rather, I could feel her looking at it, engaged, curious, from different perspectives, as she would the things she painted. No shadows, no light. No light, no shadows.

I tried to "pay my way" by consulting with her on business, in particular her approach to time management. She really wanted to understand time. It was a concept that baffled her. For example, if she needed to have 10 paintings ready for a show in 20 weeks, I would try to explain that meant she had to do about two paintings each week. She was fascinated by the idea—she'd even laugh and tell me how great I was at "figuring stuff like that out." She just didn't really grasp what it had to do with her—which she demonstrated every time another of her self-imposed deadlines faded into history.

I felt safe there. I felt I had more to offer than just my pain. Occasionally, I think I was even pretty good company. My depression was still the elephant in the studio. But its feelings about the moment were no more important than those of the other wild things running around in my head, let alone the flowers she was painting.

Another long-term friend, after realizing just how bad I was, started coming over every Tuesday evening. He kept his own bottle of cognac at our house for the occasion, and on arriving, would pour himself a healthy shot. Emboldened, I might counter with a thimble of Jameson's. Then he'd ask me questions about what it was like. A lot of questions. Having spent years exploring drug- and alcohol-induced mental anguish—in himself and others—he was genuinely interested. He had no agenda. In fact, he admitted he kind of liked me better this way. Being able to talk about it freely in an almost clinical way helped give me a little separation from it. I looked forward to his visits.

Then there was my partner in business and crime (once or twice literally)—whose family is as close as you could be to ours without the DNA. My experience was particularly hard for him because we worked together several days a week and talked almost every day. My behavior unsettled the very rhythm of his life. We had spent many years honing our own personal, ever-evolving, often-scathing comedy routine in which no fools, including ourselves, were ever suffered. It had always been the way we "processed" the bewildering behavior of other humans. Now it was the way we managed to find ways to incorporate even my most abject states into our lovingly biting verbal slingshots.

But, deeply concerned and acutely aware of fluctuations in my tone of voice, he had to find ways to help me maintain a veneer of functionality, especially in front of colleagues and customers—without forgetting I was holding on by a thread. Efforts for which I remain grateful to this day. Once, cowering in the back of his car—he and his wife up front—acutely aware that they were suffering my despair almost as much as I was, I said, "Well, let's not institutionalize my psychosis." The irony of which didn't escape any of us.

∽

What about mom? Kids going through an emotional trauma should be able to count on their parents for support. By the time you're 85, however, you don't expect having to worry about a 55-year-old son with the stability of an 8-year-old. Especially when, for many years, you've relied on *him* for the occasional emotional lift.

My mother accomplished a lot in her life. She worked for many years as a social worker in the days when most women still stayed home with the kids. She was one of the first female trustees of an Ivy League University. Plus, she put up with my father for 47 years...an act of courage that was admired by him and all who knew (and loved) him.

Until very shortly before she died, she was independent and

active. Every month or two, however, she'd call and say, "I need a David fix." She'd been doing it ever since my dad died in the early 1990s. *Translation*: I feel a little down and I need you to cheer me up.

The phrase always made me cringe. Now, it made me want to run for cover. Still, I couldn't blame her: it wasn't that long a drive, she only wanted me to stay for a night, maybe two, and she took me out to some of the best restaurants in town. Plus, she liked to stay in bed late, reading the paper, drinking her coffee, not coming out for a late breakfast until 9 or 10. By then, I'd usually walked off at least the top layer of frenzy and could sit more or less still and have a more or less sane conversation. Bike ride, nap, good dinner, some TV...By 10 P.M., I'd successfully negotiated another day of madness. It was kind of like reverse "respite care" for Wendy who could have a few days of real peace, without worrying about me being off in some cold-water motel in Kentucky, pounding my fists into the cushion.

Maybe for some people, depression is linked to stuff they have to work out with their parents. I can't speak for them. Mine didn't have that kind of psychological underpinning.

That may be hard to believe in this confessional age, but my mother inadvertently proved it: Toward the end of her life, as she reached the stage where she was functional enough to drink a little wine at dinner but not to go to the bathroom by herself, friends back home started encouraging me to see if there was anything my mom wanted to say before she died. Leftover psychological stuff. It felt artificial to me. But one day she confessed, "I feel like I'm on a merry-go-round and don't know how to get off." Figuring I might as well take advantage of the opportunity, I carefully asked if there was anything she wanted to say while she could still say it. Her response? "Oh David, don't be morbid..." (To get the full flavor, you had to hear it with the full Providence accent: "Don't be maw-bid.")

Instead of making me feel guilty for not being able to be there for her during my madness—as any self-respecting Jewish mother should be able to do—she actually managed to concoct a little Jewish guilt of her own for passing along some of her dolorous Romanian DNA. Her brothers, my uncles in particular, strike me, in retrospect, as kind of old-world depressives—barely "worthy" of the name—who'd like to smile more but don't know exactly what to smile about; as if it were a skill that wasn't really taught in their family.

My father's family of voluble, sharp-tongued Lithuanians was the opposite. As kids, we never knew whether the spot-on and often cutting one-liners exchanged between siblings and in-laws were grounded in love, annoyance, or humor. Eventually, we too realized that all three were important ingredients in the traditional familial *tzimmes,* and slowly learned the fine art of trying to keep them in balance.

As far as they were concerned, my mother was a saint. After all, she had spent all those decades simultaneously enjoying my father's intelligence and wit, enduring his volubility and temper, and worrying about his health (first heart attack at 43) and affection for Scotch (Dewars on crushed ice with a twist of lemon).

Maybe I was just bringing both sides of my genetic demons out of the closet. Maybe my mother felt subconsciously that it was a necessary thing I'd done *for the family* and that she *should* do her part to exorcise them with me. Family meant a lot to her.

And so, while I didn't have a helluva lot of emotional support to offer her at the time—and my spontaneous humor was often more tragic than comic—she continued to call, every month or so, and say, "I need a David fix." And I would cringe. And I would go. And I would amuse her as best I could. While she would make feel me at home as only a mother can.

Sometimes a little denial is a good thing. In fact, sometimes it's a subtle and profound form of acknowledgment and acceptance.

In terms of family, the holidays are the best of times and the worst of times. Particularly for those struggling to make it until the turkey/Klonopin/whiskey kicks in. (Don't try this at home...or anywhere else for that matter.)

At least you don't have to deal with the everyday stresses of work. When it's just you and the family, it seems perfectly reasonable to say, "I think I'll go to my room and take a little rest," as opposed to, "I think I'll skip this meeting, go to my office, close the door, and hide under the desk."

On the other hand, you usually have to deal with the stresses of being with a lot of people who haven't seen you all year. This involves masking your symptoms in entirely new ways—unless you want to spend all weekend watching mom and close relatives give you deeply concerned, if furtive, looks.

I assure you, however, that a lot of those "looks" are in your imagination (along with a familiar toxic brew of other paranoias). You may *think* you're broadcasting your fragile state at full-volume. But, for the most part, it's muffled by the cacophony of conversation, laughter, china, turkey, TV, and the occasional frustrated expletive.

I remember my traditional Thanksgiving walk with my brother in 2005. It was the first time my nephew joined us. Being able to pepper him with questions about school, sports, music, and the latest technology gave me a lot of "cover." My brother did see through some of the act. But, even now, he admits to not really understanding what I was going through until he started reading my descriptions of that time.

Rest assured, even people who can tell there's something wrong have a hard time figuring out how serious it is, especially when you respond with the Traditional Depressives' Holiday Disclaimer:

> *Yeah, I had a bit of a hard time a while back, but things are getting much better. In fact I just started [choose one or more]...*
> - *doing yoga*
> - *seeing a new psychiatrist*
> - *planning a trip to the south of France.*
> - *writing, painting, weaving, sculpting, baking, and/or having sex again.*

NOTE: When reciting this disclaimer, always speak quickly and finish the run-on sentence with: *"...So hey, how are you doing?"*

Talking to kids is another issue altogether. A friend with a seriously depressed wife and two young children wrote me how he could hardly bear the thought of his kids having to feel the weight of their mother's moods any more than was absolutely necessary. I'm sure it was no easier for her.

Based on the many autobiographies that reference—or are substantially based on—a parent's mental illness, it seems that children are far more affected by what's really going on than what you pretend is going on. I doubt kids can ever avoid the natural tendency to develop defense mechanisms, whether it's to withdraw into their own world, lash out in anger, match your moods swing for swing, or come up with some other creative response. In some cases, they try to parent you. While humbling, this might be, to some extent, unavoidable...particularly in single-parent homes.

Maybe the best you can do is to remember that it's your depression, not theirs; a thought that can be particularly helpful when your kid does something so annoying it triggers an explosion of some of that intense agitation, frustration, and/or rage you've been harboring. Regular outbursts like that can easily take a bunch of therapy sessions for a kid to get over—now, or when they're all grown up and find themselves behaving the same way. I'm sure that every parent, kid, and family is different. And that "age-appropriate" is more than a buzzword. There are a lot of professionals with much more experience than me dealing with this issue. One wrote me:

> Sometimes I suggest that the person going through the depression could (especially with younger children) refer to it in the third person. Something like: "My black cloud wants to visit with me pretty strongly right now, so I'll just have to go and be with it for a while. It's okay, it'll pass, but right now I'll have to go and be with it." And partners can do a lot to help by reinforcing this. I think age-appropriate openness and honesty is key.

I can't vouch for the approach personally, but the image is spot on. Depression *is* like a whole other person. It *does* feel like a black cloud. I sure struggled hard not to make it seem like the whole of me. Next time, I'll give it a name. Maybe I'll call it Dante. That'll teach him.

∽

Fortunately, at the time of my breakdown, our daughter Emily was in her mid-20s. She knew I was having a rough time. But also that I'd had rough times before and pulled through. Since she lived a few hours away, there wasn't a whole lot she could do besides visit occasionally, be sympathetic on the phone, and exchange occasional emails in which I provided updates in language so articulately restrained that it concealed, to some extent, the tempest underneath. Plus, we are both familiar with the power of self-medicating with humor. It's a drug we share whenever possible.

It was probably more important for me than her that I tried to "own" my states. It's one thing if you can't manage to act normal with friends. They can make you a cup of tea, give you a hug, make sure you're safely home, and call to check in later. It's way more discomfiting to show that kind of weakness in front of your child, whatever age he or she is. Having him or her feel like they need to parent you undermines the very structure of your relationship.

There are whole books written by and for people in their 50s and 60s about how to deal with sick parents in their 80s and 90s. Certainly when my parents were dying, my brother and I had to take on some traditional parental roles, from balancing the checkbook to dealing with doctors. That's to be expected. But there aren't as many roadmaps for dealing with a successful, high-functioning middle-aged parent who's suddenly been reduced to a dysfunctional blob. In fact, in those cases, most people write books about how their parent's trauma traumatized them!

Emily was beyond the age at which I was concerned about my depression causing her irreparable subconscious psychological harm. Still, there was no reason to flaunt it. Whenever we talked or wrote, I did my best to tell her that I was feeling better and that the latest medication (vitamins, acupuncturist, or homeopath) seemed to be helping—i.e., don't worry about dad.

I found a certain distinct comfort in being with her. We could both intentionally act as if things were relatively normal, without pretending that, in many ways, they weren't. It was as if we had a tacit agreement that we'd give it our best shot for as long as we were together. Since our love for and acceptance of each other was, and is, unconditional, if my sadness or agitation won out—if I got weepy or "needed to get going"—well, we'd just deal with it. In the meantime, I'd ask her about what was going on in her life the way I always had. And, in truth, I'd be genuinely interested in her responses. It got me out of my skin and made me feel comfortable in it at the same time.

Still, there was only so much either of us could do. I remember one specific evening that she called and, while she and Wendy talked, I prepared myself with some positive news about something I'd written or someone I'd seen or even a funny story about her grandmother. But, as soon as I picked up the phone and heard her voice, I choked up. Big time.

At that moment, it didn't matter that she was 25. It didn't matter that I was 55. It didn't matter how much we loved each other. I was so emotionally entangled I couldn't get out of my own way long enough to say hello...or even goodnight...to my own daughter.

As much as I hurt, that hurt even more. DNA runs deep.

Still, fundamentally, one of the "gifts" of a psychological firestorm is how it affects your relationships. It could be as simple as your favorite barista remembering your name and smiling a little brighter when you walk in; or the people at work realizing that deadlines aren't as stressful as they used to be; or friends sensing that you're more open, curious, and (especially in my case) way less critical.

And, as for the people closest to you, it can transform your relationships in ways that neither of you could have ever imagined.

Married to the Madness

Everything nourishes what is strong already.

—Jane Austen

⁓

DSM Axis 4: "Severe; wearing on marriage." (Psychiatrist's notes, March 2007.)

Living with a depressive can be brutal. Just brutal. Their emotions can suck your mildest enthusiasm into a black hole deep enough to give Dale Carnegie pause.

Often, Wendy had no choice but to get out of harm's way. Going to work was a lot easier than being with me. Having dinner alone with friends was a whole lot more fun than dragging me along—even though the specter of my absence could cast more of a pall than my just showing up and making the best of it.

Even the well-meaning, "How was he when you left? How's he doing today? This week?" could get tired after a while.

And, while I'm sure she was a little concerned that day I loaded my VW van with clothes, notebooks, road bike, maps, and madness, and drove off to parts unknown, I'm sure part of her gave a little sigh of relief.

Fortunately—at least in terms of her ability to understand and hang in there—she'd been down similar paths. In the early 1990s she began to see that many seemingly disparate aspects of her life fit into an overall pattern of serious depression. As she wrote at the time:

> *Imagine living in a house with lots of rooms. Some you live in every day, some you use once in a while, and some you might not go into for months at a time. Depression is like that room you go into rarely—but it's still a part of your house and you know exactly what's in it and what everything looks like, and when you're inside that room there's no denying it's real and that you most definitely are there.*

Like me, she had found ways to self-medicate for many years. And also, like me, she found those techniques increasingly ineffective. After several grueling tries of various medications, she found one that worked with minor adjustments for many years.

That experience helped her keep her own sanity while watching mine crack; helped her endure the ups and downs, tentative hopes and heart-breaking disappointments of the briefest respites and most promising cures; helped her to continue to have faith that it would pass.

What choice did she have? Just as I couldn't imagine either committing suicide or living the rest of my life like this; she never imagined either getting a divorce or living the rest of her life like this.

"Do you want to...?" You don't realize how often you ask your partner that question until, for weeks and months, all you get back is a stream of desultories: "Okay." "Sure." "Fine." "Whatever." "I don't know." "Maybe." "Why don't you go by yourself?"

"You want to go for a walk?"

"Okay. I guess."

"You want to go visit Emily?"

"Sure. You mean Saturday? I don't know. Well, you decide."

"Maybe we should take a trip. Just get on a plane and go somewhere?"

"That sounds like fun." Said in a tone of voice that says the opposite. Not to mention the deep undertone of claustrophobic anxiety that goes with the idea of getting on a plane.

"You want me to meet you downtown after work for dinner and then we'll go home and have wild sex?"

"Okay." "Sure." "Fine." "Whatever."

Sex is, of course, a topic of its own. Suffice it to say that, regardless of the physical ramifications of major depression, frequent sobbing isn't exactly a turn-on.

In all the cases above, you'd fake it if you could. But you can't. Despite the best of intentions…the strongest wish to make your partner happy…no matter what you do or say…or even how you perform, you feel impotent in every sense of the word, in every cell of your body. And there's no place to hide.

All I could do was try to keep the worst of my wailings for times when I was alone. All Wendy could do was walk beside me and intervene when things got totally out of hand. There were many of these little interventions, but one stands out.

It was one of those kaleidoscopic fall days in 2006. When the maple leaves are taking off and the oaks are hanging in there, showing intimations of what's to come. The kind that are particularly humiliating to someone who knows rapture when he sees it but is unable to go along for the ride. Wendy had gone off somewhere and I'd stayed behind to work outside. After purging as much dirt, sweat, and jagged edges as I could, I'd gone in to take a shower.

There was no hot water.

I'm pretty good at figuring things like this out: tracing wires and pipes and ductwork; silencing rattling refrigerators; investigating doors that don't latch; and even programming remote controls. My fixes are usually amateurish, but they work.

In this case, I couldn't find anything wrong. I grew frantic. I was paralyzed by the decision of whether to call an electrician, plumber, oil company, or psychic. Embarrassed by the thought of having to confess my helplessness to a professional. And, oh my God! It's Sunday! I can't call today! (You had to be there…in my head, that is.) The thought of Wendy coming home and learning there was no hot water was devastating. The more irrational I became, the more irrational I became, the more irrational I became. I finally just went out to my cabin and started screaming.

When I heard Wendy's car pull in, I walked to the house and greeted her, babbling about this apocalyptic systems failure that had befallen us. She went to get a sleeping bag, walked me out onto the grass, helped me get in it and lie down in the sun. A few minutes later she came out with a pillow and cup of tea and watched over me for a while. Then she went back in the house, called the oil company, and got the hot water fixed.

ᖫ

A friend once wrote me what it was like for him to live with his severely depressed wife:

> *Marriage is so tricky because naturally there are issues that come up which are not caused by the depression, but I'm so sensitized at this point, it is almost impossible to separate the two. Without going all 12-steps, I gotta say that it's important to accept that there's a problem. We now discuss freely which aspects of her behavior are "normal" and which are not. I don't even know if it matters whether we successfully identify which is which, it's therapeutic to have the discussion with the third entity (her mental illness) sitting at the table.*

It *is* really hard to determine what's the depression and what's everyday partner stuff. There's such a natural inclination to resist the diagnosis and/or try to just deal with it—remain silent, try not to react, redefine roles—that it can remain the elephant in the living room, dining room, kitchen, back porch, and bedroom. In some cases, for years.

In that sense, Wendy and I were "lucky." Even though it had been years since we'd last spent any serious time with the elephant (and didn't exactly welcome him with open arms), denial wasn't really an issue. We became hyper-alert to every shift of his floppy ears and every restless nudge of his trunk.

He lumbered along with us on walks in the woods. He went for rides with us in the car, sat behind us at movies—eating popcorn and peanuts, of course—and hovered in the background when we visited friends.

Even now, we don't let our guard down completely. We probably couldn't even if we wanted to because we've developed such a fine-tuned sense of each other's emotions. Which, in many ways, is a good thing. We don't have to tell each other when we feel a little off. We just say, "Don't worry. It's not chemical." And hope we're right.

When one or both partners is a depressive, marriage can be a tenuous and often tentative prayer, a partnership that endures by sheer virtue of broken hearted determination and stubborn unwillingness to choose the alternative. And, undoubtedly, a host of other elements, from children and finances to karma, pride, faith, hope, and even a little fear of the unknown. As a similarly psychotic friend wrote me: "My spouse ought to get some award for patience and tolerance."

There's a tendency to admire partnerships that survive the virulent extremes of depression. But any relationship that passes through this crucible is transformed. Whether the people stay together or not is their own private, intimate decision that nobody else is in a position to judge.

There are support groups for spouses and families, including the requisite *Depressed Anonymous*, a 12-step program "for men, women and children whose lives have been affected by a family member's depression. Members share hope, strength and experience in order to grow emotionally and spiritually."

There are also plenty of online forums for people with severely depressed partners: including the *Bipolar Significant Others Bulletin Board* (isn't the adjective in the wrong place there?) and Mental Health Matters where they suggest you start by selecting a disorder, a phrase that sounds like a "Sophie's Choice" to me.

There are also many therapists for whom it's a specialty. While we never considered turning to them (perhaps because we had our own strong network of trusted friends and advisors), I'm sure they can be extremely helpful. It's important to realize that the person you're living with *can't* just snap out of it. And, just as important, that the frustration, exhaustion, and hopelessness *you* feel is real, understandable, and forgivable. Because even if your partner is working with an experienced, sensitive psychiatrist whose treatment seems to be going in the right direction, the two of you still have to continually find ways to survive the ups and downs, tentative hopes and heart-breaking despairs of potential cures.

Unfortunately, unlike alcohol and drugs, partners of depressives don't even have the option of either getting an award or doing an "intervention." They can't lock depression away or flush it down the toilet. They have to leave you or live with it. Ultimately, their only real cure is yours.

Therapy

The process of achieving a mature personality with
an extreme minimum of defensive character armor ordinarily involves
major (and stormy) personality reorganization.

—HERBERT FINGARETTE

ᆺ

IT'S KIND OF AMAZING that I've managed to get almost all the way through Purgatory without mentioning the word "therapy." One reason is that, while I have had a good deal of experience in my life with therapy—individual, marital, and some group, I've never gone through any classic Freudian, Jungian, Transactional, Gestalt, or other formal analysis.

But the real reason is that, while I certainly think I earned an advanced certificate in primal scream, therapy wasn't a major part of my Purgatory. This isn't as odd as it seems. An increasing number of psychologists believe that, in the case of major mental illness, it's best to deal with chemicals first and personality or karmic issues second.

We all got issues. We all have things we're afraid of, people we're trying to please, ways that we feel we've been wronged. Send me a self-addressed stamped envelope and I'll send you a list of mine. (But you better hurry...since I emerged from my breakdown I've been crossing them off as fast as I can!)

At its best, therapy can help us identify the recurring patterns of thought, reaction, and behavior that keep us going in circles. It also helps us recognize and understand the triggers for those patterns, and ways that maybe we could do things a little differently next time around.

Often we're completely unaware that these patterns exist. Sometimes we have realized they exist but don't want to mess with them because the cure might be worse than the disease. Other times we'd love to be free of them but don't know how. And sometimes we know how but just can't seem to do it.

While I may not have done all that much traditional therapy, I have done a good number of what you'd call personal enhancement workshops. They've forced me to take long hard (or, sometimes, short and easy) looks at some of the things in my life that hold me back, and learn ways to be less at their mercy. While occasionally disturbing, grueling, and/or humiliating, for the most part these workshops have been fascinating and made life a lot more interesting...also, in most cases, more fun.

Regardless, whatever work I did before or during my depression certainly stood me in good stead when I emerged. Partly because I was able to enjoy the fruits of this work, but also because I was not only more aware of, but also less susceptible to, the ways familiar patterns of insecurity and worry could trigger more serious episodes of anxiety or depression.

Having been "reamed out," as a friend put it, there were fewer "sticky" places in there that could grab hold of the smallest worry and transform it into a major neurosis. I realized not only that I didn't need those things holding me back, but they weren't really all that interesting any more.

Ever since Socrates pointed out the importance of *knowing thyself*, people have seen the connection between self-knowledge and self-transcendence. Between being aware of who you are—in particular, how your mind, heart, and body tend to respond to different things—and being able to see your place in the whole thing with compassion and dispassion.

Some spiritual traditions teach that self-knowledge comes before transcendence. My experience is that it's a dynamic. The more you know yourself, the more you're able to step back and see that you're not the center of the universe—or at least no more than anyone else is.

At the same time, the experience itself was enlightening, and if anything, made it possible to better integrate the work I'd done previously into my everyday life. As if all my understanding from 30 years of personal and spiritual work had been waiting for conditions to be right to come fully into the light.

With all due deference to people who are considered spiritual "masters," I would say that we all continue to get caught, Velcro-like, on stuff over the years. Those are the steps on our personal Purgatories. At the same time, as Dante discovered, the lighter your load, the easier it is to climb.

While I didn't focus on doing therapeutic work during my illness, that doesn't mean it wasn't being done. At the time of my breakdown, I was more than five years into a writing project in which various characters from history appear in my everyday life: from Agamemnon in our local coffee shop to Harriet Tubman on a park bench in Berkeley at the birthplace of the 1960s Free Speech Movement. My old new friends included the famous, the infamous, and the virtually unknown. Kings, queens, musicians, scientists, artists, philosophers, explorers. There was no need to include a writer. *I* was the writer.

I wouldn't "channel" these people. I'd just imagine them in my life today. And, as with many writers of fiction, at some point my characters would take on lives of their own, occasionally taking over mine in the process.

Under the circumstances, I was more than willing to lay some of the blame for my mental instability on their doorsteps, figuring if I could get them to come to their senses, they might help me come to mine. For example, the Babylonian emperor Nebuchadnezzar had a big-time breakdown at the end of his life. Godfrey de Bouillion—the man who led the First Crusade—was definitely not a happy camper (although I sensed his depression was more situational...all that blood in the name of God). Similarly, the zeal of Torquemada, the first "Grand Inquisitor" of the Spanish Inquisition, suggests some significant mania, imposed upon big-time anger issues.

I was particularly suspicious of Chopin—who had spent a lot of time trying to get my attention the previous spring in Paris when Wendy and I visited his grave at Père Lachaise and then attended a piano concert of his music later that evening. He had a lifelong pattern of behaviors that were diagnosed after-the-fact as classic manic-depression.

Then there was the simple issue of whether it was a good idea to let so many egomaniacs (in the best sense of the word) run roughshod over my consciousness. Talk about issues!

Still, since I was spending so much psychological time in the past lives of *other* people, I had to at least entertain the idea that my sickness might be connected with, well, some past life of my *own*. Especially when one of my friends of the New Age persuasion claimed she had a vision that in a past life, I had been a scribe in ancient Egypt, and was strangled to death just before sunrise because I was about to spill the beans (or whatever they spilled back then) about the Sun God not being the be-all and end-all of creation. She suggested that the reason why I'd wake every morning at 4 A.M. with my heart racing and throat chakra vibrating was related to this incident; in other words, through my writing this time around, I was about to reveal certain troubling truths—on behalf of my characters—and I was afraid that some people wouldn't be happy to hear them.

Discussions of past lives have a tendency to veer into timeless narcissism. All I know is that I now write and speak far more freely than I did before. Whether that's because my *ad hoc* primal screaming purged some psychological trauma in *this* life, or some subconscious process helped me deal with a past one, that's about as good a therapeutic outcome as any writer could hope for.

Strange Obsessions
and Glimmers of Light

Though this be madness,
yet there is method in't.

—HAMLET

⁓

FOR MOST OF 2006, I was simply miserable. I couldn't write for more than 15 minutes at a time. I couldn't make people laugh. I couldn't finish the simplest projects. I felt totally stripped of my personal power.

Now, years later, I have the temerity to present my experience as an everyman's version of Dante's journey. Back then, I not only felt I wasn't getting anywhere, I felt I was regressing. I not only felt I wasn't learning anything, I felt I had forgotten what I thought I'd known before.

I still believed that there must be *some* meaning behind it, but only because, even in my most existential moments, I couldn't believe that it was totally meaningless. I still believed it would end, but only because I couldn't imagine the alternative.

One day, I had a long talk with a friend who sympathized, using words that took my breath away: "Yeah, man, the universe will whore you out…It will run you ragged. The universe doesn't put things in a human perspective."

He encouraged me to find whatever protection I could—be it comfort food, crystals, or simple walks in the woods—and hold on tight. Like everyone else, he insisted it *would* end. But by the fall of 2006, having tried various combinations of vitamins, minerals, herbs, amino acids, homeopathic remedies, acupuncture, meditation, bodywork, meditation, and chicken soup, I pretty much threw myself back at the mercy of prescription drugs.

My psychiatrist's plan was to start by calming the anxiety and then slowly build up an antidepressant behind it, careful not to re-ignite the anxiety. Which made sense, since the same strategy had worked so well in 1999.

We started on BuSpar—an anti-anxiety drug that, at certain dosages, helped a little, but at others made me more anxious. We added Depakote, a bipolar drug. It briefly stopped the madness, and gave me a few days of normalcy before I returned to agitation as bad as before.

Valium remained my late-night drug of choice, but I also gave various over-the-counter and prescription sleeping aids a try—from Tylenol PM to Lunesta. But, as before, the problem wasn't getting to sleep, it was staying asleep. So I'd end up feeling sedated but unable to sleep, drugged and wide awake at the same time. All the different parts of my body were going at different speeds. People were beginning to ask me with increasing frequency how suicidal I was.

That's when my doctor first suggested that the best course might be to check myself into an inpatient psych facility for a couple of weeks—get all of the meds out of my system in a safe environment, consult with some specialists, and then try again.

The writer in me wishes I had taken him up on it—after all, some of the best writing of the last fifty years has been about going in or out of mental institutions, including *One Flew Over the Cuckoo's Nest*, *Zen and the Art of Motorcycle Maintenance*, and *Darkness Visible*. Of course, from that perspective, my survey of twenty-first-century treatments for depression should also have included electro-shock treatment (ECT).

But that's the writer in me. The guy who was getting increasingly desperate in late 2006 was pretty freaked out at the thought of being institutionalized.

While slowly nudging the Depakote dosage up to standard therapeutic levels, we replaced the BuSpar with Seroquel, which is primarily indicated as a schizophrenia drug. It had some uncomfortable side effects—particularly dry mouth and some weird visual shakiness, but calmed me down enough to stop taking Valium. I even began to remember having dreams—which, as I understand it, indicates reduced mania.

Eventually, we seemed to have found a decent combination of Depakote and Seroquel. I still felt like a zombie. And was still a bit shaky. But it was a start so we tried lifting my mood with a little Effexor—which works on both serotonin and norepinephrine synapses.

Within a few days, I was as agitated as ever and had to start taking Lorazepam three times a day to calm back down.

We began to discuss inpatient psych again.

∞

So, what did I do all day? Looking back, I wonder the same thing. Even on the days when you feel almost human, you can't walk away from agitated depression. Wherever you go, there it is.

Even though I eventually lost 25 pounds, I did eat. Even though I feared waking up in the morning, I did sleep. Even though I lost most of my interest in TV, I did watch some. Even though I wasn't all that functional, I did manage to work a few days a week. Even though my words were primarily monosyllabic, they did come out of my mouth. And even though I wasn't much fun to be with, I did have some fun with people, and I like to think vice versa.

Figuring a few small victories at home might prove that there was a bright side to having a fairly dysfunctional husband, I started a variety of long-delayed projects: Washing every window in sight. Cleaning up the basement. Sorting through boxes of memorabilia. Matching all the socks and throwing away the orphans. Most of these projects never got done. Although I did make some progress on the socks.

There were, however, a few projects I did finish—with a feeling of accomplishment way out of proportion to the physical labor involved. Projects that felt as symbolic as they were practical. Projects that still remind me in an oddly fond and visceral way, what it felt like to do them. And, how, in the midst of it all, I could almost always find glimmers of hope.

∽

Project #1: Stepping Stones. April, 2006. The stepping stones to my cabin don't lead straight to the cabin. And they're more than a step across—unless you take giant steps.

For many years, I didn't understand why Wendy asked me to put them like that. Particularly in the spring when I often have to hop-step to avoid the saturated ground after rainstorms. Many muddy shoes and vaguely annoyed thoughts later, I've finally seen what she saw back then: that while nature doesn't really abhor a vacuum, it is slightly baffled by straight lines. And, although it's bemused by human dreams of creating order out of chaos (Dewey's decimals be damned), it can't help but follow its own mysterious, decidedly non linear logic.

Back in 2006, I didn't care *where* she told me to put them. I just wanted to be overwhelmed by weights heavier than my heart. As soon as the ground dried out, I began going around the property with my lawn tractor and cart to gather rocks from 6 inches to 9 inches thick, with one flat side at least 18 inches wide. Rocks that had been cast aside by glaciers or farmers sometime in the last ten thousand years. I even copped a few from a tumbled-down stonewall out back. But only ones that had tumbled down on our side. Stealing rocks from stonewalls around here is akin to rustling cattle out west. But I figured a few from our own land would be forgiven by the Gods, and hopefully, the neighbor whose border we share. I bring it up only because it's an example of the kind of thing I'd worry about with Talmudic obsession.

Unlike the borderline boulder I'd wrestled with after my road trip (and which, in better times, eventually became the front step of my cabin) these stones were all in my weight class. As long as I kept my knees bent and back straight, I could lift them high enough to rest on my thighs and then leverage-pivot them onto a cart and bring them over.

Setting stones may be physically exerting but isn't very mentally taxing:

Position rock on ground. Outline ground with spade, staying a few inches back from the rock so you'll have wiggle room. Set aside rock. Remove sod. Dig/scrape soil until hole vaguely mirrors contour of the rock. Place rock in hole. Rotate back and forth a little. Try to convince yourself it's perfect. Realize it's a little high or low, here or there. Remove rock. Repeat. Repeat. After 15 to 30 minutes, tell yourself it's good enough and move on.

It sounds simple. But to my mind it was high drama, requiring several more essential steps:

Decide exactly where to put the stone. Eyeball the depth exactly on the first try. Debate with self whether it looks exactly right—that is, like it had risen gently out of the ground after that last glacier and was getting ready to settle comfortably back in place until the next one. And, most importantly, worry about what Wendy, friends, neighbors, and casual walkers-by would think. Would I be exposed for the incompetent hole-digger and stone-paver that, clearly, I was?

Most of the time however, I didn't care what anyone thought. All I cared about was digging deeper into the ground, moving rocks I could barely move, and the feeling that I could purge my psychosis with sweat.

∽

Project #2: The Footbridge. June, 2006. We also have a seasonal stream—about 8 feet across, that runs between our house and the cabin. Shortly after we moved in, I built a platform bridge to cross it—just 2 x 4's nailed onto 6 x 6's. Occasionally, during the spring runoff, it had rained so hard I had to clear the leaves and gravel that were damming the upstream side. The rest of the time, it did just fine on its own.

One day in late spring 2006, the rains were so strong, the waters actually lifted up the bridge and deposited it 10 feet away on the lawn. Instead of just putting it back, I realized I should build a small arched bridge so the spring runoff could run underneath.

I thought about this bridge a lot. I mean, a lot. I mean, a *real* lot. As I drove and biked around, I looked carefully at other small arched footbridges. I studied pictures in books. I measured the span several times a week because I kept forgetting the numbers or where I'd written them down. I settled on a width and then realized it wouldn't be wide enough for my lawn tractor. I decided to put in railings and then realized that the lawn tractor cart might occasionally be loaded with sprawling saplings and brush and the railing would get in the way.

Occasionally, I'd try to reason with myself: "Dave, calm down, it's just a little footbridge." But the other voices in my head refused to listen. Eventually, through extraordinary engineering insight (which is to say I found some graph paper), I realized that if I bought three rough-cut 2 x 12's that were eight feet long—no, better make it ten feet; no eight feet will be fine; no ten feet, just to be safe—I could cut arcs in the tops and bottoms, nail down some planking, and be done with it.

But where could I get rough 2 x 12's? And, if I went up to ten feet how would I transport them? Did I need to dunk them in a high-powered preservative? Was there something less toxic to use? What about the arc? It looked good on graph paper, but what would it be like to walk across? Most, importantly, how the hell was I going to layout and then cut eight-foot arcs in a 2x12? Okay. I think I got it! But wait…I'm going to have to dig up a couple of those stepping stones I just put in! I could go on and on. And did.

Eventually:

1. A friend not only knew where to get the boards, but convinced me that if I used hemlock, the bridge would last a

long time even if I didn't use preservative. Of course, it took two weeks before we were able to be in the same place at the same time as the sawmill guy. But eventually I drove the boards to my house—sticking out of the passenger-side window with red flags on the ends, like hostages trying to get the attention of passing cars.

2. I figured out how to mark the curve. I laid the 2 x 12's against one wall in the basement, put a nail in the floor on the opposite side, tied a long string to the nail, and attached a pencil at the other end. After fiddling with the length of the string a bit, I was able to draw roughly similar arcs on all three boards.

3. I convinced another friend that someone as unstable as me could be trusted with his Sawzall.

4. I bought brand new ripping blades.

5. I cut the arcs—which, while not easy, was enhanced by my demonic mood.

6. I got the first friend over to help me prop up the three 2 x 12's as I laid a few 2 x 4's on top to hold them steady.

7. I nailed the rest of the 2 x 4's down. And only bent a few nails in the process. Although, I did end up a couple of 2 x 4's short, of course…

I walk across that bridge almost every day. From where I live to where I write. And back. Over the last few years, the water, as is its nature, has started eroding the banks below the ends of the bridge. So, a few weeks ago, I reinforced that area with heavy rocks. I still need to put some flat rocks under the ends of the bridge. It'll never be *completely* stable. But what is?

∽

Project #3: The Invasive. July, 2006. From my perspective, humans are the only truly invasive species. After all, an "invasive" is described as a "non-native species whose introduction causes or is likely to cause economic harm, environmental harm, or harm to human health. These species grow and reproduce rapidly, causing major disturbance to the areas in which they are present." Need I say more?

One of the more common invasives around here is the multi-flora rose (*Rosa multiflora*)—a beautiful, crawling vine, full of tiny fragrant rose flowers. Crawling is a polite word for it. This vine can overwhelm just about any tree or bush it gets its prickly tendrils around. I didn't really get what the big deal was until one day I biked past a neglected field that had mutiflora growing in one solid mass all the way up its hillside. Still, it's not quarantined in Vermont. Just on the watch list. Dwight Miller, the aforementioned late great patriarch of the orchards that surround us, used to watch it all the time. And, in his inimitable ADHD way, tried to control it using a combination of his beloved "Brush Hog," Yankee wit, and, if all else failed, benign neglect.

We had one major multiflora rose on our property which had begun to envelope a tree that, at the time, I thought was a young multi-trunked black birch. Over the previous few years, I'd grown kinda guilty about letting the vine keep growing. Not just because it looked like it was subjecting the tree to a long, slow strangulation, but because I knew that birds were happily eating the berries and depositing the seeds in Dwight's orchards.

In 2006, "feeling kinda guilty" meant "thinking obsessively and feeling overwhelmed with guilt."

After consulting with Dwight, I learned that the vine propagated through its roots as well as its seeds. So I couldn't just cut the thing down, I had to dig up the roots—which were busy underground doing the same thing as the vines were doing up above.

I started by pulling away all the vines I could without ripping my arms to shreds. Then I went at the thing with a shovel and pick axe, following the distinctive roots—inside they're a bright mustardy color—until I was confident I had removed every single trace of this "unwanted" plant that had invaded our personal piece of paradise. I don't remember how long it took. In my memory, it was days, weeks, months. So it must have at least been a few hours.

Eventually, I was done. Having spent an extraordinary amount of time sweating mentally and figuratively over a project that really could have been ignored—or taken care of with a chain saw (and a brief yearly follow-up) in less than a minute.

I've always been good—some might say too good—at identifying with plants, animals, and inanimate objects. In any event, looking at that multi-trunked tree, freed at last from its crown of thorns, gave me a feeling bordering on freedom...release. I hadn't felt that way in a long time.

I learned later that the tree I liberated was a Japanese Bayberry, which is also considered an invasive. But, I don't worry so much about things like that anymore...even though it sure seems like there are a lot of berries on the thing...even though a few small seedlings appeared last year in the middle of a cluster of ferns 100 yards away. I just dig them up before they get out of hand.

◌

Project #4: The Septic Tank. Yes, the Septic Tank. November, 2006. Every old house has its rituals. You learn them one by one. When to get the chimney cleaned. How to install the idiosyncratic storm windows on the screened-in porch. Which pipes lead where and—most important—where the shutoff valves are. If you have a septic tank, where it is and how often to get it pumped out.

Setting a series of heavy stones in place to make a walkway that didn't quite lead where I wanted it to go gave me pause.

Building a footbridge from the house to the cabin—connecting a narrow stream but wide psychological divide—gave me hope that one day I would get to the other side.

Digging down deep to get out all the roots of an allegedly invasive and definitely thorny bush, reminded me it wasn't easy to get free—but that it was possible.

The symbolism of having our septic tank pumped, however, simply made me smile. Still makes me smile.

I knew where our septic tank was—at least I had found a treasure-type map with obscure symbols and bad spelling. But, six years in, I still hadn't had it pumped. And November 2006 was the perfect time. I wasn't doing a whole lot to contribute to our little family's health and welfare. And, while I wasn't sure that having the septic tank pumped would necessarily endear me to Wendy, I knew that by then she (and I) appreciated any gesture at normalcy.

This is how to get your septic tank pumped: (1) Call septic tank guy. (2) Make appointment. (3) Find septic tank. (4) Dig gently until the top is exposed. (5) Wait for septic guy to show up.

Five steps that anyone old enough to pick up a phone and a shovel should easily be able to do.

It *wasn't* easy. Not for me. Steps #1 & #2 were the hardest. Primarily, because I had to speak coherently on the phone *and* commit to being home and functional on a specific day at a specific time— ready to deal in a grownup way with a total stranger who was holding a rather large hose with a rather large diameter that could suck up everything within reach.

Having dodged the appointment bullets, I had to bite the next two: find it and dig. Frankly, I didn't know what to expect. I went online (seriously!) I wanted to get an idea of how deep it might be…what diameter…how you actually got the top off…questions that, really, you don't need to know to expose the top of a septic tank.

Imagine my euphoria when I finally hit pay dirt…actually, pay cement! Imagine my pride when the guy with the big hose came and I was able to show him the top, exposed for all to see. Imagine the relief I felt when I confessed I couldn't get the top off, and he said no problem—that was his job!—at which point he materialized a special long, hooked, iron rod designed specifically for this purpose. Imagine the thrill of standing there shooting the breeze, and then some, with this consummate professional; calmly asking obsessively detailed questions about sewage:

"So, how often…?" "What's the deal…?" "What's that for…?" And, "What's the worst…"

I'm going to spare you the answers…okay, fine, the answers are:

(1) Depends how many teenagers live in the house, (2) Whether you're grandfathered, (3) Gray water, and (4) Dental floss.

∽

At the top of Mount Purgatory, after ridiculing the stammering and stuttering Dante for being so clueless, Beatrice takes pity on him and lets an ethereal woman named Matelda bathe him in the River Lethe in order to erase the memories of his sinful life. (More on that later!)

Similarly, as I, stammering and stuttering, thanked the septic guy and watched him drive away, my irreverent inner adult looked at my manic inner child and suggested, with a devilish grin, that we too had been cleansed.

To take serious liberties with Dante's last lines of *Purgatory:* "I returned from this most holy of waters regenerated, just as trees are renewed with new foliage after harshest of winters, more than ready and willing to mount unto the stars."

Life wasn't going to get much easier for a while, but my sense of humor was recovering.

HEAVEN ON EARTH

I WAS THOROUGHLY OVERWHELMED
AND THOUGH I MOVED MY LIPS AND TRIED TO SPEAK
NOT A SINGLE WORD CAME OUT.
WITH HARDLY A PAUSE SHE DEMANDED,
"WHAT ARE YOU THINKING? ANSWER ME!
YOU MUST OWN UP TO YOUR SINS BEFORE
THEIR BITTER MEMORIES
CAN BE WASHED AWAY IN THIS RIVER."

Purgatory, Canto XXXI (7-12)

For Dante, even the Garden of Eden is in Purgatory... a place where you have to pay some final dues before being allowed into Paradise. It's here that Dante finally sees Beatrice. Instead of the rapturous reunion he's been dreaming of all these years, she puts the hammer down. She insists that he admit that he's guilty of all kinds of sins and random idiocies—particularly the fact that back when they were mere children, he mistook his puppy-love fantasies of her earthly flesh for the radiance of God. She also explains that the only reason she went to the trouble of sending Virgil down to get him was a touch of pity and, more important, that one of her jobs was to reveal The Truth to some half-decent poet so he could go back and share the good (and bad) news with the rest of humanity.

After a while, you wish he'd tell her to, well, shut up! Since when did beings of pure light become such nags? Enough already! But no, Dante just takes it as pitifully as an adolescent who's been caught by his dream girl satisfying his more carnal desires with a girl "on the wrong side of the tracks." He keeps groveling. And not just for one purgative scene. But for canto after canto. Even into Paradise where he simply trades in guilt for self-deprecation.

Oddly, back here on earth, this is the period when Dante begins to act a little more empowered. He's around 50 years old. Still in exile. Still wandering the roads of Italy, following the path of his own private purgatory. While usually less than 100 miles from Florence, he remains a world apart.

But, then he gets a message from back home. The City Fathers say he can return. But there are two catches. One, he has to pay a large fine. More significantly, he has to admit he was wrong. He refuses.

Here's a guy who walked stooped over on the First Terrace of Purgatory in solidarity with people guilty of the sin of Pride, but he still has too much pride to make a simple apology?

Actually, you couldn't pay him enough to go back to Florence, let alone have him pay you. And as for being wrong, those people don't have a clue what it *really* means to confess. Plus, Dante's no fool. He knows now that his reputation is growing, the Florentines want to claim him for their own. Even after he dies, they spend years trying to get their hands on his remains.

To paraphrase Elvis Costello, Dante would have been disgusted. Now he's just amused. He doesn't have time for this any more. He's no longer dreaming about going back. He's dreaming about going *forward*.

But before Beatrice is willing to escort him into Paradise, he has to drink from the waters of the rivers Lethe and Eunoe. The first, as we just mentioned, washes away all his recollections of his sin. The second firmly implants the memories of how good he's been (which might imply that you have to be in total denial to get into Heaven).

How can you write about things you don't remember? This conundrum has vaguely troubled Dantean scholars for many years. Some point out that Beatrice was really just saying he had to forget his *own* sins—to hold firmly to his own goodness in order to have the clarity and stamina to rake everyone else across the coals. Others suggest that since his memory was good and he was allowed to hold onto his strengths, he can remember his memories...an argument that, if nothing else, explains why I wasn't cut out for academia.

All I *can* say is that after major cataclysms—whether inner or outer—you are literally no longer the same person. Many aspects of yourself—fears, troubling memories, resentments; all those little things that you feel have been tucked away, holding you back, making life more difficult in so many different ways—have been dislodged. This is your opportunity to let those "sins" go, while setting more firmly the foundations of your life going forward.

It would be nice to think that a quick dip in two rivers would take care of all this. I suppose, in the case of "spontaneous enlightenments," that may happen. But I daresay for most of us it's an ongoing process. We may only have a few "major cataclysms" in our lives, but we always have opportunities to acknowledge, embrace, or make light of our thousands of unnecessary sufferings. In other words, ours is not one long descent into Hell and another long climb up Mount Purgatory. Rather, we go a few steps forward and then some back. Admittedly, for many people, there seems to come a time when they just hunker down for the duration. But, whether for the first 10 or first 100 years, for just one or many lifetimes, our pilgrim's progress is an incremental process as we slowly get lighter and lighter, clearer and clearer.

The Labyrinth

It begins. It ends. It ends. It begins.

—PAUL REPS

౨

A CENTURY BEFORE Dante began writing *The Divine Comedy*, some French monks 750 miles away were laying out *their* vision of a spiritual journey.

For most religions and spiritual traditions, that journey leads to some ultimate goal. Whether it's Heaven, enlightenment, a blissful merging with God, or a better life next time around, the general direction of the journey is *up there*.

With all due respect to Jules Verne, the depths of the earth are fathomable. Every kid knows that...eventually you get to China. Or in Dante's case, somewhere off the east coast of New Zealand. But the sky...that's truly beyond any fathoming. If there's a great beyond, it's *up* there.

Dante provided as powerful an image of this as anybody ever has. Down, down, down into the depths of Hell. Until you burst through to the other side, behold the Mountain of Purgatory, and start working your way *up* toward Paradise.

In our ecumenical age, followers of just about any religion or spiritual path will graciously acknowledge that there are many paths that, ultimately, take you to the same place. The top of the same mountain. All that matters is that you keep going up and not in circles. In fact, most spiritual teachers would advise you *not* to follow *my* path—the Way of Dave—which involves crisscrossing all over the place 'til you don't know whether you're coming or going.

So, what were those very Christian monks doing when they laid paving stones in the form of a *labyrinth*—a two-dimensional design that goes *nowhere*, on the floor of the nave at Chartres Cathedral in the early 1200s?

They weren't rejecting the idea that heaven is *up there*. One look at the Rose Window makes that awe-inspiringly clear. Yet, where the monks' mortal feet hit the floor—almost invisible to all those eyes gazing upward—they built a labyrinth. A labyrinth. You walk to the center. You walk out. Seemingly no further along or higher up than when you started. You can make it a kind of pilgrimage—some walk it on their knees—but you still end up back where you started.

As a living representation of a soul's journey, however, it's easily as powerful an image as Dante's. In fact, having now seen the limits of perfection, he'd probably prefer it.

The labyrinth at Chartres is the first one I ever saw. It was the summer of 1976 and I was with a group of people searching for enlightenment or some reasonable facsimile. We were there on the summer solstice because that's one of the few days the labyrinth isn't covered with chairs. It's also the day that a fairly perfect circle of sunlight falls in a certain way on a certain flagstone that's set somewhat askew.

The labyrinth didn't make much of an impression on me. Neither did the circle of light, around which my friends were crowded in the hopes of seeing the face of God. Thanks to too little sleep and too much cognac, I was in a fit of manic transcendence and saw God just about everywhere. In fact, I was beginning to wish he'd leave me alone so I could find some inconspicuous corner and take a nap.

In subsequent years, I walked my share of labyrinths. Although I respected the spiritual intentions of them, I was usually only going along for the ride. Either I was at some kind of meditation retreat where everybody was walking a labyrinth, so I walked it; or Wendy had heard about one that someone had constructed nearby and wanted to walk it, so I joined her.

By the way, labyrinths are different from mazes. This is important symbolically as well as practically. You can get lost in a maze—theoretically forever—without ever finding your way out. You *can't* get lost in a labyrinth. If you walk in one direction, you end up in the center. If you walk in the other direction, you find yourself back at the beginning.

The terms, unfortunately, are often used interchangeably. This is partly due to the famous legend about a brave Athenian prince named Theseus who decided to take on a ravenous monster named a Minotaur who had an unfortunate taste for young Athenian children and allegedly lived in the center of a labyrinth. But that was no labyrinth...that was a maze. We know this because Theseus tied a ball of string to the entry door and unrolled it behind him as he went in so he could always find his way out. If it had really been a labyrinth, he wouldn't have needed the ball of string. He could have just turned around and run like the bejeezus in the other direction.

Labyrinths have been built for thousands of years. From Rome to Scandinavia. Here in America, a major building boom began when the coming of the "Age of Aquarius" segued into the "New Age." Now you can find them in all sorts of public places—from corporate retreat centers to hospitals.

They range from simple seven-circuit labyrinths, maybe 20 to 30 feet wide to eleven-circuit labyrinths of 100 feet wide or more. The one at Chartres is only about 40 feet, which makes it almost impossible for two people to pass each other while staying between the lines. Perhaps, it was designed specifically for solitary walking. So the only person you pass coming and going is yourself.

Walking a labyrinth guides you unerringly along a series of gentle switchbacks, sometimes drawing you towards the center and sometimes swinging you to the outer circle where you feel like the trailing end of a comet looping out and in around the earth. After a while you find yourself at the center—which, for some reason, always seems to come up on you suddenly. Then you walk back out. Most people go at a leisurely pace. It usually takes anywhere from

15 to 30 minutes. Although, depending on the size of the labyrinth, a serious Buddhist doing *kinhin* (Zen walking meditation) could easily stretch it out to 45 minutes. As far as I know, the unofficial world speed record is held by an 11-year-old boy who ran in and out of an eleven-circuit, 100+-foot-wide labyrinth in 2 minutes and 42 seconds.

There are all kinds of books about the occult wisdom buried in labyrinth design and the healing effect walking one can have on your body, mind, and spirit. While it's technically considered a meditative activity, the experts insist that there's no "right" way to do it. Walk fast. Walk slow. Still your mind. Let your mind chatter away. Doesn't matter. Just walk the labyrinth…all the way into the center and then all the way out. Let the labyrinth do the work. Bored? Not to worry, you won't go to Hell if you decide just to step over the lines and walk out. (Try not to bump into anybody.)

To me, the way it works is kind of like the car I once had that came with a digital compass near the visor. To calibrate it correctly, you had to go to an empty parking lot and drive around in several complete tight circles. I think that's one of the things walking a labyrinth does. It sort of recalibrates you. I've emerged feeling calmer. I've emerged feeling exactly the same. I've emerged with my mind more still. I've emerged bursting with new ideas.

Regardless, I've always walked out a different person than I walked in.

∽

Every year, I cut a cord or so of wood to heat my cabin. Although not much wood, it still leaves behind a lot of slash which, like any guy with a chainsaw, I throw into halfhearted piles, hoping it will have the decency to decompose as quickly as possible.

In early 2005, however, a weird thing started happening: The brush began intertwining itself into orderly circles around trees. Soon—as if the elves or aliens were getting increasingly bold—the branches started wending their way around several trees and even around curves in the paths.

Wending is right. As quickly as I was creating chaos out of order, Wendy was doing the opposite. Until then, I'd always considered the idea of building a labyrinth in the woods behind our house to be one of her artistic visions that might be inspired, but would never see the light of day.

The intertwining branches thing changed that. Not only could I finally see what had been in her mind's eye all along, but I realized that clearing the area, collecting branches, and laying out the circles would require a combination of light mental focus with a reasonable amount of physical activity—which was, at the time, definitely my kind of job.

More important, I superstitiously hoped that building one might reconfigure me in some way or, at the very least, buy me enough spiritual credits to make a persuasive argument to Dympha (the patron saint of the mentally ill) that she should perform a miracle on my behalf.

In late 2005, shortly after my breakdown, we began building our laby-rinth. As soon as we decided to build one, I knew the perfect place. While most of our land is a mixture of maple, beech, oak, aspen, and hemlock ranging from adolescence to old age (100+), there was a small plateau covered with baby beech saplings crying out to have a labyrinth built on it. (I hear these things.)

My first job was to cut enough of those saplings for us to lay-out the circles without continually having our eyes gouged out by twig-size branches. Remarkably—considering I usually went out equipped with nothing but a chainsaw and an abundance of nervous energy—I showed remarkable restraint. So much so, that even now I occasionally remove a few more saplings to make the paths a little easier to walk without losing the forest feel.

Most projects that Wendy and I work on together begin with a uniquely creative glimmer in Wendy's mind's eye. I translate this glimmer into a blast of activity that, while corresponding vaguely with her vision, does more to tell her what she *doesn't* have in mind than what she does.

Whenever a decision has to be made, I focus on how to make it as quickly as possible so I can get back to work as quickly as possible…figuring I can always double back to fix things later. Wendy's focus is to keep looking, waiting for the right solution to appear. Because, from her perspective, once you've committed to a specific course of action you may never be able to repair any unforeseen damage, thereby falling further from perfection with every step.

Still, contrary to all laws of our respective human natures, we've worked together successfully on many "projects," our marriage being far and away the most impressive.

Back in the late fall of 2005, as both the days and I became progressively darker, we did the preliminary work. This involved a lot of stakes, strings, branches, and pauses, as we (she) evaluated the aesthetics of different path widths and overall dimensions.

By the time I got back from my road trip out west the following spring, Wendy had realized there was no reason the outer paths couldn't veer off a little, a few feet down a bank. So, over the next month I worked in fits and starts to shift the preliminary circles outward, extending the width eventually to more than 125 feet, about three times larger than the one at Chartres. We weren't trying to show off. In fact, we've almost never shown the labyrinth to anyone. And, with a few years of neglect, it will dissolve back into the earth, a whisper of its former self. Rather, even the most irreverent voices within me will admit that the labyrinth was already there…we just had to see where it was so we could lay branches on top of it.

On Mother's Day weekend 2006, the rains came. And came. Ending that perfect spring and culminating in epic floods in New Hampshire and Massachusetts.

We didn't have any floods in Vermont that time, but the rains kept coming. We had only four sunny days between Mother's and Father's Day in 2006—not the best weather for a depressive and the death knell for most lilac blooms, apple blossoms, as well as my work on the labyrinth. Walking around in damp woods, slowly picking up and laying down sticks just wasn't my idea of fun—especially since that year's crop of black flies, mosquitoes, and deer flies all developed an uncommon fondness for the skin I was trying not to jump out of.

That November, however, after laying the stone pathway, building the bridge, uprooting the *Rosa multiflora* and, most importantly, having the septic tank pumped, I returned to the labyrinth.

Intuitively, you'd think you build a labyrinth by laying down paths. Actually, you make the circles and then figure out where the "cuts" are. Then, to make the turns, you just round the branches from one border onto the adjacent one. Trust me, it makes sense.

And so I dragged and collected branches, cut a tree here and there, and made circles of branches, with bigger logs on the outside; Wendy joined me occasionally, or more often, worked separately, adjusting my work.

One day in late December 2006, diagram and compass in hand, I hammered stakes at the north, south, east, and west nodes and began making the cuts and curves. When Wendy came out to look, she felt something was off. It took a little while for her to realize the problem: I was working based on magnetic north as opposed to true north.

And so, at high noon on one of the shortest days of the year, I marched with uncommon confidence out to the labyrinth with an old Boy Scout handbook, an old-fashioned watch with hands, and a 12d finish nail. (The Boy Scouts use a toothpick, but that's 'cause, unlike me, they usually aren't prepared with a 12d nail.) After I moved the stakes, Wendy came out to see if I'd earned my Merit Badge. She still looked at the north node rather suspiciously, but I held up my Boy Scout handbook and she yielded to superior wisdom.

We only had a few inches of snow in January, so we kept working, building up the circles so they would still show in gentle circular ridges when the heavy snows came—as long as I got out early enough to pack down the path.

The heavy snows finally came shortly after midnight on Valentine's Day 2007. By the time it was light enough for me to see out the window, there were already a few inches on the ground. I quickly put on a random assortment of sweatshirts, ski pants, and woolen hats, strapped on some snowshoes, went out to the labyrinth, and stomped it down.

We went out several times during the day, the blizzard winds sweeping paths away within a few hours of our making them. Once, I inadvertently crossed a border that had been flattened by the wind, and got totally turned around. So I had to carefully retrace my snow prints to the beginning and rush back into the house to get our diagram.

You got the image? A 50+-year-old guy, late in the afternoon of a blizzard, sweating inside multiple sweatshirts, baby icicles hanging from his woolen hat, intently peering through whipping snow at a diagram of a labyrinth, frantically trying to reconnect the dots before losing the true path for the rest of the winter.

It took me a while. But I did it, even using my glove to sweep away the error as best I could so it wouldn't show up as a glaring blemish on the perfection of the universe. I walked in and out once more to make sure. By then it was almost dark, so I went back in the house, lit a fire, and had a drink with Wendy.

I felt pretty good.

The snow stopped overnight—almost two feet for us, three feet in other parts of Vermont. The next day, I went out early to make sure the labyrinth was still visible. It was.

Relieved, I stood at the beginning and walked in. I had to be careful in a few places—certain parts on the southwest quadrant aren't as protected by trees and still tend to get buried more easily.

But I made it.

People have different rituals at the center of labyrinths. Usually of the prayerful variety. Even I tend to turn in each direction (true, not magnetic), close my eyes, take a deep breath, and then open them. That's what I did this time. Turning finally back towards the opening on the north side of the inner circle and closing my eyes.

When people talk about being heartbroken, it's usually because they've lost something *outside* themselves. The death of a parent. The end of a relationship. A lost opportunity that may never come again. My heart was broken. But the only thing I'd lost was *inside*. And he, *that* guy, was never coming back. He might look the same. He might even act the same. Hopefully, he'd be as funny as he used to be. But he wouldn't be the same.

I opened my eyes, kind of smiled, and shook my head. A slow smile. Kind of wry, kind of relieved. A small shake. First a little to the left and right. Then up, down, and straight. I was a little weepy as usual. My body felt fragile and exposed. But I was smiling.

I had finally made it to the center of the labyrinth. Now all I had to do was find a way to walk out.

PARADISE

ALL OF YOU FOLLOWING ALONG
IN YOUR LITTLE BOATS, SO EAGER TO HEAR MY SONG
AS MY SHIP KEEPS FORGING AHEAD:
TURN BACK TO YOUR SHORES!
DO NOT COMMIT YOURSELVES TO THE OPEN SEA.
BECAUSE IF YOU LOSE ME, YOU'LL BE CAST ADRIFT.
I'M SAILING ON WATERS THAT HAVE NEVER BEEN
TRAVELED BEFORE...

ᕰ *Paradise, Canto II (1-7)*

A T THE BEGINNING OF *PARADISE*, DANTE DOES SOMETHING few other authors have ever done: he urges anyone who's managed to follow him this far to stop reading. Because he's going places no one's ever gone before, and if they can't keep up, they'll probably end up lost in a bewildering maze. (Maze, not labyrinth.)

Certainly, there are practical reasons for him to do this. Copies of *Inferno* and *Purgatory* are starting to circulate, and he's wary of criticism. (You don't like it? That's 'cause you don't get it.) It's also a shot across the bow at all those powerful people who won't be exactly pleased when they find out where he's placed them. Well, they better think twice before seeking revenge, because Dante's about to experience Divine Grace, and he's taking no prisoners.

But his warning is also a colossal act of arrogance that's perfectly in keeping with his own custom blend of wisdom, pride, and stubbornness. He wants this to be a book unlike any written before. And it is. He wants it to be one that the multitudes will acclaim. And it will be.

Unfortunately, in the centuries that follow, fewer people will read *Paradise* than Dante's other two books. And fewer, still, will understand it. His goal is nothing less than rapturous consummation with All That Is, but he makes it perfectly clear that he is the *only* living human who'll get to do so. Everyone else will have to get the word secondhand. From him. After years of railing against his exile, he essentially exiles himself.

Paradise is, indeed, where Dante pulls out all the stops—mentally, creatively, and spiritually. He can't worry anymore about whether anybody else can connect the dots. He'll have enough trouble connecting them himself. So, having warned his readers of the dangers that lie ahead, he blasts off into and beyond Ptolemy's nine spheres of heaven. Along the way, he's questioned and lectured on the four theological and three cardinal virtues by a pantheon of historical all-stars—pagan and Christian alike: Saints Thomas, Peter, Francis, Bonaventure, and Augustine; King Solomon; Emperors Trajan, Justinian and Henry VIII (whom he hoped would take over Italy); several nuns, his own great-grandfather, Adam, Eve, the Virgin Mary, and God Himself, who appears in a flash of LOVE and LIGHT.

The result is a conglomeration of Medieval, Greco-Roman, and Egyptian cosmology, philosophy, and morality, grounded, with some poetic license, in traditional Christian theology. A vision of the righteous hierarchy of all things that has the trappings of a full-blown episode of mania. Sometimes the book reads like a doctoral dissertation, albeit one written on peyote: The thesis is magnificent, the insights are truly radical, and the language is so transcendent that, when necessary, it can easily overwhelm mere logic or common sense.

I see why he warned us to turn back. I'm exhausted just writing about it.

The problem is that, although many serious literary critics—and Dante himself—consider *Paradise* his greatest achievement, far more people still think his trilogy is called "Dante's Inferno." (A convention I followed in naming this one.) In other words, most of us *do* turn back. But not because the seas are so treacherous—from my perspective, it's *way* harder to read about what happens to people in hell—no, we turn back because *the story is over.*

Until now, behind the often-didactic morality tale, lies an epic myth: Man has mid-life crisis. Man reluctantly begins quest for meaning. Man meets old wise man who says he has been sent by man's one true love to show him a way out of this vale of tears. Driven by a combination of desperation, chivalry, and desire, man follows old wise man through realms of confusion, sorrow, and toil…literally hellfire and damnation. Finally, man reaches the Garden of Eden and sees girl of his dreams. In this case, her name is Beatrice…a woman he's been obsessed with ever since he met her at a neighborhood party one evening in 1274. Back then, he was only nine. She, eight. But, for him, that one glance triggered a lifelong yearning for beauty, light, transcendence, and, undoubtedly, some far-more-carnal desires.

If *The Divine Comedy* were a traditional novel, this would be the climax. After 40+ years of dreaming of this woman—not to mention the ultimate two-day walkabout on the wild side—Dante is surely more than willing to call it a day...or preferably, a night. Who can blame him? If he followed a classic storyline, he and Beatrice could now "live happily ever after"—unless, unfortunately, he arrives only to learn she's already married somebody else, or he shows up breathlessly as she breathes her last. The moral would be: "it's worth sacrificing everything for what you love," or "timing is everything," or "you better hope love is immortal because, otherwise, you missed your big chance."

Instead, the story is only two-thirds over. Beatrice remains very much "alive," but still divinely out of reach.

This is where Dante is *really* sailing on waters that have never been sailed on before. Having completed a remarkable picaresque novel, he starts writing a textbook. *About a place where everyone's happy all the time and nothing really happens.* Oh, there's some celestial singing, of course, and a lot of convoluted discoursing on transcendental matters, but the souls in Paradise really don't do anything. They're all perfectly content with being totally aligned for all eternity with God's will and living in exactly the place that He intended. Nobody is the least bit upwardly mobile. To be so would, well, defeat the whole purpose. Although, if it makes them feel any better, according to Beatrice, they *are* closer to Him, they just *appear* not to be to Dante. Huh? Don't ask...it gets worse.

From our earthly point of view, there's something immensely unsatisfying about Paradise. There's no dramatic tension. Nobody even learns anything except Dante. *He* has to take a crash course in all of creation. Beatrice and the other inhabitants spend countless cantos deconstructing—with a tinge of Zen-masterly impatience—virtually everything he knew before, and then reconstructing—with a tinge of professorial long-sufferance—a world view that reconciles contradictions that no living rational mind would dare try to reconcile. Most of these discourses come down to explaining why if God is perfect, everything else isn't. (Although, of course, it is.) Explanations that, for the most part, would truly only make sense in a late-night college "bull session."

As they arrive at the Empyrean (the highest level of Paradise) Beatrice drifts away to return to her rightful place in the Celestial Rose. The great contemplative St. Bernard then takes over and directs Dante's gaze to the Virgin Mary herself who is at the pinnacle of the Rose, surrounded by thousands of angels. Bernard beseeches her to let Dante look directly into the Light. The thousands of angels join in his prayer. Mary grants his wish.

And what is that wish? Nothing less than being allowed to use this precious, once-in-*anyone's*-lifetime opportunity to understand the scheme of all things and where he fits in it. This is a question we *all* struggle with and he's going to get to ask it. Of God Himself! Maybe there is a climax to this story after all!

Sure enough! God answers his question…in a bolt of lightning, no less!

Unfortunately, at that moment, Dante is abandoned by memory and words themselves. For a writer, the ultimate exile.

After experiencing all he can possibly experience, and learning all he can possibly learn, and meeting thousands of spirits who know and accept exactly where God has placed them, we're still left to wonder, what is *Dante's* place? And more important: what's ours?

Miracle of Miracles

Suddenly I understand that I am happy.
For months this feeling
has been coming closer, stopping
for short visits, like a timid suitor.

—JANE KENYON

Pharmaceutical wonders are at work
but I believe only in this moment
of well-being.

—JANE KENYON

෩

IN LATE FEBRUARY 2007, an odd thing happened. Wendy and I were on the phone with Emily. Which, in those days, meant me lying on the bed with the extension to my ear while they talked. I had nothing positive to contribute to the conversation. I didn't even try. But I liked listening.

Toward the end of the call, Em started talking about a cat that some friends had to give away. They'd just gotten two dogs and the cat was totally freaked out. She said he was the most affectionate hunk of cat she'd ever been with. He'd curl up—all 20 or so pounds of him—against the nearest human body and respond orgasmically to even the mildest petting. Scratch his belly, and he was toast.

She encouraged us to take him.

I said yes right away.

We were all kind of shocked.

It was the first definitive decision I'd made in a long time.

Clearly Tito needed us. And the feeling was way more than mutual.

Over the next few months, I spent a lot of time with Tito. It was like he could take all 220 amps of my high-frequency agitation and step it down to 110 or lower without skipping a beat. For him, all that mattered was the scratching. The fact that I was dumb as a post and as wired as a fur brush made me the perfect companion.

On the Ides of March 2007, I ran into a friend on the street—a fellow sufferer in complete remission—who asked me how it was going. Being known for my articulate way with words, I answered the way I usually did back then… I started crying. Told her we were thinking about second opinions, about inpatient psych, about… about… about…

"Okay, that's enough," she said. She didn't mean my crying. She meant the madness. "Call this guy. Make an appointment. Today."

The next day she called and I told her I couldn't get an appointment for a month. "No. He's going to see you in a couple of days," she said, like it was a done deal. "I'll call." She made it happen.

And so, on the first day of spring, March 21, 2007, I sat in a different doctor's office with Wendy, my head down, eyes averted, again trying to describe how I felt.

Within a month, I began to feel the Titanic turn around. And just in time.

∽

I know there are cases in which people feel immediate results from a medication, but, painful as it was, I accepted that it might take a while for me to work my way to the surface.

At the time, I was taking Depakote, Effexor, and Valium. I no longer really knew which was doing what, but little if any of them were doing much good.

I left the office with a prescription for Klonopin to replace the Valium, instructions for going off the Effexor, a plan to start on Cymbalta, and a special tri-fold five-week starter pack that held precise blister-packed dosages of Depakote and Lamictal... steadily decreasing the one while increasing the other. I wish I'd saved it as a kind of mnemonic device. Because over the next month, that innocent little pharmaceutical package was as powerful as any totem. There was something reassuring about it. Like someone in some lab somewhere had figured out exactly what I needed down to the merest milligram. No longer was I taking a pill or two every day and hoping for the best. I was following a precise bread-crumbed road to salvation.

Toward the end of the appointment, the doctor suggested— that's putting it mildly—that I stop drinking.

"How long?" I asked.

"A month," he said, and then paused. "Then another month."

"Uh, okay,"

"Then another month."

"Uh, okay ... you know I really only have a beer or glass of wine a night. It's the only thing I can confidently look forward to every day."

"Six months in all would be good."

"Uh..."

"I mean, you're strong minded. Don't beat your head against the wall. If you have one you have one. But it will give us a purer trial...a clearer picture of how the meds are affecting you."

I stopped drinking. Until one cold raw day in Nova Scotia, five and a half months later when I celebrated my newfound humanness by ordering a shot of Jameson's. Just one.

On March 26, 2007, I wrote: "This is the first morning that I've woken up in months...literally months...when this living thing doesn't seem like such a bad idea after all."

On April 3, I wrote: "I'm borderline better this A.M. I'm finding a little balance between keeping my head clear and optimistic and my body relaxed. Sure slept a lot last night."

On April 22, I cracked completely. But it was different. It was as if I was slowly becoming broader and deeper—able to hold the flood within the banks instead of being overwhelmed. Later that day, Emily sent me an extraordinary email that took my breath away and left me with a deep yearning to be whole again.

On April 29, I wrote: "The most important thing is I'm starting to have ideas again. I used to have to carry that little tape recorder because so much was pouring out. Now it's just a little pocket notebook to jot the occasional one down. It's a start, an important one. It connects with the 'beautiful urgency' of writing, as someone said (maybe me!) I still have to be a little careful. I start to think about all the phrases I want to craft and the books I want to write and I get overwhelmed. Still, it's comforting to be able to look ahead. And I'm much more confident that, when the time comes, the words will be there."

On May 5, I stayed in bed until 10 A.M. Sure, I was visiting my mom's and had stayed up talking to her until midnight...which I never did at home. Sure, I woke up at 6 A.M with a little agitation— the little agitation that used to be a big agitation. Sure, I took a little nibble of Klonopin. But, the fact was I stayed in bed for ten whole hours. To most people, that would seem ordinary at best and lazy at worst. For me, it was a major triumph over the vagaries of time, space, and adrenal glands.

On May 7, I began using the phrase "significantly better" in emails and conversations.

On May 10, I wrote to a friend: "I don't say, 'David's back.' I say he's forward."

On May 11, I did my first new writing in months—(as opposed to desultory editing just to keep busy.) It was like my vision was coming back.

On May 21, I felt a strong dip, but managed not to follow it down.

On May 25, I felt confident enough to tell Emily I felt better and to make plans for my birthday since Wendy was going to be away.

On May 30, I crashed again. For about an hour. Screaming and dry heaving in the cabin. As bad as ever. Why? Why? Was it because I didn't feel I needed the Klonopin to sleep anymore so I'd skipped a couple of nights? Was it because I'd gone for a really hard bike ride the day before? Regardless, I came in the house, took .5 mg of

Klonopin, and lay down quietly. After an hour or two I was okay, shaky but okay.

On June 8, a tie rod on my lawn tractor broke. As I was crawling under it to see what was wrong, I felt a twinge in my back. I'd pinched a nerve. To both events, I said, "Oh well." I simply called the repair place about picking up the lawn mower. (So the grass will grow a little, so what?). And arranged appointments with a chiropractor and massage therapist. (So my back/leg will hurt for a little while, so what?) The fact that neither upset me all that much was thrilling. Like I had found a way to sneak out of the darkness and none of its resident demons had noticed.

On June 15, I turned 55. Emily came down. I had something to celebrate.

On July 8, I wrote a friend: "I'm doing very well and enjoying the simple pleasures of just being able to write emails, read junky mysteries, watch baseball, work on our labyrinth, go for bike rides, etc. I'm even moving ahead with my writing. There's a lot of work to do, but I look at it now as a 'feast' to engage in slowly, rather than feeling compelled to get done as quickly as possible. It's like I'm learning how to be in the world again."

Crazy Wisdom and Creativity

The question is not yet settled,
whether madness is or is not the loftiest intelligence...
whether all that is profound does not spring from disease of thought.

—EDGAR ALLAN POE

What makes Paradiso so difficult is that it is dedicated to its own
impossibility. Language is forced to reveal its shortcoming.

—HARRIET RUBIN

ॐ

WHILE MOST PEOPLE don't end up writing masterpieces during periods of manic-depression, they often do things that make their friends think, "they're out of their minds." They blow all their money in Las Vegas; get passionate about collecting golf balls; drop out of school; leave their spouses, etc.

While mental instability can trigger or be triggered by all of the above, it's rooted, fundamentally, in some imbalance *inside* oneself—like there's an internal gyroscope spinning out of control. These people aren't *out* of their minds, their minds are *out* of kilter. Depending on the adjustments they make—medical or otherwise—this behavior recedes and, in many cases, is integrated into who they are.

Maybe that's why people have such a hard time recognizing underlying depression in others. It's one thing when you sit on your bed all day, head in hands—like those sanitized images from the TV commercials—in that case, the diagnosis is pretty easy. It's even easier when you walk down the street ranting and raving about how you saw Jesus drinking coffee at Dunkin' Donuts. But when you manage, at least to all appearances, to keep that chaotically whirling gyroscope out of sight, most people are fooled most of the time.

Sanity is simply the ability to function in your particular culture and society without pushing the envelope too far. Something that is far different—and often far more sophisticated—in an ancient tribal culture than it is on Wall Street.

Insanity (which should really be called un-sanity) is an inability to accept the story of reality that is being put forward by the overwhelming majority.

One of the hallmarks of *my* generation is that we *couldn't* accept the story of reality that was being put forward by the overwhelming majority. Back in the 1960s, when psychologist R. D. Laing said, "Insanity is the only sane response to an insane world," novelist Kurt Vonnegut said, "A sane person to an insane society must appear insane," and filmmaker Akira Kurosawa said, "In a mad world, only the mad are sane," they were preaching to the choir.

We eagerly followed their lead by immersing ourselves in any form of psychological, psychic, religious, or spiritual exploration we could get our hands on or heads around. And there were many. In particular, we had ready access to LSD and other drugs that could cause temporary (hopefully) psychosis *and* to "secret" spiritual techniques from the East that had never before been widely available in America.

By making the experiences of both temporary enlightenment and mental illness available even to those who weren't so inclined, these developments made us question our fundamental assumptions about sanity; and in the process, become aware of the seamless continuum between insanity, sanity, and spirituality.

In a legendary story from the 1960s, one day Baba Ram Dass (formerly Richard Alpert, Timothy Leary's Harvard colleague) finally convinced his Indian guru Maharaji to take some LSD. For the next several hours, he waited patiently for his master to start "tripping his brains out." All that happened is that Maharaji's smile got a little brighter. Similarly, when Aldous Huxley took some LSD while on his deathbed, he smiled and said, "Just as I thought."

My study habits during freshman year in college reflected this unconventional way of discovering the "secrets" of the universe. Before writing an important paper, I'd procrastinate as long as possible and then scan the required texts, highlighting or making margin notes on random passages that interested me. Then, about 48 hours before the paper was due, I would take some hallucinogen.

In the hours that followed—while trying to ignore troublesome thoughts about my love life and images of campus dogs who had a disturbing tendency to turn into man-eating wolves—I'd have insights that connected many of the most important ideas in the assigned books with seemingly relevant facts from the realms of current events, historical trivia, existential philosophy, avant-garde French movies, and quantum mechanics.

After a fitful sleep and a few cups of coffee, I could usually put together an "A" paper. Seriously. I was already a good writer, and by then, ideas were mere playthings.

I tell this story not to encourage anyone to follow my example. (Which is more likely to lead to dismissal than high honors [sic].) But it's important to point out that for many people in my generation, Dante's deep, I daresay, hallucinogenic attempt to encompass all of the known and unknown universe in one vision made what he was trying to do as revelatory as the words he ended up using to do it.

There's a comprehensive and insightful history of LSD called *Storming Heaven*. The title alone explains why many of us took hallucinogens. In large part, we did not use the drug "recreationally" (unless you parse the word as "re-creation-ally.") Instead, between being taught to dive under our desks to avoid nuclear attacks, watching Kennedy get assassinated on TV, and seeing our contemporaries disappear into the quagmire of Vietnam, we were afflicted by a profound hopelessness about the future, and willing do whatever it took, regardless of the cost, to figure out what the hell we were doing on earth, a.k.a., the meaning of life.

LSD seemed to offer a way out of this earthly hell that we'd somehow been born into. For a few bucks, we could explore the limits of Dantean cosmological insights, complete with visuals worthy of William Blake. We were only in our late teens or early twenties, but we were storming heaven and hell-bent on unlocking its mysteries.

Still, within hours or days, the drug usually dumped us unceremoniously back in the darkest of woods. While a few found themselves in disassociated—yes, insane—states from which they never recovered, many of us ended up dazed and confused but deeply, urgently, curious.

And so we began a lifelong search to integrate what we'd seen and sensed into our ordinary lives. Deep study, meditation, and other spiritual practices—frequently accompanied by long periods of depression and even addiction—often played significant roles in our purgatories.

Our generation forced its way into parts (and configurations) of the brain that are rarely explored. We went all the way out to the limits of our individual and group consciousness in order to find our way into the limits of our being. We learned to walk into the labyrinth and then out of the labyrinth. Into the labyrinth and then out of the labyrinth. Realizing and releasing attachments and gathering insights along the way.

In some traditions the result is often called "crazy wisdom."

In our tradition, it's usually called one or the other. Or sometimes, "creativity…"

Major depression and/or mania—frequently accompanied by serious indulgence in drink or drugs—are often associated with creativity. Baudelaire, Dickinson, Van Gogh, Nietzche, Woolf, Plath, Rothko, and a host of rock and roll stars. I mean even Bert on Sesame Street has mood swings.

From manic visionary biblical prophets to brilliant, stark-raving-mad artists to tragically suicidal writers, the mentally ill have a prominent place in the cultural history of humanity. And their treatment—whether it involves being worshipped, ignored, put in straightjackets, burned at the stake, or given Pulitzer Prizes—speaks way more volumes about the society and times they lived in than it does about the creative people themselves.

It's remarkable how much more strangeness you can get away with if you incorporate your madness into an art form. In fact, although you might not put it on your resume, occasional periods of dramatic brooding or frenetic bursts of creativity might help you on your career path. Certainly they're no barrier to making high-priced art, playing in a rock band, writing award-winning novels, starring in TV shows, or, as I pointed out before, even being the creative director of a small ad agency.

By the time Dante was forced into exile, he was a well-established poet, essayist, and politician. It must not have been all that much of a surprise when word began to filter back to Florence that he was working on "something big." But if he had been able, or later chosen, to return, he could probably have blended back into society with relative ease.

Instead he was out there. Somewhere. Doing something that could make folks back home a little wary. (Think of politicians in the Soviet Union wondering what Solzhenitsyn was writing during the 20 years he lived in an obscure Vermont town. Or the entire New York literary world wondering what J.D. Salinger was doing right across the river in an equally tiny New Hampshire town.)

Back home, the exiled creative may be able to retain a special kind of romantic mystique.

On the road, however, without the support of his family and community, the reality isn't always as romantic. Because, in addition to the uncertainty about his living situation, he has to wrestle with his creative angels and demons all on his own.

If Dante wasn't afflicted with at least a touch of depression before he left Florence, it's hard to imagine him escaping it after he left. I see him at his writing desk, looking out the stone arched window in the home of his current patron. I see him envisioning Hell in his memories of the politically restless streets of Florence and Rome; envisioning Purgatory in the November days of gray pouring rain; envisioning Paradise in the shifting colors of a spectacular sunset over a grove of olive trees. All while wondering if he can ever go home. Wondering, more importantly, if he will ever be able to complete his masterpiece. Wondering, most importantly, if he is truly worthy. Worthy of paradise. Has he really paid his own dues? Has he really expiated his own sins? Is he really strong enough to transform his own earthly passions into heavenly bliss?

I'm sure there were days in which he had doubts. *Many* days. I'm sure there were days when he didn't put a single word on paper. *Many* days. I'm sure there were days when he wondered how he could possibly go on. *Many* days.

If Dante wasn't afflicted with at least a touch of mania before he left Florence, it's hard to imagine him escaping it after he left. I see him waking in the middle of the night in some strange bed in some strange villa, having finally caught a glimpse of that rhyme he's spent days looking for; thinking, perhaps with a devilish grin, of the perfect person to put in that level of hell; remembering a really good Augustinian one-liner that might untangle an unruly philosophical puzzle he's been wrestling with. He's wide awake now, writing until dawn. Which comes, it seems, only moments later.

I see him riding along back roads, under a Tuscan, Lombard, or Reggiano sky, hurriedly getting off his donkey and rummaging in his saddlebag for something to write with and a scrap of cheap paper (they'd invented some rough stuff by then); only to realize later that day, when he's back with a glass of wine by his side, pen poised over vellum, that the canto in question still doesn't hold together.

Writing was as much about memory as craft back then. Dante certainly didn't have to have as prodigious a memory as Homer's. But neither did he have access to the kind of written references Shakespeare had. Or, for better or worse, the seemingly limitless editing *and* reference capabilities we modern writers have. He had to carry an extraordinary amount of material in the back of his mind, while working on rhymes in the front, juggling and jostling those words into place… only writing them down after they'd clearly earned the right to see the light of day.

In one important way, however, the relationship between writer, words, and vision has never changed. Just as I suspected that the labyrinth Wendy and I made was actually already fully formed, waiting for us to lay branches upon it, I suspect that Dante could see many cantos ahead in his mind's eye, but had to struggle mightily to imagine and remember the words that were supposed to fill them. Sort of like doing an entire New York Times crossword puzzle—the Sunday one—in your head. No cheating.

That's the real power of hypomania. It's not the stream of one-liners that zoom across your neural pathways—it's the speed and transcendence of connections. The way that thoughts tumble over each other and fit into place in ways that feel *so* right while, simultaneously giving birth to new ideas that explode faster and faster in more and more directions.

The "suffering" of mania, particularly in times when it's fueling the creative process, is that it all happens so fast that you can become frantic that if you can't keep up with your ideas, you'll "lose them." It's probably not true. Those labyrinthal patterns are still firmly in place. But that fear can make you, well, crazy.

∽

We assume that mountain climbers write their memoirs after they've come down the mountain, that prisoners of war write their memoirs after they're freed, that lovers write theirs after the romance has ended—or at least have the decency to wait until the next morning. It's as if their memories, their ability to "relive the moment" can be trusted. But we have an image of depressives—poets and artists in particular—hanging on to sanity by a thread (if at all), creating powerful, elegant, revelatory expressions of their experiences in real time. As if anything less would lack authenticity.

Rest assured, our experiences are as seared in our minds as they are in the minds of mountain climbers, prisoners of war, and lovers. We can revisit them at will. Our "authentic voice" may now be different from one that spoke to us during our madness. But, in retrospect, *that* voice often sounds one dimensional. Maybe that's why Beatrice made Dante forget what he'd seen in order to write about what he saw. He needed the wisdom of the entire experience before he could write page one.

One bright, sunny winter morning in 2006, I sat in front of the large Palladian window in my cabin. Five inches of heavy snow had fallen the night before, transforming even the most ordinary surfaces into shameless exhibitionists. The evergreens were having a friendly competition to see who could hold their snow weights the longest. The hemlocks easily outlasted the white pines. I wrote:

> *There have been two 5" snowfalls in the past few days. And very little wind. The hemlocks hang laden with snow, like tired old handmaidens with brooms attached to billowing aprons. A large puff of snow makes a slow motion swan dive from the top of the tallest pine, setting off mini white explosions as it floats through lower branches to the ground. Snow dominos.*
>
> *What's particularly...humiliating seems too strong a word... about depression is that I'm looking at what has to be one of nature's most amazing little performances, and all I can see is darkness.*

Five years later, I can still vividly remember... I can *feel*...the guy who wrote those words. I remember exactly where he was sitting, exactly what he was seeing, and exactly what he was feeling. I'd like to tell him to stop equivocating. I want to tell him to put the pen down, drop the pad to the floor, and curl up into the little ball he feels like inside. Humiliating was *not* too strong a word. Humiliating, frustrating, overwhelming, tragic... none of them would have been words that were too strong.

If you're cold, sick, and starving, melancholy makes sense. I wasn't cold, sick, or starving that day. I was just disconsolate. It made no sense then. It makes no sense now. Depression always trumps the mind's ability to reason with it. But not the mind's ability to be aware of it.

As a friend wrote me back then:

> *Those that have never felt those states…you can feel how they do not quite get it, even though their concern is welcome. And even those of us who do feel those states, can, between episodes, wonder what all the fuss was about.*

Sometimes while writing this book, I've been concerned that my attempts to wrestle these elusive feelings into submission may actually give me too much distance from them…as if this all happened to *him*, not me…that I'll become one of those people who now "wonders what all the fuss was about."

Then a morning like this one—years later, here and now—will come along. A morning when I'm doing just fine and enjoying what I'm doing. A morning when, at the same time, the memory is right there, hovering over my right shoulder like a forlorn angel looking for a home. Fortunately, I don't have to give him one. But he can stay right where he is. He can keep me honest.

I did do a lot of writing while in the depths of depression. Mostly turgid. Occasionally sublime:

> *Next to the woodshed, I have this huge, knotty, maple stump. I refuse to stop trying to split it—even though I'm burning twice as many calories trying to do so than I'll ever get burning it in the stove. I just keep going at it, hoping a seam will open up so I can stick a wedge in and start blindly whacking away some more. You'd think I could choose a path of lesser resistance…just roll the thing back down the ravine and find something more suitable for the woodstove. But I can't escape the feeling that if I could just get through it. Dear God, if I could only just get through it.*
>
> *My cabin has become little more than a projection of the abyss itself…*

I also did some writing while in the throes of hypomanic, melancholic agitation. Mostly chaotic. Occasionally inspired:

I keep writing. All these years. Sometimes it seems brilliant. Sometimes it seems banal. Almost like thumb wrestling. You put your thumb down. It's a trap, of course. But the more you relax it, the more you're ready. Blink and you're caught. Fly fishing at its best. Catch and release. And so I settle into a riff that feels real profound. I'm thinking I'm saying things that really have never been said before. And yet, a moment later, I'm claiming that I'm this bumbling, self-deprecatingly amused 21st-century guy, who, through no "fault" of his own, has become a messenger of the divine. In between, one-liners fly off my fingers trying desperately, urgently, eagerly not to telegraph who's who...and just as hard to blend one voice with the other. (There is no other.)

People want you to be something. Fast? Slow? Despairing? Delirious? Make up your mind, Dave. I know. I know. I appreciate that. It's just that I am not something. I'm this mercurial bundle of energy that can travel in a heartbeat from unfathomable despair to equally unfathomable ecstasy faster than a speeding bullet. And just when you think, you know, ahhh...there he is; he's gone. I'm neither proud nor not proud of that. But I know it's who I am and no longer feel there's any need to apologize for it.

So you work on something for years and years and maybe the whole point is just that it's reminded you and evolved you to be you. That it's a mirror you've been carrying around to remind you who you are. And good hologram that you are, and the world is, a person could read one page or hundreds upon hundreds of your pages and be equally enlightened. And so you walk into a Barnes & Noble or a Borders and you say oops, did I just walk into a recycling center? What is all this stuff? Give me a cappuccino, maybe two, and get me the hell out of here; thinking about the days when a new Vonnegut or Updike or Oates or Kesey or Lessing or Pynchon, or Styron would come out and it would be an event. Dylan, particularly Dylan, or the Beatles or the Stones or the Dead would come out with an album and it'd be an event. And you'd stare at the back of the album cover while listening to the music and wonder: "Who are these people?" "What do they know?" Because if they knew something that could lead you to heaven, you wanted to know it. You wanted to know it so badly, you'd put on those old Koss headphones, take all the drugs you could find, and listen to it as loud as you could in the desperate hope that it would catapult you to a place where there'd be no more pain of unknowing.

In both cases, the images are powerful. And, appropriately, there are four times as many words in the manic piece as in the depressive one. But if I'd written this whole book while in either state, it would have been less accessible, less multi-layered.

Whether melancholically "profound," or "brilliantly" rich, first drafts are like falling in love. In the thrall, they feel so all-encompassingly, solipsistically rich. But, by the light of day, they don't stand the glare of scrutiny; the glare that our human nature eventually shines on everything, stripping it of its mystery long enough to make sure you've truly captured that thought, that feeling, that moment. I'm certainly not suggesting that rapture needs editing. You don't have to burn those love letters you wrote when you were 16. But, down the road, there's nothing wrong with a little maturity. I mean, without Shakespeare, Romeo and Juliet would have just been two kids in love.

Still, imagine how suspicious I was when my psychiatrist assured me that medications wouldn't dampen my creativity... they'd make it more mature. Mature? For me, that implied a lack of *intensity*. A medicated distance that people are always warning you about. Imagining my creative life without at least some profound contemplative melancholia was like imagining I had different parents. It's not that I wanted to be depressed all the time. I *certainly* didn't want to end up committing suicide like a shocking number of the people mentioned before. It's just that I was concerned that I'd...well...get a little vapid. Surely, as a serious writer, I still needed to spend a respectable amount of time stumbling blindly in the darkness, questioning my very reason for being.

But, while I still loathe using the word "maturity" in relation to myself in *any* context, he was right. I know that, for many bipolar and schizophrenic patients, medications replace wildly creative visions with lethargic stupor. I'm one of the luckier ones. They haven't dampened my waves of creative thought or my enthusiasm for getting them down on paper. They just make the torrent of words easier to manage, arrange, carve, and shape. They help me listen to the reader as closely as I listen to myself.

Peter Kramer, the well-known author of *Beyond Depression,* goes a few steps further to argue that people suffering from one or more flavors of mental illness would have been more creative without suffering them in the first place. He says that since the relationship between melancholia and creativity has been ennobled since ancient times, we can't imagine life (especially the arts and philosophy) without it. Kramer can imagine it. Having seen so many of his patients' creativity emerge after years buried under the chaotic thinking of depression, he turns our whole understanding of what it means to be a profound creative thinker inside out... with depression definitely on the out.

As usual, I come down firmly on both sides. I'm curious about the implications of having never been depressed. But I'm not yet ready to tell my fellow dysfunctional manic melancholics to find another line of work. In terms of creativity, we're just here to serve: to reflect the world as we experience it. In a way, it doesn't matter what that world is or even how we experience it. Our job is to just keep polishing our own particular mirror.

Creativity isn't limited to one particular state, medium, or reality. As far as I'm concerned, the more the merrier. The emotional arc from deep depression through everyday emotional balance to psychotic mania is so seamless, I defy anyone to determine what it means to be in a "creative state." The fact that, over the last twenty years, we've *unsuccessfully* tried, through text messaging, to reduce human emotions to a few hundred emoticons is a testament—a welcome one, in my opinion—to our infinite complexity.

Writing, music, art, dance come from the whole of us...whoever we are, wherever we are, whatever time we live in, whatever medications we may or may not be taking.

Creative spirits play the hands that are dealt them. They couldn't have it any other way even if they wanted to.

∽

At the very end of *Paradise,* Dante appears to give up: "O how my power of speech falls short of my vision." A moment later he's smote by the "love that moves the sun and the stars." As we said, having been charged to reveal all the secrets of the cosmos, when Dante finally gets to the punchline, he claims that his words fail… that even his creativity is subsumed in the light of pure Love.

But the story has actually just begun. Beatrice didn't send Virgil down simply to lead Dante to this pinnacle purely out of the goodness of her heart. She needs Dante. She needs him as much as he needs her. God needs Dante as much as he needs God. Because, although Dante might not dare make a big deal of it—he's only the second human in Christianity *to ever be sent back down by God Himself* to show humans out of the darkness.

Words give Dante power. A power that, in some strange way, even God doesn't have (at least without some kind of human intermediary). A power so great that Dante's words are still resounding and evolving in human consciousness; still, as Bob Dylan says, "glow like burning coals."

The philosopher Jacques Derrida says, "writing captures only what has happened, not the eternal unfolding present in which the reader can experience exactly what the author experienced." (Especially, you'd assume, when what the author experienced was God.)

However, it's too easy to say that when push came to shove in those final explosive cantos, words failed Dante. That's not what happened. Actually, he failed words.

Fortunately for us, it was only temporary. Even though Beatrice had him cleansed in rivers that washed his memories away…even though God rendered him speechless, Dante's remained a writer. Seven hundred years later, he's still a writer. That's his place. Not even God can take that away.

Depression and Spirituality

Someday you'll look back at the experiences that you are having now
and say, "May I never have to do anything like that again,
but if it's what it took to get me here,
I wouldn't have had it any other way."

—ANONYMOUS

WHILE *The Divine Comedy* can be seen from the perspective of manic-depression or creativity, it is best known as a glorious spiritual journey. Indeed, many people who consider religion or spirituality to be a major focus of their lives say that their quest began when they became lost in their own version of Dante's dark wood (or "dark night of the soul," as St. John of the Cross put it in the sixteenth century). Even Eckhart Tolle, the author of the best-selling *Power of Now* books tells the story of how he experienced his spiritual awakening after years of alternating depression and anxiety.

That's why I suggest, only partly in jest, that some kind of emotional breakdown may be as direct a path to the experience of enlightenment as six years under a fig (bodhi) tree, forty days and nights in a desert, seven-day *sesshins* at a Zen Center, three-day vision quests in the middle of nowhere, and/or beating yourself up by trying to put your attention on the NOW.

The role that deep depression often plays in spiritual or personal transformation has led many people to suggest that we should meditate, not medicate away the pain...that those dark nights are part of being human—in fact, one of the most meaningful parts of being human. Whenever I read words to this effect, I wonder if the writer knows (or remembers) what major depression really feels like. It hurts. Okay? It hurts.

To be fair, meditation can be an excellent therapy for anxiety and depression—whether it involves following your breath, chanting, repeating a soothing mantra, reciting a heartfelt prayer, watching a sunset, or just lying on the ground and looking up at the clouds. However, few would recommend withholding medication from people with headaches, broken legs, heart disease, or cancer, arguing that if they'd just suck it up and transcend the pain, they might reach some kind of enlightened healing. But, for some reason, we're worried that madness, meditation, and medication don't mix?

During my twenties and thirties, I spent countless hours (actually, probably only ±4,000, now that I think of it) sitting with my legs crossed, watching my breath, and trying to still my mind. In the process, I frequently had moments of madness and transcendence—occasionally simultaneously.

So, at first, I believed that I could handle my breakdown with a kind of equanimity that most people couldn't even dream of. That, even in the midst of my darkest night, the Real Me would remain detached, fully aware of its own True Self, like a Zen master sitting on his meditation cushion in the midst of a hurricane. But as I learned early on, you can't get up from the cushion and walk away from agitated depression when the bell rings.

This inability to calmly bear witness to my mixed states just intensified my feelings of inadequacy. When a fellow traveler kindly and curiously asked why I didn't just "sit with it," in the way we'd both been trained, I wrote back:

> So you ask, what about simply being in the now, sinking fully into the moment...no matter how uncomfortable? Yes. I agree. I want to. Lord knows, I want to. But I've learned that trying to do so is now, for me, at best a prayer...because the experience invariably continues whether I'm "trying" or "not trying."

As strange as the "uselessness" of my traditional spiritual practices were in all this, those whom I turned to for what I considered
a bigger picture—one in which enlightenment is just one aspect of
spirituality—weren't much more encouraging. I wrote:

*It's surprising and frustrating that virtually all the people I now go to
for guidance encourage me not to do anything. And not to feel guilty
about doing nothing. They say I should certainly take care of myself,
eat good food, get outside—regular healthy human stuff. But that
sometimes it's fine to just take some Valium and pull the covers over
my head. Patience, I hear again and again. Just patience. "Resistance
is futile," they've all said in one way or another. Watch "bad" movies.
Read "bad" books. Just be patient and let the storm pass through you.*

*What a mysterious path for someone like me, huh? I mean, how
the hell is the universe going to respond to a guy who's constantly
equivocating, shuffling his feet, saying it doesn't matter, and crying
every chance he gets? There must be something I can DO. Can't I at
least be the one who surrenders?*

*No, they're saying. They're saying that the idea of my trying to
"do" anything, in the sense of "I" have the "power" is, in this case, a
little off the mark. That's not the lesson.*

*At least when I rest in the bright light they all assure me is coming,
I'll be under no illusions that I brought myself there through sheer
force of my own creativity, intelligence, insight, or efforts. I'll know,
in my bones, that it was and is, rather, through sheer grace I am
again able to experience the unspeakable joy of being alive, of being
grateful, and of having compassion for all other beings.*

∽

One of my more energetic alternative healers referred to the energy called kundalini in her attempt to describe what the heck I was
going through.

In keeping with our Western define-divide-conquer attitude toward virtually any experience, most of us equate the concept of
kundalini with the mastery of specific sexual techniques. Which,

considering what you can learn just standing in most supermarket checkout lines, makes you wonder why all our heads aren't exploding with energy that we've recklessly raised from the base of our spines...with or without the help of some willing partner.

Not to throw a wet towel over this impression, but at least from the perspective of several centuries-old spiritual traditions (primarily Hindu), kundalini is in everyone. It moves in different ways and to greater or lesser degrees depending on the person and the circumstances. For some people it stays fairly dormant. For others it bursts forth as a result of specific exercises or some random configuration of internal, karmic, planetary, or other factors.

Whether you try to manage this energy by doing special breathing exercises, having intercourse in complex positions, or screaming in desperation, the result is usually transformational. Because, as my friend explained, kundalini energy is really fiery. It tends to rage out of control, consuming everything in its way until you end up all shiny and new—if you live that long. (One could argue that the prime cause of some suicides is uncontrollable kundalini energy.)

This is something Dante understood. Because, in addition to one helluva episode of manic-depression and a traditional spiritual journey, *The Divine Comedy* can also be seen as the most famous kundalini experience of all time. In just three days—the poem takes place between Good Friday and Easter in 1300—Dante is completely transformed from a bumbling writer to God's right-hand man. In the process, he suffers deep despair, is frequently scared out of his wits, and walks through fire until nothing remains except him and his Lord.

☙

One of the most classic meditation practices is simply to focus on the famous *koan,* "Who am I?" By doing so, meditators are able to become aware of their many disparate "selves" (e.g., the one who's a perfectionist, the one who's never on time, the one who feels misunderstood, the one who'd rather be doing *anything* but meditating!) By getting a little distance from all those unruly selves, you can sometimes collect them in a way that gives you a sense of a "higher" Self.

When you're really depressed, it's easy to be aware of all those selves without even trying! In addition to your run-of-the-mill selves, there's the painfully sad self you constantly feel imprisoned by, the self who's bursting at the seams, the passably sane self you manage to project out in the world, the panic-y self who's watching all this with increasing horror, and some quiet self, barely sensed, seemingly impossible to reach, who maintains a distance, a wonder, a curiosity, and even some hope in the midst of it all.

Many people who are successfully treated for depression say, "I feel like myself again." At first, whenever I had a brief respite and, ultimately, when my meds started working, that was my experience. But for me, and I suspect for many others, that was soon replaced by the sense that I felt like someone very, very different—a Self who was no longer so swept away by what all his "little selves" were doing; in fact, who appreciated them for what they were and the equally important roles they played in his life.

Yes, depression can be excruciating. Yes, if I have a relapse, I will try everything I can to find a cure. Yes, it pains me to think of those who aren't fortunate enough to find relief—in particular, those who find relief only in suicide. But it's important for those mired in the illness to know that their lives are not being wasted... that their experiences are as valuable as those of the happy...that these are not "lost years."

We don't need depression to be creative or spiritual. At the same time, we are creative and spiritual even when in its grasp. That creativity and spirituality may not be apparent to the world, or even to ourselves, but it's there.

For sufferers, this fact may provide a modicum of reassurance that what they're going through is not a sign of weakness or indulgence; that there's not something "wrong" with them. It just hurts. For those whose life's mission is to treat or eradicate this disease "once and for all," the same fact may be a helpful reminder that, until they succeed, there is still great wisdom for those who endure it.

I had profound insights and moments of deep contentment before, during, and after my episode—in good times and bad, even during long existential but-not-depressed dark nights. As I emerged in mid-2007, I would sit on our porch staring out at the trees, overwhelmed by the delicious sensation of just sitting on our porch staring out at the trees. Psychosis certainly isn't a one-way ticket to cosmic consciousness. In fact, all too often, it's a one-way ticket to something far different. But I wouldn't be where I am today—I wouldn't even be able to sit still long enough to write these words—unless, one way or another, the storm hadn't passed.

All I know is that if we are to make war on depression in ourselves or in others, we first need to make our peace with it.

☙

Back when I was in my deepest *extremis,* I started signing virtually all my emails LOVE (all caps). Not in business correspondence, of course, or messages to anyone I thought it would make uncomfortable but, for the most part, I stopped making that subtle delineation between "Best," "All the Best," "Cheers," and even "Love." Instead I steadfastly clung to "LOVE."

It was more a prayer than a sentiment…a gesture toward human contact, bursting forth against all sensate-ness from that place where I was incapable of experiencing. To say that I'm more loving since my breakdown not only seems kind of melodramatic, it doesn't really capture the experience. I still get annoyed. I still get frustrated. I don't walk into a group of people and feel equal and unconditional love for all of them. (Although, I admit, it's no longer a very hard sensation for me to have for a few moments if I put my heart, mind, and body to it.)

But as I moved through this process, compassion for the suffering, sadness, or even idiocy(!) of any and all people and things backed and filled behind me, fueled by my complete and utter gratitude for even the briefest respite.

I feel that my internal chemistry has changed…that I've been rewired. That I'm simply incapable of making the inner connections that you'd need to be really pissed off…to think that someone is really a complete and utter idiot.

If I learned anything "spiritually" from the experience, it wasn't about living in the moment (I'm still as all over the place as ever), or about self-awareness (I still have so many selves to be aware of, it's hard to keep track!), it's about being more open, curious, and yes, I daresay loving, than I could have ever imagined being. This feeling is very different from "non-judgmental" as I used to understand it. It's more a knowing in my bones that everyone has a place in the big picture and that place is as legitimate and as important as mine. I no longer say (or think), "Well he has a right to his opinion." Of course, he has it! Who was I to even suggest I could give him that right? What makes me superior enough to put on spiritual robes and say what someone else's journey should look like?

I also had no choice but to learn about one of the greatest spiritual "barriers" we face. A barrier that's less noticed and more pervasive than I ever realized. One that's impossible to avoid when you're brought to your knees, especially if you follow the "official" Depressive's Mantra that a friend of mine developed. It throws down three gauntlets:

"It will pass." (Okay, that's hard to believe, but I'll keep it in mind.)

"Be kind to yourself." (Would love to, if I could figure out what the hell it means?)

But the last? "Ask for help?" (Ouch.)

Feeling love for everyone around you is easy compared to *receiving* love *from* all around you. But when you're in the state I was in, you don't have a lot of choice. And that's one of the most humbling and healing spiritual lessons of all.

Bottom line, we're all spiritual beings. Just like we're all physical, emotional, and mental beings. I understand why Dantean hier-archical structures are important for many people to maintain a sense of order in their spiritual pursuits. And I suppose that certain people have a brighter spiritual light (to people who see those kinds of things)—in the same way Babe Ruth might have had a brighter physical light, Einstein might have had a brighter mental light, or Mother Teresa might have had a brighter emotional light.

But, I think it's really healthy for all of us to realize that we're just as spiritual as the next person. And not just when we're in the church, temple, mosque, or meditation hall. Spirituality shows up in all aspects of our lives—everybody's life. I don't have to turn off my spiritual light in order to study genetics, fall in love, or play power forward...although I may have to grow a few inches to do the latter.

Until my breakdown I thought I knew what spirituality looked like. And it simply didn't look like a guy who was so agitated he couldn't even finish washing a window. I didn't fully accept the fundamental truth that every step on the path, "forward" or "back" is as "spiritual" as the one before.

One afternoon, Emily sent me a Mary Oliver poem, and I spent the whole afternoon repeating the refrain on and off to myself: "What blazes the trail is not necessarily pretty. What blaz-es the trail is not necessarily pretty. What blazes the trail is not necessarily pretty. What blazes the trail is not necessarily pretty."

Another day, a friend sent me a tape by a channeled spirit named Abraham. I couldn't look at the screen while it played... something about the woman who channeled him made my head hurt...although many things made my head hurt at the time. But one thing Abraham said has stayed with me through the years. A woman stood up to ask a question and said she couldn't ask it without crying. Abraham said, "Well, you can either not ask the question or ask the question while crying."

During my breakdown, I had a lot of questions. Those words

helped me ask them without resistance—without questioning
that what I was going through was as valid a human experience
as the President's, the Dalai Lama's, or the homeless guy who
hits me up for coffee money every morning. We find our jewels
where we find them.

THE DIVINE COMEDY

PAY CLOSE ATTENTION TO WHAT I'VE TOLD YOU,
SO YOU CAN TEACH THOSE WHO STILL LIVE IN THAT WORLD
WHERE LIFE IS MERELY A RACE TO DEATH...

Purgatory, Canto XXXIII (52–55)

YOUR WORDS ARE PLANTED IN MY BRAIN AS
FIRMLY AS A SEAL ON WAX.
YET THE HARDER I TRY TO FOLLOW THEM,
THE FURTHER THEY SOAR OUT OF SIGHT.

Purgatory, Canto XXXIII (79–85)

W HAT DO YOU DO FOR AN ENCORE? YOU'RE 55 YEARS, a few months, and a week or so old. You've been breathing life into the greatest story ever told for twenty years, somehow integrating seemingly every last bit of your worldly and other-worldly wisdom, even as it morphs and grows by leaps and bounds.

Fourteen thousand lines. No word processor. No outlining program. Not a whole lot of paper to take notes on. You're don't even have a permanent office!

What do you do when you wake up the next morning?

In Dante's case, he didn't have to worry about that very long. His current patron in Ravenna, Guido Novello da Polenta, sensing that he was at a bit of a loss about what to do next, gave him a challenging, but straightforward mission. To go on one more road trip: up to Venice to negotiate an agreement with the Venetians about sharing control of the Adriatic.

Dante wasn't any more successful than he'd been back in 1300 when he tried to find some common ground between Rome and Florence. Not only did Venice spurn his offers, they made him return by a more circuitous swampy route. He came down with malaria. Fortunately, his daughter Antonia recently had come to Ravenna and joined a nunnery... taking the name Beatrice, of course. She was with him when he died.

Beholding the Stars

It scarcely mattered whether he was happy or unhappy,
he was alive and he was fully aware that he was alive
and that was enough.
—ERICH MARIA REMARQUE

CO

M Y RECOVERY CONTINUED through the summer of 2007.
Like a tree straightening up after having been bent this way
and that by fierce winds from every direction. Breezes would still
come along, sometimes strong ones, but in the process of holding
on so tight for so long, my roots had grown deeper and stronger.

I'd usually wake up at 5 A.M. And fall back asleep until 6. I'd
begun to keep a thermos of tea next to the bed and would spend
the next hour sipping the tea, maybe dozing, mostly scratching
our new cat, and letting myself dream, just thinking quietly about
things, waiting for some idea that sparked something and got me
interested in the day.

It seemed that every few days or week brought a quiet mile-
stone. I went bike riding early one morning with my friends again.
(I'd been riding by myself for most of the season… usually in the
afternoon.) On another morning, I got up, took the tea with me
out to the cabin and put in a few hours of work. I found I could
start a small project and neither abandon it nor force myself to
finish it by some arbitrary deadline. Occasionally, I'd find myself in
the middle of a mild skirmish or major battle with my still-skittish
brain and—whether by working out, nibbling on a pill, or just stepping back—find a way to make peace.

There was something almost exhilarating about being with people. Being able to sit through a dinner or stand and make small-talk was a shocking breakthrough in interpersonal skills. I could make people laugh again. I could help people see things differently again. It was as if I had my own one-person cheering section in my brain applauding my efforts, encouraging every step, like you would encourage a baby to walk.

Late that summer, I was at a party, seeing many people again for the first time in years. I began a long conversation with an old friend about our shared experiences as "depressives in recovery." As I began to explain my understanding of how the disease worked, I began to talk faster. Soon, I'd begun to rant a little. Just a little. I watched it. It was kind of fun. I didn't feel out of control. But, toward the end of the conversation, he said, "Well, you're still as much of an egomaniac as ever, Dave."

The comment didn't just make my heart sink. It made the whole of me sink. I knew, and Wendy reassured me, that he mistook celebration of self with obsession with self. But I could see how he made the mistake and, in the process, resurrected the dichotomy I'd experienced my whole life between what I wanted to say and how people might react. Fortunately, that dichotomy continued to be slowly revealed for the paper tiger it now was. As that new sense of acceptance worked its way into every corner of my formerly hypercritical self, my observations increasingly came out in words that, while equally insightful, weren't threatening. Weren't downright mean.

Yes, I can be as caustic as ever. Yes, I can be as funny as ever. But it's entirely different.

As I was emerging in the summer of 2007, I read William Styron's *Darkness Visible*. When Wendy asked why that, of all books, I said: "It's like having a confidante."

It was such a relief to read someone who took a clear-eyed, literary, and—of all things—sane look at the mixed states I knew so well. Styron captured the desperation without sounding desperate. He captured the anxiety without sounding manic. While he occasionally lost his sense of humor, he didn't lose his sense of irony.

Bottom line: he got right inside the madness and ripped it open, so the allegedly sane could see the guts of the thing.

Even in the midst of my experience, I wanted to write about it; I wanted to understand it; I wanted it to have meaning. Because, as bad as I got, I knew that I was still a writer—husband, father, son, brother, friend—first and a depressive a distant second. Writers tell stories. It's what we do. In the process, we maybe be indulgent, vapid, resolute, or wise. Often all in a single paragraph. (That's why we like having good editors.)

The more intimate the writing, the more difficult and important it is to maintain the authenticity every writer strives for—what people call "finding your voice." I'd call it "aligning" not finding. Like when you hit the "sweet spot" on a tennis, squash, or golf ball. Something inside you just lets go and leaves you in a rare balance with the task before you. But, you have to "find" it over and over, stroke after stroke, sentence after sentence. In the case of memoir, you're definitely dealing with a moving target. It's too easy to be swept away by the drama of the thing, or stay safely on the banks. Both keep the reader at arm's length. Both leave the writer and reader with a vague sense of unfulfilled longing.

I'm no longer sure that's any but a theoretical problem. I have no interest in dragging anybody kicking and screaming into the experience itself. If you want to be really sad, I'd suggest *Of Mice and Men*. For agitation, there's nothing like having a few books about global warming on your night table. And for mixed states, just root for the Red Sox.

What books about mental illness *can* do is make the experience so human that it's no longer necessary for you to hold it at that arm's length...or vice versa. Deep depression can at times be as contagious as laughter. Fortunately, most people are immune to the former—or at least can be quickly "cured" by the latter.

I've chronicled some wild emotional swings here—including some written while in the belly of the beast. I've also tried to provide a comprehensive overview of the disease, although I do occasionally indulge in some plain-English versions of medical jargon. Like a poor-man's William Styron, it's *my* attempt to get right inside the madness and rip it open, so the allegedly sane can see the guts of the thing...and also reassure the clinically ill that there is intelligent life on the other side.

ॐ

In late August of 2007, I took off for a final trip in my 1990 VW Vanagon. After three years and ±50,000 miles of travel together— both around town and the country—our relationship was symbiotic, if not co-dependent. It wouldn't be fair to say it broke down all the time. It didn't. (Although it had every right to, considering how many of my worries, screams, and tears I'd subjected it to.) But it frequently did need major upkeep, as the various systems that were new two decades before decided they'd had enough of life on the road. We're talking the usual: brakes, wheel bearings, head gaskets, transmission seals, starter, fuel pump, alternator, thermostat, and odometer (don't worry, I told the truth when I sold it). There were also odder things that I didn't even know cars had: the rear main seal, AC Inverter, torque converter seal, plastic cooling pipe, and all the gas vapor hoses. Throw in some regular oil changes, tune-ups, and tires and altogether I'd spent about $10,000 to keep a $9,500 car running for three years.

That was nothing compared to the parts of *me* that had worn out at the same time. Those couldn't be measured in dollars and cents. Fortunately, I had no desire to ever replace them.

I didn't know exactly where I was going. I mean I'd kind of decided I was going to Cape Breton on the northeast tip of Nova Scotia, because I'd heard that its Cabot Trail has some of the most beautiful bike riding in North America. But as far as specific routes and way stations, I was going to make it up as I went along.

It was a pilgrimage of sorts. A chance for the me, the van, and the psychosis to make peace with each other. We had become acutely attuned to each others' idioscyncrasies over the years, and had learned to find a kind of perverse comfort in their familiarity. But it was time for us to give each other a wry smile, a poignant hug, and be on our ways.

Years ago, I used to do two- and three-day retreats occasionally. Alone somewhere, sometimes fasting. But, eventually, I realized that just wasn't my path to peace and quiet. For me, it was and is still traveling. Alone. Driving for hours, listening closely for faint sounds of disquiet from my heart or my van. Sitting alone in coffee shops and restaurants—the noise of oblivious strangers balancing the noise within, leaving me free to observe both.

Sleeping in a pop-top camper in a Walmart parking lot in Portland, Maine, is probably not on many people's lists of things they must do before they die. But, if you really want to experience the wondrous bizarreness of life on earth, you might consider it. Because the experience of waking up at 3 A.M., sliding down off the sleeping loft, and staggering into the starry asphalt night to pee is an image will forever have a place in my personal Ripley's Believe-It-Or-Not.

I can't quite remember how I ended up in a Walmart parking lot that night. (I still wasn't drinking, so that's no excuse.) I had spent the evening wandering around the Portland waterfront, ending up in a sushi restaurant where I watched a few innings of a Red Sox game at the bar, while three Japanese chefs effortlessly slivered recently dead, but still vibrant fish. They seemed oblivious to the game (as did the fish) until they heard the announcers get excited. Then they would glance quickly at the TV. After they did this a few times, I realized that all they cared about was whether the play involved their countryman Daisatsu Matsuzake, who was pitching that night.

I left well before the game was over, stopped at a Whole Foods for supplies, and drove around for a while trying to pick a cheap hotel. By then it was past 10 P.M. I had to be at the docks at 7 A.M. for a ferry to Nova Scotia. So, when I drove past a Walmart, I pulled in. All three of us—me, the van, and the psychosis found this decision rather odd.

But, you know? That was okay.

The trip was filled with a series of similar mundane, but, for me, potentially mind-bending unexpectednesses. There was no way I was going back to Hell. But I still had to take a few more steps up my customized Purgatory-Lite, climbing through some terribly ordinary experiences that previously would have left me buzzed and distraught. It was humbling. But the whole two years had been profoundly humbling. I could handle a little more.

I got seasick on the ferry. I've never been seasick before. One minute I was inside the cabin reading a book, trying to get a good-looking woman to glance my way. The next minute, in an act of digestive and karmic retribution, I was clamping my mouth shut trying to keep my entire breakfast of trail mix from covering my shirt. I went to the bathroom, cleaned up, got a cup of coffee and spent the rest of the ride shivering out against the back railing with the cigarette smokers and choppy waves.

But, you know? That was okay.

When the boat docked five hours later in Yarmouth, Nova Scotia, I walked down to the van, trying to keep down the dread that it wouldn't start, thereby bringing the entire disembarking system to a complete halt, as annoyed vacationers glared at me and my poor camper.

I got in the van and turned the key. It started, I sighed, and we drove off with a sense of accomplishment far greater than would have been called for by anyone else. With maps on my seat, I began driving south and east, occasionally on the highway, but usually on Route 3, the original shore route.

When it started to get dark, I decided to stay in a campground an hour or so away from Halifax, Nova Scotia's capital, figuring I could get up early, and stop there for a good breakfast...maybe even spend a day.

The campground was dank with grey sea air and many of the people had fires going. I walked around slowly, smiling and nodding at them and receiving smiles and nods in return. People smile and nod a lot in campgrounds. But no one offered me any marshmallows so I went back to the van to read the literature they'd given me when I checked in. The major "tourist attraction" was a fishing village called Peggy's Cove, once known for its huge glacial boulders and well-photographed lighthouse, but now visited mainly because it's where Swissair Flight 111 crashed in 1998. I decided to pay my respects. So the next morning, I drove out of the campground, turned left, and drove forty miles or so wondering how I'd missed both Peggy's Cove and Halifax. Turned out…I should have turned right. In spite of frequent stops to ask locals who seemed as lost as I was—and consulting maps that made it clear that to go north and east along the shore, you often had to go south and west—I had retraced my steps for more than an hour. And, ultimately, spent three hours going 15 miles.

But, you know? That was okay.

It was noon by the time I got to the memorial for the flight, where I spent a few minutes of quiet contemplation surrounded by people who were talking loudly about what it must have been like, and gee they didn't know *that* many people died, and I wonder how often people who lost relatives must visit the place. Quiet contemplation isn't what it used to be.

Dictating notes and feeling profound, I went up to the lighthouse and ate breaded salmon. It burned the top of my tongue and seemed so bland, it probably came from British Columbia instead of the ocean a few hundred yards away.

By the time I left Peggy's Cove, it was raining heavily. While I was trying to decide which exit to get off in Halifax, I felt a familiar jarring in the back of the car. I didn't even have to stop to see if I had a flat. I managed to get off the highway and pull into a gas station. The rain was getting torrential.

But, you know? That was okay.

I got a little air into the tire with one of those fix-a-flat cans and drove slowly to a tire place a couple of miles away, had a new tire put on, and took off again. Two hundred miles later, I arrived in the town of Mabou, halfway up Cape Breton Island. I followed a sign to the local campground. When I asked the owner how much it would cost, he said $10. When I pulled out my credit card, he said $20. Somehow that made me feel right at home. I gave him the cash, set up my camper and went into town.

Mabou is most famous for being the home of the Rankin Family, one of Canada's most long-lasting and award-winning folk musical groups. They own a restaurant in Mabou called the *Red Shoe Pub* that's, naturally, well known for its live music. There wasn't any music that night.

I sat down and when the waitress came over to see if I wanted to start with a drink, I opened my mouth to say coffee and the words, "Jameson's, on the rocks" came out.

But, you know? That was okay.

The next morning, I started talking to the guy the next campsite over. He was from Michigan and, it turned out, also a road biker. He came there every year to ride in the Labor Day Cabot Trail ride and told me there was a lot of good biking around Mabou, too. We went on several long rides over the next few days. He even managed to convince me to go to a Céilidh (pronounced Kay-lee), a traditional evening of music and contra-type-dancing, with people from 6 to 100. For the next several hours, I was flung unceremoniously from person to person as they tried to keep my hapless feet from ruining the entire rhythm of the thing. Most of them laughed. One woman in her 80s made it wordlessly clear that people like me were the bane of her existence.

But, you know? That was okay.

I went for a long bike ride myself the next day. I got lost and dehydrated.

But, you know? That was okay.

I never even made it up to the Cabot Trail—thereby missing one of the most not-to-be missed biking experiences in America.

But, you know? That was okay.

And so it went. Three days later I started home, following the northern shore route. That evening I arrived in a town called Parker's Cove as the sun went down in a blazing sunset. I didn't really see that sunset. I was driving around lost, looking for a campground, and the low contour hills just inland kept blocking my view. As I finally found the place and paused to see the spectacular colors, they all dissolved into pre-midnight blue. I'd missed yet another celestial vision.

But, you know? That was okay.

I got to the ferry the next morning. Took it to Bar Harbor. Spent a few days biking and eating, and now, drinking. I was getting a little lonely. I was beginning to wonder how long I had to stay on the road in order to make it an official "last breakdown road trip." I still had a knack for obsession. I wanted to do this right. I was still anxious about leaving any psychosis on my plate.

Eight days after I'd left, I gave myself permission to start heading home. I spent a night in Camden at my cousin's. The first night in a real live bed since I'd left. We talked for a long time that night and the next morning. Family stories that ranged from warmly hilarious to vaguely troubling.

The next day, around noon, I finally drove home. Down Route 1 to Portsmouth, NH and then Route 4 over to Concord, to Route 9, to Route 123. Familiar roads all. Road that I'd driven many times over the last 30 years, in a whole lot of different cars and a whole lot of different moods. I got on Route 91 at Exit 5 in Westminster/Bellows Falls. One exit from home. Seven miles later, just before my Exit 4, I had a flat tire. I pulled over and jacked the car up. As I wiggled the tire off, the car fell off the jack and almost tipped over on to me.

But, you know? That was okay.

∽

Four years later. A winter morning, 2012. 6 A.M. I'm sitting too close to the woodstove, waiting for the cabin to warm up. Legs really hot, fingers really cold. Coffee already lukewarm.

I'm feeling kinda off. For good reason. Last night I was troubled by some stuff. Outer, not inner. No big deal, just little things. So I decided to take the *Law & Order* Cure.

This famous non-prescription treatment involves pouring a glass of wine or beer, sitting down in front of the TV, picking up the remote, turning on the USA Network or TNT, and watching successive episodes of *Law & Order* —one after another after another, until your mind is a blur of strange murders, the even stranger people who may or may not have committed them, and the deeply troubled detectives and lawyers who struggle to preserve some semblance of justice and sanity in the midst of it all. Detectives and lawyers—or, I should say, actors and actresses—who have perfected looks of tragic poignancy that would make any depressive proud.

This treatment, although pleasant, is usually just a short-term solution. It's usually followed by twisted dreams during the night, a headache the next morning, and the realization that I just gotta do whatever it was I was avoiding the night before and get on with my life.

I'd like to go back to sleep, but I have too much caffeine in me. So I start looking around. My cabin is a mess. I still have boxes of childhood stuff that I've been meaning to sort through (i.e., throw out) since my mother moved out of the home we grew up in and made me take them. Which was almost twenty years ago. I have drafts of novels, piles of paper, and half-filled notebooks scattered all over the place. There are things pinned to the wall I haven't looked at in months. There are paper clips on every surface, photos in frames that have fallen over, tangles of wires near every outlet, little organizing contraptions that haven't organized anything in years.

Five years ago, this scene of chaos would have been enough to break my heart. It would have sent me back under the covers, out on a manic bike ride, rummaging in drawers for a Valium or sleeping pill, or calling every alternative therapist I could think of to see if they could possibly see me today, preferably this morning, preferably *right now.*

Today, thanks to three different medications and, undoubtedly, many mysterious forces beyond my control, I have other options. I can sit still and keep looking around. I can have an idea. Then another. And another: Okay...I'll move this here and that there and clear off that surface so I can start organizing this material here, and, in a show of remarkable courage, throw away every stray paperclip I see...

Then I start thinking about writing this little piece. And *then* about going in the house and getting another cup of tea. And *then* coming back out and writing something else. And *then* having breakfast. And *then* taking a nap! Gee, I'm feeling pretty good. I'm feeling *inspired*.

All pretty trivial. But, for someone with a history of depression, there's nothing trivial about it. Because, at least for me, the opposite of being depressed isn't really being happy, it's being *inspired*. Full, as the etymologists would explain, of *divine* breath.

☙

I used to think of the period from October 2005–October 2007 as my "lost years." Now, I think of them as my "lost-and-found" years. I look pretty much the same as I did in 2005…a little grayer in the beard…a few more lines in the face…I don't bike quite as fast as I used to…I've put back on the pounds that I lost back when my metabolism was constantly on overdrive…people tell me I'm as smart and funny as ever (Phew.)

So, beyond brain chemistry, astrological alignments, midlife crises, and raging kundalini, why did this happen? In the spring of 2007, as I began to return to my version of normalcy, I wrote Emily:

> *It's been a year and a half. And it's coming to an end. At a pace, of course, that isn't fast enough for me.*
>
> *Why have I had this experience? I've said this before…probably to you…but I think it began with a perfect storm: changing careers (not being interrupted every 15 minutes with someone's question); hormonal changes (fyi: male menopause is real); a let-down after six months of extreme creativity which segued into a sense of being overwhelmed by my writing projects; and, to some extent, not getting the right drugs at the right time. I say, "to some extent" because I have learned and changed so much during this period that I think only now is it the right time for me to be getting the right drugs.*
>
> *Then there's just my nature. I think I wanted to explore this. I think I wanted to understand certain limits. I think I wanted to dive down and bring to the surface some things that maybe, otherwise, would*

hold me back from the next phase of my life. I know that I'm much, much more understanding, compassionate, and non-judgmental than I could even imagine. And, as I get better, I can feel other, more subtle things coming up. Ways I respond to what people say and do, fears I've had, that I can begin to let go.

And there's been this other thing. It has to do with letting myself be loved and cared about. By mom and you. By friends. Even by doctors. While your email last week was, simultaneously, the most elegant and heartfelt/rending, there have been others, from various friends, that have just made it clear how much they care about me. Even people who just want me to be better and really don't like talking about these things ask me how I'm doing and listen to me talk about it in depth. Softening yourself to allow that in also softens the way you look out.

I think about how many people go through this without that support. I think they often get hard and brittle. And maybe break.

That's my story, Emily. It's 11 A.M. Sunday morning. I started before 9. It's hard to believe it's taken me almost two hours to write these few words, but I wanted to get them right. I like to get things right. But you know? Maybe that's okay.

∞

A few hundred years after Dante died, people began calling books with sad endings "tragedies," and those with happy endings "comedies." That's why his masterpiece had that rather odd descriptive tacked on to its name. But remember: his original title was *The Vision.*

Vision is about looking *forward*. That's why all three books end with the word "stars," even *Paradise* where, by definition, all distinctions are rendered meaningless. Yes, even in *Paradise,* Dante is still looking *forward*. Because, brilliant as his masterpiece is, Dante knows he's really still telling an old story. He's just telling it better than anyone ever told it before. And telling it. And telling it. And telling it. If only he could tell it once and for all. Certainly he doesn't want to go through all *that* yet again. And he wouldn't wish it on us either! He's ready to move on.

In other words, all this time that I've been looking *back* on my experience…all this time that I've been looking *back* at *The Divine Comedy,* Dante's been looking in the other direction. Past me, past all of us, and beyond. *Forward.*

No copy of *The Divine Comedy* written in Dante's own hand has ever been found. While, for emotional and financial reasons, he had started passing around *The Inferno* as early as 1314 and *Purgatory* a few years later, he was undoubtedly holding back *Paradise,* waiting to do his own complete three-volume "authorized" edition only after he had written the whole book. But, by then, he might have been too tired, felt it was too late, or that it didn't really matter. Because even though transcribers undoubtedly let their own prejudices creep in (who could resist casting their own favorite political or religious enemy into eternal Hell?), the poet's genius was so refined, intricate, and yet inviolable, that its multiple levels of ever-evolving meanings remained intact—and the most profound ones remain invisible.

The legend is that Dante actually never "released" *Paradise.* He never gave the entire manuscript to his patron—which he always did before letting it into the world. His children easily found most of it after he died. It was sitting on his desk, right there out in the open. He'd been working on it just a few days ago, before he'd been bedridden with malaria. He'd arranged it in a nice tidy stack, the way writers do to punctuate the completion of anything from a chapter to a whole book. But it was missing a few final cantos. One morning, several months after he died however, his son Iacopo claimed he had a vision that they were hidden behind a wall hanging. And sure enough they were.

Dante was only 55. He hadn't planned on dying anytime soon. Figured he had plenty of time for a last read. He probably told Iacopo where those pages were…in case something happened.

It's hard to let go. But, whether you're transformed by outer events, inner cataclysms, or just the inexorable passage of time, there's no going back. And how far you can go forward is limited only to the extent that you are able to be renewed in your own rivers Lethe and Eunoe. Limited only to the extent that you can make firm in yourself what you are now and let go of what's held you back in the past. Limited only by your vision.

> You have seen the temporal and the
> Eternal fire and arrived at the place
> Where I can no longer point the way.
> I've led you here with skill and art,
> Now, follow your own bliss, let that be your guide,
> For you have overcome steep and narrow paths.
> See, there, the sun that shines on your forehead,
> Behold the grass, the flowers, and the bushes
> That, here, the earth produces by itself.

—PURGATORY, CANTO XXVII (127–135)
*Virgil's last words to Dante
before Beatrice becomes his guide.*

ᴄᴏ

Psychiatric Notes

ᴄᴏ

T HE FOLLOWING IS A RUNNING CHRONOLOGY of my doctors' notes from 1999 through 2007. I've been on the same medications since then and go only every six months or so to check in.

Although I've seen a few different practitioners—professional depressives use the phrase *pdocs*—I present them as if they were one doctor. I have a great deal of appreciation and respect for all of them.

As you can imagine, their notes are virtually indecipherable, so I've incorporated some of my own notes from those appointments and translated their jargon, abbreviations, and hieroglyphic scribbles as best I could. You'll get the idea: (1) Medication is a long and winding road. (2) It can be *really* hard to hang in there. (3) It's worth every step when it works.

Interestingly, when compared to other things I wrote at the time—and the observations of friends—I seem to have over-dramatized or under-dramatized my condition at any given appointment. I think a lot of psychiatric patients do that. It may have to do with how you feel about the drugs you're taking and whether consciously or subconsciously you want to keep taking them or go off them. Also, that you really don't realize how "out there" you were until you're back—something friends and family appear to have realized all along.

January 27, 1999
[First ever visit to a psychiatrist.] *Wife's urged him to come for a long time. Recurrent depressions. Can usually use vitamins and exercise. This*

fall, exhausted...[those strategies] not working. Works all the time, anxious. Wakes up early both wired and exhausted. "At recent meeting felt I just couldn't do this." Next day, presentation to client, "almost ranting." Coworkers said, "out of control." Some A.M.s have to play racquetball to get energy out—others just dragging. Alcohol...usually wine. He went off it years ago for a few years. In past, depression for several days to weeks. Mania—usually hours—great times. Can focus and be productive. Borderline crying but can't. Frantic drive. Can hyper-concentrate if no stimulus.

Sleep—goes right to sleep. If wakes, can go back. Gets up 5-6 A.M.. Not rested this winter. Naps don't work now. Can be irritable. Concentration either on or off—15 minute cycles now. Memory? No long term. Yes at work.

Sadness, yes. Some hopelessness. Not suicidal. Has to be busy. Frantic drive. Sex drive okay but less so. Hyper as a kid. "My mouth caused problems."

Diagnosis: Major Depression. Rule Out Bipolar. Trial of Wellbutrin.

February 8, 1999
OCD helped by meds (not really depression and anxiety). Some side effects at first but less now. Relaxed this weekend and didn't work all the time. "I don't have to go on a tangent and worry about things. Can say no." Still sad and anxious but better! Wife agrees—the layer of manic-ness is gone now—he can see problem and work on changes. Able to slow down and "stop the train." Continue Wellbutrin another 10 days then consider medication for anxiety.

February 22, 1999
Off caffeine a week. No change. Still wakes with a chest buzz. "Think I'm getting better." Feels Wellbutrin helps but still fragile. Hard for him to stop taking on any new obligations from others. Much worse A.M.. Better during day. May warrant going up on the dose.

March 11, 1999
"The same." Much more relaxed and less compulsion but more sad...will

still burst into tears Monday before work. Mood was better for two days doing Wellbutrin 2x day. Helps with anxiety and obsession. Not depression. Continue Wellbutrin. Add Celexa 10 mg three days then 20 mg.

March 22, 1999
Stayed at 10 mg Celexa. Jaw ached—fading some now and he felt better. Does get lift but fades. Relief from ADD. Depression is more prominent. No stomach upset. No impotence. Worth continuing Celexa trial. He's still sad...not looking forward to Monday A.M.s. Co-workers still see difference from Wellbutrin. Continue trial. Then go up to 20 mg Celexa 2x Day.

March 30, 1999
Phone: He'll go up to 40 mg Celexa.

April 8, 1999
Somewhat better on 40 mg Wellbutrin still working. Relaxes better and can stop and do things. Better mood. Sleep's fine. No big side effects. A little spacy and yawning. No other side effects. A little loss of mood past few days. Wife worries he'll get compulsive again—people are easier around him—he finally can sit still and watch movies or play card games. Energy to only plan a small garden at new house. Good diet. Several cups coffee/day. Takes B vits daily.

April 21, 1999
Seen with wife. She sees major improvements in depression since adding Celexa. Calmer. Likes staying in bed in A.M. Not as driven. Still gets things done. Much better mood. Minimal side effects. Mild shakiness, yawning. Clearly better since upping Celexa to 40 mg. Sustained response.

May 18, 1999
Survived the move to new house! Meds working well. Minor tremor. Blood pressure 118/76. Can't complain. Doing well. Wife and co-workers agree. "I can go out to lunch and not feel I have to rush back. I enjoy work, biking, working on house, etc. Work piling up—a busy time." Sustained benefit.

July 20, 1999

He says, "Best two months of my life." Except for 36 hours when he felt it was all coming back. But he survived and recovered. Work's fine. Busy again, but "I can leave work at work and go home." A complete turn-around. Not exercising compulsively. Continue meds. Wellbutrin SR 150 mg 2X Day. Celexa 20 mg 2X Day.

September 28, 1999

Great. "2nd greatest 2 months of my life." Vacation w/wife on Lake Champlain. First vacation since depressed. Sustained relief. He'll continue this regime through the winter. Possibly go down in spring.

January 20, 2000

Still great! At times forgets A.M. dose…no loss of benefit. And he's willing to continue thru winter. Still office politics a problem but he's coping.

April 30, 2000

Missed Celexa one day—tears and down the next. Work's fine. Home's fine. Asks for tranquilizer for plane flight. Prescribe 10 Xanax .25 mg.

July 10, 2000

Doing well. Work's okay. Feels a little scattered on Wellbutrin—sometimes skips pm Wellbutrin. Still feels absentminded but tolerable. Plans to take January off from work to write.

October 10, 2000

Taking B Vitamins helps. Feels meds interfere with his ability to recover from exercise some, but tolerable. Some up and down mood but okay. Thinks Wellbutrin helped with his compulsiveness. Celexa with mood. He wants to consider going down in spring.

January 19, 2001

Plans a month working at home. Built a small cabin house to work. Starts Thursday. Tried Alpralozam [Xanax] for flying. Went okay. Not sure he needs it.

October 24, 2001

Almost went off meds in August—was on ½ pill each. Then crashed and back on in September. Going to sell his business. Will stay on as creative head. Took Jan 15-Feb 15 off. DSM Axis I: 296.32 Major Depressive Disorder/Recurrent - Moderate. Axis IV: Moderate: Management responsibilities. Had to fire an employee. Current GAF (Global Access of Functioning) 80.

May 27, 2003

Phone message asking me to call in an Rx for Celexa. I'll call him back. Thought he was off. Have him make appt.

June 18, 2003

By summer 2002 was off all meds and okay. In fall 2002, thought maybe he just had S.A.D. Felt he didn't need Wellbutrin. Restarted Celexa, In April 2003, tried to wean off again but in a month felt worse. So back on Celexa 40 mg. Finally kicking in. We discussed options. Would like to try Lexapro 10 mg and then go up to 20 mg. Will phone report.

July 28, 2003

Doesn't like Lexapro. Asks to return to Celexa.

May 21, 2004

Lexapro didn't seem to work as well, so back to Celexa. In winter 60 mg; summer 40 mg or 30 mg. November is too late to go up on dose. Will go up in late September or October. Ending 3-year contract with business at end of the year. Has another part-time business. May go on a road trip in spring.

March 28, 2005

Took year off to write. Travelled for a month through South and back. Going to France. After he left business went down to 40 mg Celexa and felt okay. Maybe after return from France he'll go down to 20 mg. Maybe off in summer. Cautioned re withdrawal effects.

October 17, 2005

Phone: Started taking Celexa 20 mg again. Feels wired. Only change is Chinese herbs. He'll stop the herbs and see how he feels. Phone report.

October 25, 2005

Phoned: Anxious. Valium helped. Crying jags.

October 26, 2005

Seen with wife. Went off Celexa in summer and did fine. Started Celexa 20 mg ten days ago, and then to 40 mg. PCP gave Valium for business trip but just couldn't go, so cancelled. Each A.M. since Celexa has terrible feeling in pit of stomach. Vibration. Can't sit still. Lost 5+ pounds. Weighs less than in 10 years. Agitated, emotional, tearful. Not suicidal but could understand how it happens. Got off Celexa. Already getting better. 5 mg Valium until he feels like himself. Once he does, restart Wellbutrin but lower dose. SR 100. Then phone report. Will not go up on Wellbutrin or return to SSRIs until we speak.

April 6, 2006

Prescription from primary-care physician: 40 5 mg Valium.

July 18, 2006

Phone call for renewal of Valium 5 mg. Rarely needs it but wishes to have it available.

August 3, 2006

Had two weeks fairly fine last November after discontinuing Celexa. Since then, he wakes restless, stomach restless/anxious. Crying jags every 3-4 days. Took Wellbutrin 150 mg March/April. No change. Assessment: Depression NOS. Anxiety NOS. Doubt bipolar (he's sleeping.) Try BuSpar 5 mg. 3x/day. Valium as needed up to 3x/day.

August 8, 2006

Message from him on answering machine. Couldn't hear all of it but sounds like he's getting some relief at low dose of BuSpar but having trouble getting the dose up. Poor sleep if he takes it too close to bedtime.

Left message to take his time going up on the dose...to not go up if having side effects.

September 6, 2006

May wake 1 A.M. but back to sleep, then awake 4:30 with sudden jilt like adrenaline rush. Then has a sense of agitation and obsessiveness. Try going up to 10 mg BuSpar 3x/day.

October 26, 2006

More anxious on 15 mg BuSpar so back to 10 mg again. He still wakes up 4 A.M. wired—takes 10 mg Valium and can stay in bed 2 hours. Once up he'll have to be very active, take steam, sweat, before able to relax. Celexa triggered this in October '05. He's never felt really himself again since. Weight down 10-15 pounds. 135. His journal notes: "Essentially, there's nothing I want to do. Every time I think I hit bottom I'm out on a mountain bike sobbing or lying in bed panicked at 4 A.M.." Hypomanic. Dysphoric mania. Will try Depakote.

November 3, 2006

"Depakote really works." Feels a little subdued but okay.

November 17, 2006

First week on Depakote, the spells stopped. Second week dropped back into deep depression—now back to agitation. First week the explosion episodes stopped. Felt normal. When depressed in the past, wasn't agitated. But now wakes with sense of dread. Bipolar depression? Off BuSpar. Add Seroquel 25 mg to 50 mg to 100 mg to 200 mg. Continue Depakote and Valium. Contingency—DHMC [i.e., Inpatient Psych Unit/Dartmouth-Hitchcock Medical Center].

December 1, 2006

Seroquel stopped the worst of the symptoms...the madness. At 200 mg he dreams again. Wakes once but back to sleep. Side effects: dry mouth, felt odd, eyes jittery and unsteady. "Don't feel like myself." No more Valium. Can stay engaged when busy during the day. Depression's there but no tears. Still 1250 mg Depakote and no side effects. Tired and can't sleep during the day.

December 26, 2006
"I'm better—not amazingly so but better." A.M.s *still not great. He's tried going down on Seroquel. 200 mg works but 150 mg has fewer side effects. Seroquel "gets me through the night." We'll go up to 1500 mg Depakote.*

February 8, 2007
On 1500 mg Depakote he got more shaky. Went down to 1250 mg. No change in shakiness. We'll back to 1000 mg Depakote and follow. Tremor may mean the agitated and manic state is continuing in which case would have to go up on Depakote/Seroquel again. He's down, blunted, sad today.

March 8, 2007
Feels better on 1000 mg Depakote and 50 mg Seroquel. Then thought maybe go down further and start with an antidepressant. But still wakes up anxious. Used Wellbutrin and Celexa before. Lexapro didn't work for him. We'll use Seroquel as needed for sleep. Try Effexor for depression/anxiety. If doesn't work revisit 2-week Inpatient at DHMC.

March 13, 2007
Phone: Really agitated on 37.5 mg Effexor. Lorazepam 1 mg 3x/day.

March 21, 2007
[Full Review] 54y mwm w/ long history of confusing symptoms of mood vacillation, depression, seeming ADHD, etc., throughout life with never really having sustained remission of symptoms. Predominant symptoms is melancholic depression w/hypomanic episodes complicated by alcohol self medication. Feather away Depakote and benzodiazepams over time. Also address alcohol.

Cymbalta: go 10 mg to 15 mg to 30 mg. as tolerated. Lamictal 25 mg. Continue Depakote ER 500 mg 2x/day. [There's a "Starter Pack" for the transition from Lamictal to Depakote.] *Stop Seroquel and Lorazepam and Effexor. Switch to Clonazepam 1 mg.*

March 28, 2007

First *A.M.* after Lamictal w/Cymbalta was first time he felt good waking. Good eye contact, brighter affect, calmer, relaxed. Responded well and tolerated meds. Positive response to bipolar depression approach.

April 11, 2007

The symptoms haven't really changed in terms of start of day. "I look forward to the end of the day...most of the day I'm sort of flat." His journal notes: "No interest in getting up regardless of bedtime, exercise, whether I drink, food. If I get up and walk, I just cry on the walk. I'm driven and drowsy." Hard exercise helps but can lead to dry heaves like last summer. Evening closest to "good mood."

Good eye contact. Calmer still. Slowly stabilizing and accepting the gradual change offered by meds. Needing a lot of psych-ease and reassurance.

April 25, 2007

"People really do notice improvement." Told him it takes time to turn the Titanic around. Focus on best times, when noticeable. Had 4-5 pretty good days. Stopped drinking since last visit. Takes a little Clonazepam at night and once in a while a nibble during the day. Mornings are tough. Good eye contact and calmer. Very good response to cross-taper Depakote to Lamictal. Continue.

May 18, 2007

A lot better. Significantly better. Two weeks ago it really kicked in. Went for bike ride and had experience of putting things in perspective. "It was such a relief, it was huge." Working, writing, muse is back. Sleep is fine, just a little nibble of Clonazepam to sleep. Lamictal 100 mg just right. Very positive response to regime. Continue.

June 20, 2007

He says things were blissful...then settled down...then he started to feel Cymbalta wasn't doing anything. Then he had one incident with low blood pressure. But only one classic attack; lasted a day...it was after he tried to do without Clonazepam. Didn't notice side effects with *Lamictal…Residual melancholy periodically. Slow incremental change.*

July 18, 2007
"Good, good…if I had any crying it was only ½ hour…writing is easier… able to sit still and read just regular stuff." Still a little tentative about doing things where might not be in control. Side effect curling hair. Good eye contact. Calm, clear. More enthusiasm, relaxed. Humor. Try bumping up Lamictal to 200 mg /day. Try feathering away Clonazepam.

September 14, 2007
Came with wife. "I went up to Cape Breton alone…big deal for me…a lot of that clearing away stuff." Has some moderate dips that he manages. "I have my brain back." Infrequent episodes vs. ongoing. "I have a lot of fun now." Low key. Continue regime and monitor. Coach, support.

November 15, 2007
"I'm like a poster child for Lamictal." Side effects: a little word finding. "I'm throwing nouns around with abandon." No problem…sleep is fine. Rarely takes Clonazepam. Doesn't oversleep as much. Much freer with writing. Happy and relieved. Looks incredibly relaxed and enthusiastic.

Annotations, References, and Random Notes

∞

Dante and Me

I am not a Dante scholar. While I've probably read most every canto at one time or another, I've never done so sequentially. Still, I've thought about him a lot. More as a mythic character than a historical one; a kind of superhuman Scribe who—like Homer before him and Shakespeare after him—appears every once in a while to gather up all the human knowledge that can be held in one brain and write it down, in order to help humanity get its bearings… establish where we are in our evolution.

I'm as interested in how these writers might see the world now as I am in how they saw the world then. As if their understanding, rather than being static, has continued to evolve, following a kind of metaphysical trajectory up to and beyond our present day. To put it simply, the *living* Dante is not the same as the dead Dante.

At one point, I had a theory that *The Divine Comedy* was not the book that Dante had actually written. That rather, it was the "public" book, an expurgated version that he created for the contemporary church and state. Perhaps, I thought, there was a "secret text" of the book, hidden in some monastery or castle somewhere, that would, like an Egyptian papyrus, eventually see the light of day.

While that would make a great plot for a novel, I no longer think that's what happened. The book we read *was* the book he wrote, just not the book he really *wanted* to write. He didn't quite dare to reach as far as he had wanted to in terms of presenting a complete picture of human experience. It was not the church that had censored him…he had subconsciously censored himself. Or, rather, been inexorably censored by his time and place.

Fortunately, whether advertently or not, he left a clue that the journey wasn't complete: Beatrice told him he had to go back and tell all us temporal humans what he'd seen.

Think of what that means. He goes back. Tells people what he saw in Hell, and Purgatory, and Heaven. And then what? Well, if he sticks to his plot...he goes back again. To witness again and tell again. In the meantime, the people who were in Hell are still in Hell, those in Purgatory are still in Purgatory, and those in Paradise are still Paradise. If we follow this logic...we are *all* in the Hell of eternal repetition.

Say what you will about history repeating itself, when you finish writing a book you want to start a new one. I see Dante, looking at his elegant script on all those ancient sheaves of parchment shaking his head and smiling affectionately at that "young" Dante. Because by now he realizes that as long as he keeps leaving us in Hell, he's stuck there too. It's time for a new story.

ᗡ

Even though I've always had this almost metaphysical affinity for Dante's eternal journey, to invoke his name for a book like this seemed a bit contrived. While I could *feel* the parallels on multiple levels, on the surface our only resemblances are that we're both Gemini writers with aquiline noses.

At first I thought, well, I'll include some academic-type essays about Dante to try to obfuscate the apparent tenuousness of the connection. But as I began to immerse myself more deeply into both *The Divine Comedy* and my own writing, the parallels began to click into place in ways that felt increasingly seamless.

Eventually, I accepted that I doth protest too much. For while, as countless books have attested, *The Divine Comedy* is the journey of one man, it is also the journey of *everyman*. Indeed, my journey through Hell (and hopefully not back), was and is every bit as important to humanity as Dante's. And so is yours. And yours. And yours.

The Dark Wood—yes, we all have been there. Limbo, we've been there, too. Hell and Purgatory, we've tasted them. And a Paradise that's beyond the forms of this earth? Beyond contentment? Beyond bliss? Well, those who know don't say and those who say don't know. Me? All I can do is say I don't know.

Translations

Not only am I *not* a Dante scholar, I don't even understand Italian. Fortunately, there are many English translations of Dante's work. At various times, I consulted ones by Henry Wadsworth Longfellow, Mark Musa, H.F. Cary, A.S. Kline, and others. The Dante quotations in this book are the result of my mixing and matching these translations, and then putting them into a vernacular that made sense to me. Heresy, perhaps. But I'm in good company.

References

Growing up in my academic household, you were only supposed to use primary sources. Looking things up in encyclopedias was a capital offense. And summaries like *Cliff Notes* were beneath contempt. Nevertheless, *Wikipedia* deserves my thanks and even a bit of my money for saving me an extraordinary amount of time when I was trying to remember for the 20TH time what year Dante was exiled or which behaviors dopamine affects. The everexpanding website *Shmoop* was similarly helpful as were the *Cummings Study Guides* (http://www.cummingsstudyguides.net/). In all cases, you need to cross-check your facts, but sites like this sure make things easier when you encounter a factual block in the middle of a paragraph.

No matter how much cross-checking you do however, there are many things about Dante that are still subject to debate…in particular, when he started and completed each of the three books, and where he traveled while in exile. Sources disagree on the former by years and the latter by miles. Paris? Likely. England? Maybe. And then there's the stuff of pure legend. Which son found how many remaining cantos? Where? How many months after he died? In this regard, my favorite source for the confusion about his travels while in exile is a review of the book *Dante the Wayfarer* which was published in *The New York Times* on December 2, 1905 (http://www.unz.org/Pub/BookmanUK-1905nov-00074).

After reading the introductions to various translations and roaming around the Internet, I pretty much settled on http://www.worldofdante.org/timeline.html for the basic chronology, because it was easy to follow and was developed by the University of Virginia's Institute for Advanced Technology in the Humanities. Advanced technology? Humanities? I hear a little cognitive dissonance there. But is it all so different from Dante's insistence on writing in the vernacular? The medium changes. The message evolves.

Beyond that, I intentionally didn't read too much about Dante while writing this book, because, as I've said, my goal wasn't to write *about* him so much as have a relationship *with* him. Since this led me to make some assertions and projections that could raise the eyes, if not ire, of Dante scholars, it's probably best if we call those those sections "historical fiction" and leave it at that.

One biography I do need to acknowledge is *Dante in Love* by Harriet Rubin (2004). When I discovered this book, I felt I had met a kindred spirit because she, like me, was more interested in the *living* Dante than the dead one.

Also her book was the one that brought to my attention the important fact that the poet called his book "The *Vision* of Hell, Purgatory, and Heaven." Anyone who likes my apparently speculative sections about Dante in this book will likely enjoy Rubin's.

Depression

There are two authors in this field that I—and most other people interested in depression—consider required reading: Kay Jamison and Peter Kramer. I was informed, illuminated, and inspired by *An Unquiet Mind* (1995) Jamison's groundbreaking book about manic-depression (including her own first-hand experience); her *Touched with Fire* (1993) about manic-depression and creativity; and her *Night Falls Fast* (1999) about suicide.

I also read Peter Kramer's *Listening to Prozac* (1993) and *Against Depression* (2005), both of which have been major forces for bringing depression "out of the closet," as an illness that can be treated with medication, and the implications of that for understanding who we "really" are. The latter book also raises the intriguing question of what human life and creativity would look like without depression.

Whenever we read a book about some kind of suffering, we experience a kind of simultaneous relief and envy. There is, however, a place in the middle, where the emotional lives of the writer, reader, patient, caregiver, and innocent bystander all have their place and are equally deserving of acceptance and respect. While there are many memoirs of depression, bipolar, and schizophrenia, William Styron's *Darkness Visible* (1990) still sets the standard. By being equally intimate and informative, he lets you into the experience without forcing you to stare or to turn away. To get a bigger picture of his experience and what it was like to live with him through it, read his daughter Alexandra Styron's new book *Reading My Father* (2012).

Neuropsychiatry and Pharmacology

While I tried to make most technical terms self-explanatory in the text, I've included a Glossary for easier reference. It includes a chart of trade and generic names that professionals tend to use interchangeably.

The only medical *text* I referred to was *DSM IV: Diagnostic and Statistical Manual of Mental Illness*, which is published by the American Psychiatric Association. As of this writing, *DSM V* is about to be released. Many libraries have copies, and there are several websites that give general overviews of the various diagnoses, including http://allpsych.com/disorders/dsm.html and http://www.dr-bob.com

I tend to triangulate between a lot of different resources in order to understand the who, what, when, where, how, and why of technical topics. After a while, however, I began to rely on certain ones. The following are my major Internet resources for understanding neurotransmitters, diagnoses, and medications:

Burke, Dr. Brian: Abnormal Psychology: http://faculty.fortlewis.edu/burke_b/Abnormal/Abnormalmultiaxial.htm

Culbertson, Fred: Phobia List: http://phobialist.com/ *(Not to be missed.)*

Dewey, Russell A., PhD: Psychology: An Introduction. http://www.intropsych.com/ch12_abnormal/five_axes_of_dsm-iv.html

Drugs.com: http://www.drugs.com/

EMC Publishing:/Most Commonly Prescribed Drugs: http://www.emcp.com/college_resource_centers/resourcelist.php?GroupID=7237

eMedExpert: http://www.emedexpert.com/compare/ssris.shtml

Enchanted Learning: http://www.enchantedlearning.com/subjects/anatomy/brain/Neuron.shtml *(As with all complex topics, children's books and websites are the best place to start your research...and often to end it.)*

Hart, Carol: Secrets of Serotonin: http://www.nasw.org/users/twoharts/serotonin.html *(My favorite comprehensive explanation of serotonin.)*

Livestrong: http://www.livestrong.com/

McManamy, John: McMan's Depression and Bipolar Web: http://www.mcmanweb.com/neurotransmitters.html *(A comprehensive blog that combines really good information with memoir.)*

Pharmacology Corner: http://pharmacologycorner.com/ *(Some very helpful short video lectures.)*

Poore, Jerod: Crazy Meds: (http://www.crazymeds.us/pmwiki/pmwiki.php/Main/HomePage) *(The essential layperson's guide to prescription drugs.)*

Prescorn, Sheldon: Applied Clinical Psychopharmacology: http://www.preskorn.com/books/ssri_s1.html *(Clarifies the history of SSRIs)*

Psychresidentonline.com: http://www.psychresidentonline.com/

WebMD: http://www.webmd.com/depression/features/the-dalai-lama-and-depression-treatment

Chapter Notes

NB: Dante Alighieri was born in Florence in 1265 and died in Ravenna in 1321.

THE DARK WOOD

Words Fail

- Epigraph: From Book 5 of Marcus Aurelius's *Meditations*. This 2nd century Roman emperor—as famous for his mastership of Stoicism as his military skills—is the kind of guy who gives brooding melancholic insight a good name. He spent many nights encamped with his troops in the far northern territories of the Roman Empire, writing down his reflections on what it means to be a whole human being...in terms of how you think, feel, and behave. I highly recommend a few passages next time you have to take a deep breath and accept that it really is what it is. Even when it's not.

LIMBO

Fifty-Three Years, Four Months, and One Helluva Week

- Epigraph: From *The Journals of Søren Kierkegaard*, February 1836.
- The BBQ place in Mississippi is called The Shed (http://theshedbbq.com). It survived both Hurricane Katrina and Isaac.
- Paris: The most famous river is, of course, the Seine. The most famous cemetery is Père Lachaise—resting place of Jim Morrison as well as Chopin. The most famous bookstore is Shakespeare & Company. Its legendary owner, George Whitman (a relative of Walt) used to serve tea every Sunday afternoon to whomever showed up until he died in 2011 at the age of 98.

Make Up Your Mind

- Epigraph: One of Sam Spade's many great one-liners in Dashiell Hammett's *The Maltese Falcon*. He uses it to describe a guy whose life was completely turned upside down when a beam falls to the sidewalk right next him and almost kills him. Spade goes on to say: "He adjusted himself to beams falling, and then no more of them fell, and he adjusted himself to them not falling.

264

HELL

Looking for Traction
- Epigraph: A friend said this to me in May, 2006. He was commiserating about my increasingly chaotic state and, after making a few mild suggestions, ended with this simple statement. I scribbled it down word for word and returned to it frequently. While on the surface, it might sound rather harsh—for me, it was a reminder that I still had at least a modicum of personal power and that I would endure.

Road Trip
- Epigraph: Theodore Roosevelt was more of a situational depressive. Or, perhaps a situational manic-depressive. For him, a major change of scene was often the best therapy. His famous line about the "black care" was written when he fled to the Badlands after the death of his pregnant wife and his mother on the same day in 1884.
- Neal Cassady was the model for the character Dean Moriarity in Jack Kerouac's *On the Road* (1957)...a dash across America that was easily as mad as mine.
- Michael Chabon's book about Sherlock Holmes is called *The Final Solution: A Story of Detection* (2003).
- The University of West Virginia Mountaineers lost to Texas in the NCAA Sweet Sixteen that year. Florida beat UCLA in the final.
- One of my late godfather Larry Spitz's best stories was about how he helped organize the textile workers in Woonsocket, Rhode Island in the mid '30s. Among other things, this involved arranging night classes in English for the primarily French Canadian workers. Larry was the real deal.
- The Susan Orlean book of essays I was listening to is called *My Kind of Place* (2004).
- Natural Foods Expo: This is a good place to clarify my "business career." Why was I at a Natural Food show? Hadn't I retired from advertising? Well, back in 1987, a friend and I started a company to import soaps and body care products. I ended up owning an ad agency. He ended up running the soap company. But I occasionally consulted, wrote, and, as indicated, went to trade shows with him.
- The poem in Brown's Park is by Joseph Brown, an ancestor of the family who created the park.
- *One man's miracle...* The "famous man" who said this was Godfrey de Bouillon, one of the leaders of the First Crusade. You won't find it, however, on any website of quotations, because he said it in a book of historical fiction that I'm writing.
- The main goal of primal scream therapy is to help patients release child-

hood trauma. Janov's most famous patients were John and Yoko Ono. Listening to the song "Mother" on their album *John Lennon/Plastic Ono Band*, gives you a sense of the technique's intensity. Janov's book *The Primal Scream* (1970) is still in print.
- For more on the Rainbow Family see http://www.welcomehome.org/rainbow/index.html
- "Sympathy for the Devil" is, of course, by The Rolling Stones. "We Built This City on Rock & Roll" is by Jefferson Starship. Apologies to the many people who still love hearing the "Pachabel Canon" and "The Rose" at weddings.
- The song "Long December" (1996) is by Counting Crows, from their album *Recovering the Satellites*.
- I'm happy to say that, with the help of a neighbor, I eventually got the rock free and it's now the front step of my cabin.

Diagnosis
- Epigraph: From Siddhartha Mukherjee's (2010) *Emperor of All Maladies: A Biography of Cancer,* a fascinating look at the disease and our relationship to it over the last few thousand years.
- Bipolar I & II. As mentioned, doctors draw the line in various places. The clearest explanation for me was when my doctor said, "If you were in a full-blown mania, you'd be bouncing off the walls, not sitting in this chair." There were, of course, times that I *felt* like bouncing off the walls, but I never did.
- There are a variety of Patient Health Questionnaires. I assume the one I filled out was a version my doctor had customized. There were, indeed, 132 questions.
- By the way, I'm serious about DSM codes. That *is* how insurance companies determine reimbursement. Insurance companies also have different policies about whether they require pre-authorizations for brand vs. generic drugs.

PURGATORY

Hard Turns and False Tops
- Epigraph: From Notebook IV in Albert Camus' *Notebooks: 1942-1951.*

The Wit and Wisdom of Neurotransmitters
- Epigraph: From an article by Peter Schjedahl called "Rule Like An Egyptian: Hatshepsut the King and Queen," published in *The New Yorker*, April 3, 2006.
- My physics professor friend (who, by the way, also takes Lamictal) wrote: *The way the molecular weight business works is: (100mg) x (1 mole/256.0926*

g) x (6.02 x 10^{23} molecules/mole) = 2.45 x 10^{20} molecules. That's not exactly explaining how it works in English, but if you track through the units you would say I have 100 mg = .1 grams of Lamictal, and 1 mole of Lamictal has a mass of (256.0926 g), so that gives me the number of moles of Lamictal that are in 100 mg. One mole contains Avogadro's number of molecules, so I multiply the number of moles I have by Avogadro's number and voilà, I have the number of molecules. 10^{6} is a million, 10^{9} is a billion, 10^{12} is a tera (big hard drives currently have 1 - 1.5 terabytes), so the 100 mg of Lamictal has 24.5 hundred billion tera molecules. I guess that goes to show molecules are very small! Even molecules of Lamictal. Who would have thought that such a small molecule could have such a big effect. This gives you the number you wanted, but it doesn't explain what a mole is, or why it's related to Avogadro's number, or how weight is related to mass, or whether gram is a unit of weight or mass, and so on. If you are interested in that stuff then there's another email.

- I do really encourage you to find one of the many representative illustrations of synapses if you want to try to follow this. I highly recommend the children's site listed above: http://www.enchantedlearning.com/subjects/anatomy/brain/Neuron.shtml. If you want to get a little deeper, check out the one from "How Stuff Works" http://www.howstuffworks.com/enlarge-image.htm?terms=nerve+communication&page=0
- The article in the June 1998 issue of *Scientific American* was written by Charles B. Nemeroff.

Prescription Medicines

NOTE: I say this many times in many different ways, but it's always worth repeating: The experiences in this book with specific medications are *my* experiences. They have little if anything to do with how you might respond to the same drugs. In that regard, I tend to avoid forums and chat rooms where people talk about their experiences. A comment that makes you feel good about what you're taking is often followed by a comment that's so scary you think you should stop right away. I admit it's hard not to get hooked on those sites…we depressives tend to have addictive natures anyway…but your doctor really is the best source for up-to-date information about responses, side effects, and so on. Although, you should never hesitate to ask for a second opinion.

- Epigraph: With the caveat above, the site www.crazymeds.com deserves a bookmark on the browser of anyone involved in mental illness. A guy named Jerod Poore writes it, and it's the most comprehensive, comprehensible, and irreverent presentation of psychopharmacology and prescription drugs on the web…and perhaps anywhere. This quote is right from his home page.
- The correct answer is the Red Sox.
- Kay Jamison devotes a whole chapter to the alleged suicide of Meriweth-

er Lewis in her book *Night Falls Fast*. This quote is on page 230.

- The reference is to Neil Young's song, "Hey Hey, My My (Into the Black)" (1994) from the album *Sleeps with Angels*.

Alternative Medicine

- Epigraph: From the works of Galen, the 2ND century Roman physician who elaborated upon Hippocrates' theory of "humors". He was also the court physician to Emperor Marcus Aurelius, which gave him the freedom and resources to write extensively on medicine.
- Dr. Andrew Weil is one of the most famous MDs to encourage people to combine western and alternative medicines for maximum health. His first book was *The Natural Mind* (1972).
- Hippocrates, who lived from 460–370 BC is known as the Father of Modern Medicine. He's most famous for his "oath" that doctors should first do no harm.
- Paracelsus was a brilliant alchemist of the sixteenth century. The idea of combining ordinary elements to make gold, however, was not the focus of true alchemists like him. Rather he combined breakthrough scientific discoveries with careful observation and traditional folk wisdom to create a new scientific and medical paradigm that, while incorporating some traditional folk wisdom, went far beyond mere "superstition."
- Dr. Patricia Slagle now offers her book *The Way Up From Down* (1994) as a free eBook: http://www.thewayup.com/ebook/ebook.htm. It really is a great way to learn about why/how vitamins, minerals, amino acids and herbs can affect your mental health. She also offers newsletters on her site and phone consultations.
- The quote from the Dalai Lama is at http://www.webmd.com/depression/features/the-dalai-lama-and-depression-treatment. As an aside: I'm kind of surprised he said it and I hope I'm not quoting it out of context. Of course he's right: compassion is a great friend during times of great stress. But, as I say in another place, to ask someone in the throes of mania to feel compassion can be like asking someone who's color-blind to see red.

Self-Medication

- Epigraph: Cookie Monster's favorite cookie is chocolate chip, although oatmeal comes in a close second. An obvious binge eater, Cookie Monster also shows clear signs of "Pica" (DSM-IV 307.52), which involves eating things that are not food, as well as memory lapses that might indicate Disassociative Fugue (300.13). Thanks to Louise Finley 's website for helping me clarify some of the fine points of this diagnosis. http://www.louisefinley.com/?cat=18.
- This paraphrase of Dylan is from "Just Like Tom Thumbs Blues" on *Highway 61 Revisited*.

Who Knows?

- Epigraph: One of Socrates' most famous. From Plato's *Apology*. No one seems to know for sure whether Socrates actually existed. That's another thing that at least I know I do not know.
- The costs I used to analyze the difference between treating someone with antidepressants versus hospitalization are based on several sources, primarily http://www.cms.hhs.gov/Outreach-and-Education/ Medicare-Learning-Network-MLN/MLNProducts/downloads//InpatientPsychFac.pdf which gives the federal *per diem* base rate for 2012 and http:consumerreports.org/health/best-buy-drugs/antidepressants.htm for the typical retail prices.
- Robert Whitaker, the author of *Anatomy of an Epidemic* (2010) also wrote *Mad in America* (2002). The wide variation between various statistical analyses as well as their cognitive dissonance with personal experiences can be pretty confounding. As I discuss later in the book, I suspect that a great deal is due to the subjectivity of when a condition of mental *imbalance* becomes one of mental illness, as well as what it means to be cured.
- The William Blake quote comes from his *The Marriage of Heaven and Hell* (1790-1793).

Visible Means of Support

- Epigraph: I seem to be "afflicted" with a Quixotic drive to find the true source of any quote I use; especially because the Internet has become filled with quotes that were spliced together to serve someone's purpose, taken totally out of context, or were never said by the person in the first place! I've made an exception in this case. I've looked unsuccessfully for a film, interview, or letter in which Marilyn Monroe actually said this. Regardless, it's such a great expression of how depressives feel, I hope she doesn't mind my attributing it to her...
- The story about brain scans that my friend told me was based on the work of Dr. Daniel Amen, http://www.amenclinics.com.
- The comments about talking to children about a parent's depression come from an email correspondence with Caroline Carr, http://www.carolinecarr.com.

Married to the Madness

- Epigraph: From Jane Austen's *Pride and Prejudice*.

Therapy

- Epigraph: From *The Self in Transformation* (1965) by Herbert Fingarette. This book, which explores the relationship between personal growth and

spirituality was a staple of psychology and religion curricula when I was in college.
- You can find more about my writing about historical characters on www. davidblistein.com.

Strange Obsessions and Glimmers of Light
- Epigraph: Polonius says this about Hamlet in Act 2, Scene 2, after one of the Prince's most eloquent pieces of triple-entendre imagery.
- Here in Vermont, stealing rocks from walls is charged the same as theft. But across the river from us in New Hampshire, there's a law that specifically says you can be fined three times the costs of rebuilding the wall, plus attorney's fees. It's an update of a 200-year-old law. See http://www. abajournal.com/news/article/n.h._ups_ante_for_stone_wall_thieves_ new_law_provides_for_attorney_fees.
- I'm pleased and proud to say that my little arched bridge survived Hurricane Irene in 2011, one of southern Vermont's worst storms in decades.
- I've mentioned our late neighbor Dwight Miller a couple of times. See http://www.boston.com/news/local/breaking_news/2008/08/obituary_dwight.html for a brief bio. Among other things, he's known for being one of the founders of Brattleboro, Vermont's annual Strolling of the Heifers (www.strollingoftheheifers.com), which has become a major celebration of locally-grown food.

HEAVEN ON EARTH

- I'm paraphrasing Elvis Costello's "(The Angels Wanna Wear My) Red Shoes" from his album *My Aim is True*.

The Labyrinth
- Epigraph: Paul Reps (1895-1990) was one of the key figures in bringing Zen Buddhism to the West. His *Zen Flesh Zen Bones* (1957) was one of the very first books about Zen Buddhism published in America. The quote itself comes from *Reps: Letters to a Friend*, a compilation of letters and drawings that Reps sent to his equally enlightened friend William Segal over the course of their 30-year friendship. I knew both men and, in the late 1970s Segal gave his collection of Reps' correspondence to some friends and myself. We self-published the book in 1980.
- The very unofficial "world record" for running an 11-circuit labyrinth is held by the much-loved Keith Wilson (1985–2009).
- For details on ways to find true north just like a real Boy Scout, see the nearest Boy Scout handbook or go to http://boyslife.org/outdoors/outdoorarticles/1739/true-north.

PARADISE

Miracle of Miracles

- Epigraph: The Jane Kenyon (1947-1995) lines are from her poems "The Suitor" and "Credo." Both are included in *Otherwise: New & Selected Poems. (1996).* By the way, one of the conditions of reprinting these lines is that they are flush left as she wrote them.
- R. D. Laing's line about insanity being the only sane response to an insane world is from his seminal *The Politics of Experience* (1967).
- Kurt Vonnegut's quote is from his book of short stories *Welcome to the Monkey House* (1968).
- Akira Kurasawa's quote is spoken by the character Kyoami in his film *Ran* (1985).

Crazy Wisdom and Creativity

- Epigraph: Edgar Allen Poe's quote is from the short story "Eleonora" (1842). Harriet Rubin's quote comes from her book *Dante in Love* (2004).
- *Of Mice and Men* (1937) is by John Steinbeck.
- The story about Ram Dass giving Maharaji some LSD is in *Be Here Now*. Originally, it was a boxed set with a booklet, poster, and twine-tied book on rough paper put together in 1970 by the Lama Foundation in New Mexico, one of the first spiritual communes in America. Over the last forty years, I've left a lot of books and records behind in various places. But this is the only one I really regret losing track of. Not because its rare-book value—but because so much of my late adolescent yearning for enlightenment was psychically imprinted in my copy. When it came out, shortly thereafter, as a one-volume paperback, distributed by Crown Publishers, it cost $3.33. It is still in print, now published by the Hanuman Foundation.
- The story of Huxley doing LSD on his deathbed is told by his wife Laura in her book *This Timeless Moment* (2000). His last words are probably countercultural urban legend.
- Peter Kramer writes about depression and creativity in his book *Against Depression* (2005).
- *Storming Heaven: LSD and the American Dream*, by Jay Stevens, was published by Grove Press in 1998.
- Before he died, William Blake (1757-1827) actually started doing illustrations of *The Divine Comedy*, see http://www.blakearchive.org/exist/blake/archive/work.xq?workid=but812&java=no, a project of the Library of Congress in conjunction with the University of Rochester, University of North Carolina at Chapel Hill, and National Endowment of the Humanities.
- Bob Dylan's homage to Dante is in the song "Tangled up in Blue" from the album *Blood on the Tracks* (1975).

- I'm very poorly read (if at all) in the philosophy of deconstructionism. But I've always liked the concept. I found the Jacques Derrida quote in Rubin's book.

Depression and Spirituality
- The Epigraph: A prophetic remark from a conversation with one of my favorite psychics in the summer of 2006.
- St. John of the Cross's *Dark Night of the Soul* is one of the classics of Christian spirituality...a poem that describes how a human can be detached from the things of this world and thereby merge with the light of God in much the same way as described by Dante.
- Eckhart Tolle's *The Power of Now: A Guide to Spiritual Enlightenment* was published by New World Library in 1999.
- While on the subject of koans and kundalini: the great Hindu guru Sri Ramana Maharshi (1879–1950) said that all you really needed to do to raise your kundalini energy was to hammer on that "Who am I?" koan until you broke wide open. Maharshi was a teacher of several of the most important figures who brought Eastern spirituality to the West...including Paul Brunton and Paul Reps.
- The Mary Oliver (b. 1935) poem with the refrain "What blazes the trail is not necessarily pretty," is called "Skunk Cabbage." It's in her collection *American Primitive* (1983). She won the Pulitzer Prize for that book.
- "Abraham" is a spirit who's been channeled by a woman named Esther Hicks for more than three decades. As with all such things, it's probably most productive to focus on the message and not worry about the medium.

THE DIVINE COMEDY

Beholding the Stars
The Epigraph: From *Arch of Triumph* (1945) by Erich Maria Remarque...one of the great existential love and war stories of all time.

Glossary

HAVING SPENT 40 YEARS traveling the highways and bi-ways of traditional and alternative medicine, I tend to casually throw words around, forgetting that they aren't familiar to a lot of people. Hope I caught most of them because I wouldn't want to be accused of being a sesquipedalian...

5-HTP: A natural amino acid that regulates serotonin levels.

Acetylcholine: A neurotransmitter involved in memory, learning, and voluntary muscular control...including orgasm! A lack may be associated with Alzheimer's disease.

Acupuncture: An ancient Chinese medical treatment based on stimulating certain points in the body with tiny needles. Often combined with Chinese herbal medicine.

Agitated Depression: Just what it like sounds...depression combined with uncontrolled restlessness.

Amino Acids: The molecules your body uses to make proteins.

Axons: An umbilical-cord-like thing-a-ma-jig that extends out from the body of the cell and has a whole lot of filaments that shoot out neurotransmitting molecules to other cells.

Ayurvedic: A traditional Hindu approach to medicine involving massage, hygiene, and herbal remedies.

Bach Flower Remedies: A collection of plant extracts developed in the 1930s by a British doctor that are commonly used in alternative medicine to treat emotional and mental imbalances. The most famous one is called *Rescue Remedy*. Don't knock it 'til you've tried it...many people find it a much milder and equally effective relaxant as prescription benzodiazepines.

Benzodiazepine: The most common type of sedative and anti-anxiety medication. Including Valium, Lorazepam, and Klonopin. They vary mainly in terms of the therapeutic dosage, half-life, and tendency to lead to addiction.

Bipolar: Psychiatric condition in which periods of manic behavior alternate with deep depression. Bipolar II is the *milder* form.

Craniosacral: A special kind of bodywork in which the practitioner makes subtle adjustments to how the "cranial fluid" is moving. The technique is used by osteopaths and chiropractors as well as massage therapists.

Dendrites: Tiny receptors on neurons that *receive* the neurotransmitters from axons on other neurons, thereby transmitting "information" (in the form of electric charges or molecular changes).

Dopamine: Raises alertness and confidence; lowers aggression, compulsivity, and paranoia. Also helps you get a good night's sleep. Parkinson's disease seems to be linked to dopamine deficit. Excessive amounts are a factor in schizophrenia. Speaking of which, cocaine and amphetamines crank the levels up really high.

Dysphoria: The opposite of euphoria. That is, manic behavior marked by deep anxiety/depression.

Enzyme: Molecules that increase or decrease the speed of change in cells. The enzymes in the brain break down used neurotransmitters in a way that corresponds to how stomach enzymes break down (digest) food.

Full Spectrum Lights: Bright lights that mimic the spectrum of the light of the sun in order to help people with Seasonal Affective Disorder.

GABA: Keeping those GABA levels up can make you feel more relaxed and less anxious. Sedatives often help GABA receptors meet their quotas. It's also the target of several drugs for psychosis. By the way: GABA stands for *gamma-aminobutyric acid*. Might come in handy next time you do a crossword puzzle.

Glutamate: Glutamate is the other side of the GABA coin. It gets the target neurons more excited. In fact, some drugs that are used for bipolar and schizophrenia may work by somehow balancing the GABA and glutamate receptors.

Hippocampus: A part of the brain that's particularly involved in memory and orienting yourself in space.

Hypnagogic: The dream-like images that you see just before falling asleep.

Kundalini: In Tantric and Kundalini Yoga, concentrated energy in the base of the spine that changes consciousness when it spirals up into the brain. In Sanskrit, "kund" means "to burn."

Macrobiotic: A therapeutic diet—and lifestyle—that focuses on eating whole grains and locally-grown vegetables, but little if any meat or processed foods.

Neurons: Brain cells. Neurons look kind of like giant squids with a whole lot of tentacles and a real whole lot of filaments coming out of each one.

Neurotransmitters: Molecules made in neurons that transmit signals from one neuron to another. The way a person feels "off" usually depends on which neurotransmitters aren't getting the job done. Even though each type has its general area of expertise, there's a lot of cross over and they tend to be willing to cover for each other when one wants to go out for a cup of coffee or take a millisecond or two off.

Norepinephrine: Gets your body up and at 'em by increasing your heart rate and blood pressure. So you feel more energized, alert, and able to focus. It's also used in heart medications. (Norepinephrine is another word for adrenaline.)

Petroglyphs: Pre-historic glyph-like images carved in rocks. There are tens of thousands of them in the Southwest alone.

PTSD: Post Traumatic Stress Disorder. While best known, and most prevalent, among soldiers returning from war, the diagnosis is also occasionally given to people with similar symptoms that have been caused by a wide range of other traumas.

Receptors: You're not going to believe this, but each of the tiny dendrites on a neuron has really, tiny, tiny doors. The doors are different shapes so they'll only let in certain kinds of neurotransmitters and thereby pass along certain kinds of messages. Usually people describe it as a lock and key kind of thing.

Rolfing: A special form of deep-tissue massage developed by a woman named Ida Rolf in 1971. Among other things, it can have a major impact on your posture.

Serotonin: The most famous mood-related neurotransmitter. Serotonin can decrease anxiety and aggression while calming and lifting the emotions. There are cells making serotonin through your entire nervous system and, as pointed out in the text, 90% of the serotonin in your body is in your tummy. Think about that next time you have a gut feeling!

Shamanism: A "magical" religion that, in some cultures, includes ceremonial use of hallucinogenic plants.

Synapse: The space between cells that neurotransmitters leap across to pass signals from one to another, eventually leading to a part of the brain that knows how to do things like "Crank it up!" or "Chill out!' Or one of a million different variations on those two messages. That is, it's all about getting the brain cells to move and shake in a way Goldilocks would approve of—that is, not too fast, not too slow…just right.

Tyrosine: An amino acid that neurons use to make neurotransmitters.

MEDICATIONS (Trade/Generic)

Every time I read about prescription meds I wish I had one complete list of the trade/generic names of the most common ones. So I finally put my own list together based on a variety of sources. Many of these medications are *not* mentioned in the book. But a similar one may be, in which case this may help you figure out what type of drug it is and what it's usually prescribed for.

As I mentioned in the book, there's a lot of mixing apples and oranges here. For example, there's a wide class of drugs usually referred to as "atypicals." Which are typically prescribed for psychosis, mood stabilizing, bipolar, and/or schizophrenia—although some tend to be prescribed more often for one condition: e.g., bipolar (Depakote) *or* schizophrenia (Haldol) or mood stabilizing (Lamictal).

TRADE NAME	GENERIC NAME	INDICATION - CLASS
Abilify	aripiprazole	Antipsychotic/Mood Stabilizer/Bipolar
Adderall	amphetamine	Attention Deficit Disorder
Ambien	zolpidem	Sleeping Aid
Anafranil	clomipramine	Antidepressant - Tricyclic
Aventyl	nortriptyline	Antidepressant - Tricyclic
BuSpar	busprione	Anti-anxiety - Azapirone
Celexa	citalopram	Antidepressant - SSRI
Concerta	methylphenidate	Attention Deficit Disorder
Cymbalta	duloxetine	Antidepressant - SNRI
Depakote	valproic acid	Antipsychotic/Mood Stabilizer/Bipolar
Desyrel	trazodone	Antipsychotic/Mood Stabilizer/Bipolar
Dexedrine	dextroamphetamine	Stimulant - ADHD
Effexor	venlafaxine	Antidepressant - SNRI
Elavil	amitriptyline	Antidepressant - Tricyclic
Emsam	selegiline	Antidepressant - MAO Inhibitor
Eskalith	lithium	Antipsychotic/Mood Stabilizer/Bipolar
Focalin	dexmethylphenidate	Stimulant
Geodon	ziprasidone	Antipsychotic/Mood Stabilizer/Bipolar
Halcion	triazolam	Anti-Anxiety - Benzodiazepine
Haldol	haloperidol	Antipsychotic/Mood Stabilizer/Bipolar
Klonopin	clonazepam	Anti-Anxiety - Benzodiazepine
Lamictal	lamotrigine	Antipsychotic/Mood Stabilizer/Bipolar
Lexapro	escitalopram	Antidepressant - SSRI
Librium	chlordiazepoxide	Anti-Anxiety - Benzodiazepine
Limbitrol	amitriptyline	Antidepressant - Tricyclic
Lithobid	lithium	Antipsychotic/Mood Stabilizer/Bipolar

TRADE NAME	GENERIC NAME	INDICATION - CLASS
Lorazepam	Ativan	Anti-Anxiety - Benzodiazepine
Lunesta	eszopiclone	Sleeping Aid
Marplan	isocarboxazid	Antidepressant - MAO Inhibitor
Nardil	phenelzine	Antidepressant - MAO Inhibitor
Norpramin	desipramine	Antidepressant - Tricyclic
Parnate	tranylsypromine	Antidepressant - MAO Inhibitor
Paxil	paroxetine	Antidepressant - SSRI
Pristiq	desvenlafaxine	Antidepressant - SNRI
Prozac	fluoxetine	Antidepressant - SSRI
Remeron	mirtazapine	Antidepressant - Tricyclic
Risperdal	risperidone	Antipsychotic/Mood Stabilizer/Bipolar
Ritalin	methylphenidate	Attention Deficit Disorder
Seroquel	quetiapine	Antipsychotic/Mood Stabilizer/Bipolar
Sinequan	doxipin	Antidepressant - Tricyclic
Strattera	atomoxetine	Attention Deficit Disorder
Thorazine	chlopromazine	Antipsychotic/Mood Stabilizer/Bipolar
Tofranil	imiprimine	Antidepressant - Tricyclic
Valium	diazepam	Anti-Anxiety - Benzodiazepine
Vyvanse	lisdexamfetamine	Attention Deficit Disorder
Wellbutrin	bupropion	Antidepressant - NDRI
Xanax	alprazolam	Anti-Anxiety - Benzodiazepine
Zoloft	sertraline	Antidepressant - SSRI
Zyban	bupropion	Smoking Cessation
Zyprexa	olanzepine	Antipsychotic/Mood Stabilizer/Bipolar

Antidepressant Classes

MAOI (Monoamineoxidase Inhibitor): Blocks the enzyme that breaks down neurotransmitters so they stay in the synapse longer.

SSRI: Selective Serotonin Reuptake Inhibitor. It keeps neurotransmitters, *primarily serotonin,* from skedaddling out of the synapse before they've done their job.

SNRI: Ditto, except it works on serotonin and norepinephrine.

NDRI: Ditto, except it works on norepinephrine and dopamine.

Tricyclic: Blocks reuptake of serotonin, norepinephrine, and/or dopamine.

*All of the above have varying degrees of effect on the "receiving side," making receptors more receptive (agonists) or less (antagonist).

Index

Acknowledgments

Thank you...

Ambrose Bierce called love, "a temporary insanity curable by marriage." Wendy and my marriage has been more like a long-term insanity curable by love. Of all our 35 years together, this book describes two of the hardest. And yet here we are. Still together. Something for which we are both very grateful, and maybe a little amazed. (By the way, the prophetic dedication is from Bruce Springsteen's song "Born to Run" which was released just a few months before we met in January, 1976.)

I'm similarly thankful to and for our daughter Emily who, while deeply troubled by what I was going through, always managed to say or write the right words at the right time. Thanks also to her husband Drew and the boys: Owen, Lucas, and little Julian—whose smile, from Day 1, has been an inspiration to us all.

I'm also eternally indebted to my late parents Elmer and Sophie Blistein who taught me to think, feel, read, and write; and believe it or not, had a set of Dante and Beatrice bookends in their ample library.

Keeping it in the family a bit longer, I want to thank my brother Adam, in particular for our annual Thanksgiving walks and talks, as well as his family—Maralin, Jonathan, and Lenna—for, among other things, helping to keep holidays relatively sane and mom relatively relieved. Also, my late cousin Rob Cutler who showed us all how to keep laughing in the face of adversity, as well as the whole extended family of Cutlers, Kerns, and Schaffers, particularly Dora Schaffer, Ronni Kern (on the West Coast) and David and Robin Kern (on the East Coast), who helped me understand—and be amused by—the curiosities of our particular gene pool.

There are so many others:

Ken Burns, for the Foreword, the Depressive's Mantra ("It will pass. Be kind to yourself. Ask for help..."), 40 years of friendship, and "24/7."

Joe Marks & Maggie Cahoon whose support, friendship, and ability to lift my spirits never wavered, day after heartbreaking day.

All my "special correspondents:" particularly Deb Delisi, Gigi Kast, and Camilla Rockwell. Our back-and-forth emails are the basis for some of the more insightful parts of this book; as are the words of Betsy Alden, Brenda Biddle, Caroline Carr, John Cadley, Noah Elbers, Norman Lerchen, Mark Semon, and Deb Shumlin.

Then there are all the people who did their professional best to help me stay within screaming range of sanity. From traditional psychiatrists to untraditional psychics, I'm indebted to them all in equal measure: Ray Abney, Ann Acheson, Laurie Crosby, Marcus Daniels, Lucinda Dee, Bruce Dow, Deb Feiner, Richard Fletcher, Jacqueline Jimoi, Julian Jonas, Spero Latchis, Carl McNeely, Marilyn Morgan, Janet Isabel Murphy, Kassie Nelson, and Susan Taylor.

A special thanks to Joe Kohout who stopped by to share his unique insights into strange states on many a Tuesday evening; Nancy Guzik who so generously let me share her space on many a Wednesday; Ann Fielder who—I think it was a Thursday—did her own no-nonsense intervention; and the late Al and Martha Morgan who let me wander into their house down the road any day of the week, pour myself a drink, share stories, watch baseball, and forget about everything else for a while.

While some of the following people may not even know why I include them, rest assured that, in some way, you helped me make it from breakdown to book—for reasons that range from well-timed bike rides and squash games to one-time conversations and long-term friendships: Charlie Conquest, Wendy Conquest, Leo Dunn, Phil Feidelseit, Sam Gearhart, Rebecca Jones, Arnie Katz, Suzanne Kingsbury, Ruth Klein, Anna Kuo, Mark Lachman, Eric Leo, Kathy Leo, Lynn Levine, Jill Lillie, Sally Mattson, Nanci McCrackin, the Miller Family, Joey Morgan, Stephan Morse, Cynthia Nims, John Nopper, Julie Peterson, Kathy Pontz, Jeff Potter, Cynthia Reeves,

Andy Rome, John Scherer, Richard Senft, Michele Slatnik, Larry Spitz, Amy Stechler, Susanna Steisel, John Stephans, Robert Stone, Jack Wesley, Tim Wick, Keith Wilson, and Tom Yahn. If I've left you out, please let me know!

I'm grateful to Hotel Pharmacy in Brattleboro, VT for understanding the intricacies of co-pays even better than the insurance companies. Thanks to Brooks Memorial Library in Brattleboro, for having the books I needed when I needed them—including three copies of the DSM-IV! And let's not forget the Windham Wheelmen (and women) and all my friends at Some Like It Hot in Putney, VT and Brattleboro Racquetsports, who kept my core strong and endorphins pumping when I needed it most.

Then there's the creation of the book itself. I have to start by thanking Eve Alintuck who believed in the book when it was only a blog and my agent Deborah Warren who believes there are many more to come.

I'm very grateful to the folks at Hatherleigh Press for helping this book survive the slings and arrows of modern-day publishing: Ryan Tumambing who figured out the practicalities, editor Anna Krusinski and her assistant Ryan Kennedy for their great sense of narrative flow (as well as firm grasp of details and deadlines), and publisher Andrew Flach who had the curiosity and confidence to take on this project.

There are two other special friends who made this book what it is:

Catherine Adams, development editor extraordinaire, who appeared as if by magic a few months before the manuscript was due, immediately embraced the vision, and proceeded to do her very best to make sure my words rose up to meet it.

Last but not least (actually first and foremost) I'm deeply and happily indebted to the incomparable Dede Cummings, whirling dervish of things book-ish—from finding publishers to designing books to getting the word out. Her ability to connect people in unexpectedly timely ways is truly remarkable.

Finally, I'd like to thank VF & Sons and all my friends out west. They know who they are…and a whole lot more.

A Note on the Type

David's Inferno was typeset in Dante, which was designed from 1946 to 1954 by Giovanni Mardersteig at the Officina Bodoni, as the press returned to full production after the Second World War. Mardersteig's goal was to create a new book face type with an italic face that worked seamlessly and elegantly with the roman. The designer was meticulous about detail, and he continued refining Dante for years.

Dante was the last and final type that Mardersteig designed, as well as one of his finest. The name comes from an edition of *Trattatello in laude di Dante* by Boccaccio—the first book to use Dante—which was published at the Officina Bodoni in 1955, the year that the Monotype Corporation of London issued the typeface for machine composition.

The new digital version of Dante, redrawn by Monotype's Ron Carpenter, is free from any restrictions imposed by hot metal technology. In 1993, Dante was issued in a range of three weights with a set of titling capitals, which are used for page titles or headings.

Interior printed by Berryville Graphics

Cover printed by Coral Graphics

Written in Scrivener

Typography & Design
by Dede Cummings
DCDesign, Brattleboro, Vermont